The Political Economy of Cambodia's Transition, 1991–2001

This book explores the three continuing, intertwined transitions which have taken place in Cambodia since the late 1980s – the transition from command economy to free market, from civil war to peace, and from single-party authoritarianism to multi-party democracy. Using a political economy approach and drawing on extensive original research, the book argues that the first transition, to the free market, has been particularly important in determining the character of the other transition processes. The reorientation of the state on the basis of personal networks of political loyalty and economic entrepreneurship, backed by the threat of violence, permitted the emergence of a limited political accommodation between the major parties in the 1990s, which provided few benefits to Cambodia's poor.

The book goes on to show how the interaction between local, state, transnational and international networks has provided different opportunities for local participation and empowerment in rural and urban areas, and suggests that the roots of a future Cambodian democracy lie in this local activity, rather than primarily in elite or international policies for state transformation.

Caroline Hughes is a lecturer in the School of Politics at the University of Nottingham. Her research focuses on the politics of resistance to, and negotiation of, international discourses of human rights and democracy in the Southeast Asia region. She has explored these themes in particular with respect to post-UNTAC Cambodia.

The Political Economy of Cambodia's Transition, 1991–2001

Caroline Hughes

LONDON AND NEW YORK

First published 2003
by RoutledgeCurzon
2 Park Square, Milton Park, Abingdon, Oxon OX14 4RN

Simultaneously published in the USA and Canada
by RoutledgeCurzon
711 Third Avenue, New York, NY 10017

RoutledgeCurzon is an imprint of the Taylor & Francis Group

Typeset in Times by Taylor & Francis Books Ltd

British Library Cataloguing in Publication Data
A catalogue record for this book is available from the British Library

Library of Congress Cataloging in Publication Data
Hughes, Caroline.
The political economy of Cambodia's transition, 1991–2001/
Caroline Hughes.
Includes bibliographical references and index.
1. Cambodia–Economic conditions. 2. Cambodia–Politics and government–1979– I. Title.
HC442 .H844 2003
320.9596'09'049–dc21
2002068233

ISBN 0–7007–1737–4

Contents

Acknowledgements

This study was possible thanks to the generosity of the Leverhulme Trust, which funded fieldwork in 1998–9 through their Study Abroad Scholarship programme, and also supported me during the writing phase from 1999–2001 through the Special Research Fellowship scheme. Fieldwork in 1995–6 was funded by the Economic and Social Research Council, to whom many thanks are also due. I would like also to thank John Vijghen of the Experts for Community Research project for facilitating further opportunities for research. The many people in Cambodia who kindly gave their time and expertise to assist me in my fieldwork are far too numerous to mention. Special thanks, however, are due to Chea Sophal, Sok Ty, Soeur Ketja, May Sam Oeun, Oeur Hunly, Nouv Phearit, Eva Mysliwiec, Ann Bishop, Jeanne Morel and Juanita Rice, for their generosity, indefatigability and hospitality. In helping me to make sense of the results at various stages, I am indebted to Laura Summers, David Chandler, Robert Taylor, David Hawke, Mike Parnwell, Sorpong Peou, John Marston, Yukiko Yonekura, Christine Chaumeau, Eva-Lotta Hedman, Vanessa Pupavac and colleagues at the School of Politics, University of Nottingham. I would also like to thank my parents, Dawn and Tom Hughes, for their financial and moral support, and my husband, Richard Brown, for his patience and advice.

Note

A number of the interviews referred to in these notes were conducted under guarantees of confidentiality. Consequently, interviewees are identified by a code letter (indicating their profession, etc.) and a number. For instance, J indicates a judge or court official. The full list of codes used is as follows:

D	National Assembly Deputy
DEM	Demonstrator
EO	Election observer
F	FUNCINPEC activist
GW	Garment worker
H	Human Rights NGO worker
I	International Organization official
J	Judge
L	Lawyer
LA	Villager, Lvea Aem District, Kandal Province
N	Journalist
OR	O'Russei market trader
S	Student Union activist
SK	Villager, S'aang District, Kandal Province
SQU	Evicted squatter
SRP	Sam Rainsy Party activist
U	University professor
V	Monk
W	SRP-produced witness of alleged electoral fraud

1 Introduction
Points of departure

Cambodia's transitions

The Cambodian state has been undergoing a triple transition since the 1980s – from command economy to free market; from war to peace; and from authoritarian rule to democracy. All three strands of transition have been intensively scrutinized and influenced by international intervenors in Cambodian affairs. All remain incomplete, insofar as the terms 'free market', 'peace' and 'democracy' are understood in the West. This study investigates the ways in which the first strand of transition – the transition from command economy to free market – has significantly influenced the possibilities for, and limits to, the other two strands. In particular, it seeks to demonstrate the ways in which the development of the Cambodian economy over the course of the 1990s has erected barriers to the emergence of substantive democracy in Cambodia.

The transition from command economy to free market took place by degrees, in Cambodia, following the collapse of the horrific experiments with total collectivization conducted by the Democratic Kampuchea (or Pol Pot) regime in the late 1970s. The restoration of privately farmed plots of land in the early 1980s proceeded to the embrace of market relations in all economic spheres in the late 1980s. This transition took place in the context of a civil war, the presence of Vietnamese troops, withholding of trade and aid from Western countries, and the struggle to rebuild a Cambodian state and to remake Cambodian society in the aftermath of the devastating Democratic Kampuchea regime during which up to two million Cambodians died.

The war that raged in the 1980s was conducted between a Phnom Penh-based regime and a resistance based on the border with Thailand. The Phnom Penh constitutional regime, initially named the People's Republic of Kampuchea (PRK) and later renamed the State of Cambodia (SoC), was installed by the invading Vietnamese army in 1979, and controlled the majority of Cambodian territory. Opposing them was a resistance formed of remnants of three earlier regimes. Dominating the resistance militarily was the National Army of Democratic Kampuchea (NADK), more commonly known as the *Khmers Rouges*, comprising the remnants of the infamous Pol Pot regime of 1976 to 1979, that had fled to the Thai border following the Vietnamese invasion. Also participating in the resistance were the royalist *Front Uni National pour un Cambodge Indépendent, Neutre, Pacifique et Coopératif* (FUNCINPEC), led by Prince Sihanouk, who had led Cambodia from independence in 1953 until he was toppled by a right-wing coup in 1970, and the republican Khmer People's National Liberation Front (KPNLF), formed of remnants of the republican government that had succeeded Sihanouk, from 1970 to 1975.

The resistance, who together formed a Coalition Government of Democratic Kampuchea (CGDK), retained diplomatic recognition in the United Nations and aid from China and Thailand, as well as humanitarian aid, directed in particular to the two non-communist parties, FUNCINPEC and the KPNLF, from the West. The PRK enjoyed the recognition of the Soviet Bloc. The international alignments that supported these warring armies served to mark the Cambodian conflict as a specifically Cold War phenomenon.

This designation appeared increasingly apt towards the end of the 1980s, when, war-weary and suffering from a decline in Soviet aid and an economic reform agenda at home, the Vietnamese army began to pull out of Cambodia. Signs of a rapprochement between Gorbachev's Soviet Union and Deng Xiaoping's China, together with the articulated desire of Thailand's premier Chatichai Choonhaven to 'turn battlefields into market-places', entailed increased regional interest in a solution to the problem. The dependence of the warring armies within Cambodia upon external aid and arms permitted significant pressure to be brought to bear upon the parties to the conflict to begin to negotiate more seriously over an end to the war.

Thus, the second strand of Cambodia's transition – the transition from war to peace – began from 1989, when negotiations began to gather steam. A United Nations-sponsored ceasefire was brokered in 1991, in the context of a wide-ranging and complex peacekeeping operation. Although unsuccessful in prompting an immediate end to the civil war, the UN operation altered dramatically the balance of internal and external forces. UN peacekeepers organized an election in which parties emerging from the four armies were to participate. Although the Party of Democratic Kampuchea refused to take part in these elections, preferring a return to warfare, FUNCINPEC and a KPNLF party called the Buddhist Liberal Democratic Party (BLDP) did participate. The result was a victory for FUNCINPEC and the formation of a coalition government comprising FUNCINPEC, the Cambodian People's Party (CPP), which represented the SoC and the BLDP. Aid was restored to the Cambodian government in Phnom Penh, and the increased power and prestige of the new constitutional regime led to the collapse of the NADK in 1999, following years of defections of units and commanders to the Phnom Penh government.

Along the way, and in response both to the changed ideological environment of the immediate post-Cold War era and to the concern that a failure to preserve the 1991 ceasefire should be offset by successes in other fields, the United Nations initiated a third strand of transition in Cambodia – the transition from single-party authoritarianism to multi-party democracy. This strand was useful to international actors who were party to the conflict in a number of ways. Firstly, it could substitute local popular sovereignty for international recognition as a basis for state legitimacy in Cambodia, by means of an election in which the population chose the government they liked the best. This would allow an end to the international disputes over the status of Cambodian sovereignty that had bedevilled, in particular, relations between the Soviet Union (backing Vietnam and the Phnom Penh regime) and China (backing the border resistance) in the 1980s. Further, it could promote a regime that would be friendly to the pro-business policies of regional neighbours. Finally, such action could promote the ideological agenda of the United Nations and Western powers in the post-Cold War world, which sought to link the promotion of democracy to the maintenance of international peace and security, in order to legitimize increased international intervention in problematic states under the terms of the United Nations Charter.[1]

Cambodia thus forms part of the unprecedented wave of democratization that took place after 1991, when many poor communist states, previously backed by the Soviet Union and which now looked to the West for aid as Council for Mutual Economic Assistance (CMEA), collapsed at the end of the 1980s and attempted to reorient their political institutions to align themselves more closely with new international donors. This wave of democratization was unprecedented not only in extent, it also saw the breakdown of earlier correlations between levels of development and transition to democracy as countries democratized in response to the imperatives of aid dependency, rather than in response to local pressures.[2] Furthermore, the move to democratization as a result of external rather than internal factors resulted in the emergence of a number of regimes in which rhetorical hyperbole regarding democratization was not matched by institutionalization of participatory political processes.[3]

To an extent this has been the case in Cambodia, whose transition has incorporated contradictory elements of political opening and repression, state accountability and repression, institutionalization and violence. Militarization, elitism, charismatic leadership and the everyday use of violence for economic and political gain have been the hallmarks of Cambodian democracy throughout the 1990s. Early optimism following a successful UN-organized election in 1993 gradually receded, as relations between the coalition partners, FUNCINPEC and the CPP deteriorated. A bloody artillery battle which took place between military units loyal to the two parties in July 1997 led to the flight of FUNCINPEC leaders and the leaders of other associated parties from Cambodia. Internationally, there was widespread pessimism for the future of Cambodian democracy.

However, in 1998, a successful election was held, in which returned opposition leaders participated. The election was accredited as free and fair by an international observer group comprised of representatives selected by a variety of governments. The CPP won the election and formed a new coalition with FUNCINPEC as junior partner. The emergence of the CPP as the senior party of government coincided with the ending of the war, as remaining NADK units defected to the government. This has prompted a new period of political stability, although it has been accompanied by concerns that, while the forms of democracy are being maintained at the turn of the century, the deepening of democracy is not being facilitated.

Approaches to the study of Cambodia's transition

Unease as to the nature of Cambodian democracy at the turn of the century reflects an uncertainty in defining and evaluating new democracies. Emphasis upon procedural definitions of democracy have been widespread during the 1990s, particularly in the study of democratization and democracy promotion. However, increasing focus on the question of how to achieve democratic consolidation, as transitions of the early 1990s continue to appear inadequate, has dovetailed with increasing concern about a declining quality of democracy in well-established liberal democracies in the West. This has prompted a refocusing upon a more normative view of democracy as pertaining not only to the observance of procedures, but also to their embedding in a political sphere peopled by empowered citizens. This new emphasis requires a view of democracy that ventures beyond Dahl's elite and minimalist polyarchy,[4] and, arguably, incorporates a more substantive vision in which democratic institutions offer not merely participation and choice to citizens, but power over policy agendas.[5]

The breakdown of previous correlations between economic indicators and democratization in the 1990s and the contemporaneous emergence of a number of regimes that have experienced an apparently low quality of democracy, despite successful implementation of democratic procedures, prompts renewed reflection upon the relationship between wealth and quality of democracy. Rueschemeyer *et al.* (1992) suggest that cross-national statistical comparisons of economic and democratic indicators imply that 'a positive, though not perfect, correlation between capitalist development and democracy ... must stand as an accepted result ... Any theory of democracy must come to terms with it'.[6] For Rueschemeyer *et al.* the interaction of three political factors explain this comparative finding: namely, the balance of class power, the relationship between state and civil society and the impact of transnational structures of power.

An interrelationship between the balance of class power and the emergence of a powerful civil society is posited by Girling's finding that

> Economic development gives rise to civil society – i.e. to new intermediate groups ranging from middle class professionals to labour organizers and party officials – which in turn creates pressures for the

> development of representative institutions enabling the 'new social forces' to take part in decisions affecting them.[7]

To the extent that new social forces promote democratization from within, the quality of democracy can be expected to be relatively high, at least in arenas in which these social forces are prominent. The power to exert sufficient pressure for democratization to begin is likely to translate into continued power to influence policy agendas once a transition has taken place. Economic development constitutes the link between the emergence of this capability and the emergence of civil society – a more complex economy permits the capture and mobilization of economic resources by non-state actors. These resources may be used to force the state to concede terrain – public forums, free media – in which public political debate can take place.

The contribution of transnational forces to democratization is more problematic. A number of studies have found that countries reorienting their political systems primarily in response to external pressures, rather than emerging endogenous forces, whether economic or political, have had difficulty in making democratic procedures work in a manner that encourages both widespread participation and empowerment, and stability. Kohli describes these states as 'follower democracies', where local conditions favoured particularist, personalist and clientelist political relations, rather than the universalist, rationalist and rights-based relations of adopted Western models. Consequently, a 'central political tendency' in such democracies is towards 'the emergence of two track polities, with a democratic track in the sphere of society and politics, especially electoral politics, and a not-so-democratic track in the state sphere, especially in the areas of economic policy making'.[8]

This reflects the focus, in international democracy promotion, on international support for tangible aspects of democracy – primarily procedures such as elections, and organizations such as parliaments, courts and non-governmental organizations (NGOs). However, these procedures alone do not constitute substantive democracy. Benedict Anderson points out that procedures such as elections are not always empowering to ordinary citizens, but, rather, can narrow the range of opportunities for political participation and activism and the range of items open for political debate in a way that delegitimates political action aimed at a broader understanding of reform. He comments: 'the logic of electoralism is in the direction of domestication: distancing, punctuating, isolating'.[9]

Kohli's analysis suggests that in follower democracies, the emergence of public terrain that offers opportunities for the ordinary citizen to engage in the setting of political agendas may be limited – although elections occur, for example, they do not offer the poor sufficient scope to pressure an elected government into redistributing economic resources. The reservation of spheres of state activity, such as economic policy making, from the intrusions of democracy, suggest that while electors are offered an opportunity to participate in the making of certain choices, the scope of such choices is strictly limited and control of the electoral agenda is reserved for elites.[10] Participation and choice are thus highly regimented.

This analysis contrasts sharply with the optimism surrounding the prospects for international promotion of democracy evident in the early 1990s. Cambodia was one of the first targets of such policies – Cambodia's 1993 elections, organized and implemented by the United Nations Transitional Authority in Cambodia (UNTAC), was one early exemplary element of what UN Secretary General Boutros Boutros-Ghali, the previous year, had described as 'peace-building' – a concept which drew upon Kantian theories of international democratic peace, and which also posited a powerful link between political participation and domestic peace.[11] The extent to which international promotion of democracy was viewed as unproblematic in the euphoria of the immediate post-Cold War era is summed up in a comment made by US former National Security Advisor Theodore Sorensen, who wrote that US professional experts had an important role in international affairs in giving instruction on:

> how to build a truly free legislature, an independent judiciary, a restrained police authority, a system of responsible local governments and a civilian-controlled defence force ... In addition to free political institutions, free economic institutions must also be in place to make economic assistance meaningful. From agriculture to banking, to transportation and energy ... the need for technical and practical advice from the US and others is enormous in these nations, north and south, making their way to freedom.[12]

The mandate for the United Nations in Cambodia included efforts in a number of these areas.

Much of the literature discussing Cambodia's transition, particularly studies of the period of United Nations authority and its immediate aftermath, adopted this starting point. It regards the democratization of Cambodia – or any other state – as not intrinsically problematic, but as requiring a great deal of fine tuning of policy and tireless international political will in order to prevent the individual choices of key political actors from 'derailing' the process.

This approach largely analyses Cambodian democracy as a function of international intervention, and frames emerging problems in the Cambodian democratization process as a critique of interventionary policies. It offers a teleological view of democratization, as a path to a predefined set of procedures, with predictable policy outcomes, with the focus on the individual agency of powerful actors – bumbling intervenors or recalcitrant local 'partners' – as crucial for understanding the tendency of the Cambodian polity to stray from the path. This view has been promoted by Cambodian politician Sam Rainsy, who regularly decries international failures to intervene more intrusively into Cambodian politics through sanctions and other measures.[13]

A second, more pessimistic, approach, particularly prominent following the shocking military battle that took place in Phnom Penh in 1997, views the Cambodian context as unpromising for democracy, and considers that the initial wave of momentum towards democratic reform produced by the United Nations intervention has been absorbed by the bulwarks of Cambodian 'culture'. Cambodian culture is regarded as antagonistic to democracy, because innate tendencies towards hierarchy, deference and intolerance of difference preclude the Cambodian people from either seeking, or being able to sustain, meaningful participation in the peaceful debate and formulation of national policy agendas. Therefore, the prospects for international pro-democracy projects 'taking root' in the local context are considered to be slim.

The focus on political culture questions the universality of either an aspiration for or an understanding of democracy. This has informed a body of literature on Cambodia which seeks to locate the shortcomings of Cambodian democracy in a view of Cambodian culture as combining a predisposition toward hierarchy and deference with an extreme intolerance for dissent. Frequently, these cultural predispositions are regarded as having both permitted and been exacerbated by the trauma of war. They are held responsible for an allegedly typically Cambodian stance of 'passivity' in the face of abuse and tyranny, interspersed with outbreaks of sudden and extreme popular rage. Such cultural traits are viewed as inimical with democracy because of the inability to maintain an appropriate level of critical debate without prompting either a retreat into apathy and deference or a descent into violence.[14]

These different accounts of Cambodia's approach to democracy imply different views of how political change takes place. The optimistic account suggests that the creation of the appropriate democratic institutions, and their maintenance by sustained international intervention, can engender a process of local 'habituation' to internationally promoted procedures and processes. This is a process described in O'Donnell and Schmitter's account of transitions from authoritarian rule.[15]

O'Donnell and Schmitter regard the early stages of democratization as a chaotic multi-dimensional chess game. This multi-dimensionality, in their view, represents stochastic noise surrounding an underlying uni-directional trend, in which political behaviour becomes regularized and sanitized over time, and players become 'habituated' to their own game. The belief that democratization is a process whereby players become 'habituated' to endogenously evolving, but initially exogenously implanted 'rules' of democracy creates a clear opportunity for international democracy promotion.

Emphasis on habituation implies that the initial motivation for the erection of democratic institutions and procedures is less important than the embedding, over time, of these procedures in the ideas and strategies of political actors. The concept of habituation also suggests the possibility that Western understandings of democratic procedures can be implanted in non-Western societies, since the form of the procedures constructed is less important than their accretion of legitimacy through use over time. This understanding of how democratization works has been important in providing the theoretical underpinnings of international democracy promotion as primarily a procedural affair.

This view is contested by adherents to political culture approaches to democratization. Larry Diamond writes that, 'the development of a democratic culture cannot be taken for granted as a natural by-product of democratic practice or institutional design'.[16] Although procedures may be implanted, they may not work to produce the hoped-for public participation in policy making, because of cultural barriers to such an exercise of popular political power. Explanations of Cambodian politics rooted in accounts of Cambodian culture have generally been pessimistic regarding the prospects for any far-reaching change in Cambodian politics at all. Studies refer to the allegedly unusually resilient nature of Cambodian culture, which is frequently portrayed as having remained unchanged in its essential characteristics for hundreds of years.[17]

Surprisingly, given the importance of political economy as a theoretical approach in the study of democratization, few studies of the Cambodia case have investigated political economy as a key independent variable. This study investigates the question of whether the impoverishment of Cambodia, following years of warfare, has prevented the substantive participation of Cambodian citizens in control over policy agendas, despite a measure of success in the international promotion of procedural democracy. This approach has been rejected, particularly by international policy makers, because it contradicts interventionary rationales which seek to delegitimate 'economic determinism' as denying political aspiration or agency to the poor. For example, US Congressman Stephen Solarz, who has long been an influential figure in US–Cambodian relations, commented after reporting on the conduct of Cambodian elections in 1998:

> I'd like to add my personal reflection on the statement that what we witnessed in the course of the past few days was an extraordinarily significant commentary on the desire of the Cambodian people to play a meaningful role in the determination of their own destiny ... Personally I'd like to say that it should lay to rest that old and now discredited notion that it is only those who are the heirs to Western civilization or who enjoy a middle class way of life, who have any interest in the benefits of a genuine democracy.[18]

The undoubtedly reasonable conviction that ordinary Cambodians desired an alternative to the oppressive and destructive armies that had ravaged the land in the 1980s underlay a powerful presumption amongst international democracy promoters in Cambodia in the 1990s, that they were working on behalf of – even in partnership with – the Cambodian people, to use liberal democratic institutions in order to restrain the excesses of the state, the parties and their venal leaders. However there are important presuppositions inherent in this view which require close examination. 'Interest in the benefits of a genuine democracy' is not differentiated here from the ability of a particular society to generate, sustain and respect a democratic process sufficiently powerful to forge new agendas that may undermine minority vested interests. The conflation of a desire for democracy with the ability to put democracy into practice immediately – with international assistance – suggests that the process of political change itself is unproblematic, given the universal nature of democratic aspiration.

This study seeks to challenge the prognoses of these theses on the basis of an approach that is informed by political economy. The political economy approach emphasizes the importance of the economy in prompting or limiting changes in possibilities for individual action that differ from one citizen or group to another. In particular, it emphasizes the importance of access to material resources for the expansion of possibilities for substantive participation in the setting of political agendas. This study will argue that the prospects for international democracy promotion to propel new democracies beyond limited procedural forms remains in question more than ten years after the supposed victory of democracy at the end of the Cold War. This is largely because international democracy promotion tends to substitute the provision of international resources to non-state actors, for the democratizing activities of non-state actors engaged in wresting resources from the state. This can lead to the substitution of international political forums – meetings of bilateral donors, or UN committees – for the emergence of a local sphere in which participation in agenda-setting is possible. Consequently, despite the best efforts of international democracy promoters, the emergence of public terrain for debate and dissent internally is not an inevitable by-product of democratization, but remains dependent upon economic relations between state and society.

In making this argument, this study differs from both the habituation and the culturalist theses. The habituation thesis – particularly as this has been used as a basis for international democracy promotion – presumes that the construction of democratic procedures, and the provision of access to them, is unproblematic, even in conditions of extreme poverty and dearth of material infrastructure. The experience of Cambodia challenges this assumption. In Cambodia, the extreme lack of material infrastructure has, in fact, caused difficulties in providing access to internationally provided resources beyond the capital city of Phnom Penh. Consequently, the country remains fragmented into numerous small and isolated village political arenas, within which the ability of the state to monopolize inflowing economic resources represents the key determinant of power.

However, a political economy approach which focuses upon the material status of a group as limiting the ability to perceive or take advantage of different political opportunities does not rule out the influence of culture, social position, ideology or individual skill and creativity as factors in political action. It merely imposes limits upon the operations of these various factors. Consequently, it offers a more flexible tool for examining individual and group actions than either the habituation or culturalist approaches. The habituation approach presumes the ability of the democracy promoters to maintain the rules of engagement without themselves becoming political actors. The role of neutral referee, however, does not accurately characterize the nature of relations between international democracy promoters and local actors.

The culturalist approach, by contrast, replaces local political actors with automatons, whose actions are regularly put down to unthinking adherence to custom. Such an essentialist view of culture suggests that culture will co-opt and transform new political actors and processes into pre-existing collective dispositions, while remaining unchanged by this extra-cultural contact. The political economy approach offers an opportunity to understand the significant changes in relationships that have been prompted by Cambodia's transitions, even where claims of cultural continuity have been used to legitimate these.

Changes in the economy offer a window through which to conceptualize changes in the structure of opportunities for individual and collective action to place grassroots grievances onto elite political agendas. Used in this way, the political economy approach gives rise to a dynamic model of political action which acknowledges both individual agency and changing cultural norms, but also adequately accounts for limits to change. At the same time, in focusing on the economy as a source of both opportunities and constraints, the political economy approach avoids a teleological account of flawed democratization either as a greater or lesser readiness to be appropriately 'habituated', or as a reversion to cultural type. Rather, an analysis of the varying manipulation of new opportunities by political actors offers an examination of trajectories in the context of constraints, to be measured insofar as each expansion of opportunities for substantive participation in political agenda-setting observed prompts a greater or lesser likelihood of further similar expansion.

Economy, democracy promotion and political change: a conceptual framework for the study of democratization

Haggard and Kaufman reject a view of democratic transition as a class action dictated by the relationship to the means of production, but they 'assume that the economic-cum-social structure constitutes an essential point of departure for understanding politics'. Equally, they maintain, 'it is impossible to derive political or policy outcomes from economic cleavages and interests without consideration of the institutional context in which groups operate'.[19]

This account combines economic, social and institutional structures to arrive at an understanding of the ways in which elites mobilize resources to maintain legitimacy. Similarly, economic, social and institutional structures together form the terrain upon which non-state actors mount challenges to the legitimacy of the state. In mounting such challenges, non-state actors contest state-sponsored political understandings and agendas that attach notions of legitimacy to particular distributions of resources and norms of decision-making while ruling out alternative visions. Through staking out a position based upon the mobilization of resources of their own, non-state actors engage in discursive struggles with the state in which such political understandings and agendas are challenged.

Such participation in the framing of new democratic agendas is a crucial aspect of democratization. This represents the staking out of new terrain for discursive struggle amid economic, social and institutional structures; it thus represents the dynamic behind the transformation both of individual perceptions of the possibilities for political action and of the cultural frameworks of political understanding shared by the group in a context of democratization. The publicity implicit in the creation of such new terrain for political contestation further prompts the replacement of the secrecy and fragmentation of authoritarianism with the plurality and openness of democracy.

The connection between the emergence of new terrains for political participation and the efficacy of collective action to promote, preserve and deepen democracy implicitly underlies a variety of approaches to democratization. By making this connection explicit, the problems of promoting democratization in an environment of ongoing surveillance and material dearth can be more clearly delineated. In order to engage in collective struggle against state-sponsored agendas and limits to political action, the creation of autonomous terrain is necessary and requires capacities for organization, resource mobilization and discussion that are in some respect independent of state power. The widening of participation in discursive struggle thus relies on the widening of access to economic resources independent of the state.

Collective action on autonomous terrain permits the discursive contestation with the state that informs a dynamic view of political culture. Alberto Melucci (1989) describes this process as follows:

> When actors produce their collective action, they define both themselves and their environment (other actors, available resources, opportunities and obstacles). Such definitions are not linear but are produced by interaction, negotiation and conflict.[20]

Economic resources form a part of the environment that is 'negotiated' by groups seeking to promote particular social projects or identities in contention with others. Melucci states that

> the propensity of individuals and sub-groups to involve themselves in collective action always depends upon their differential access to resources, such as information, access to networks and professional or communicative skills, which enable them to participate in the process of identity-building.[21]

This view of political change avoids the determinism of Marxist approaches to political economy, offering due weight to individual agency, while at the same time acknowledging the importance of the material sphere in providing the material basis for collective resistance. In the context of international intervention, political change thus takes two forms – the infusion of resources that can assist in the construction of autonomous terrain from which to challenge the state and the infusion of international discourses into locally contested frameworks of meaning. These infusions take place via a process of 'borrowings and refusals' which accumulate to form a 'trajectory'.[22] Such a trajectory emerges as a function of individual creativity and skill in co-opting and manipulating international ideas in the context of a broader struggle over the nature of new political terrain.

Such manipulation has been regarded as a malevolent force in the politics of international intervention. For example, James Mayall comments that complex UN intervention has frequently resulted in 'the manipulation of the UN by undemocratic forces in the countries where it operates'. Mayall regards 'unscrupulous politicians' as the chief suspects in this manipulation.[23] However, this normative understanding of manipulation rests upon two doubtful presuppositions. Firstly, it fails to note that manipulations of UN mandates are as often conducted by idealists in pursuit of ideals as by unscrupulous politicians in pursuit of power. Such idealists include voters and NGO activists, as well as pro-democracy leaders and even UN staff themselves. The ideals they pursue include democracy along with other moral goods such as peace, justice and prosperity. Secondly, it suggests that the implementation of a UN mandate *without* local input in the day-to-day interpretation of the mandate could possibly be democratic – a doubtful proposition if democracy is viewed broadly as a process of empowerment and participation, rather than narrowly as the seamless implementation of pre-defined procedures.

This study, by contrast, views the response of local actors of all ideological persuasion to international intervention as a process of reorientation, with a view to the co-optation and manipulation of newly available international resources, in pursuit of a diversity of ends, both scrupulous and unscrupulous. It views this process as both inevitable, productive and empowering. It is pro-democratic, insofar as the net effect, however marginal, of all the various manipulations that occur is a broadening of opportunities for political engagement in agenda-setting by the full range of political actors, particularly the poor. Thus, while international intervention to promote political processes of democracy is usually instrumental and influential in altering the direction of intervened polities, finally the process of democratization is endogenously defined through a variety of means, both violent and non-violent, and empowered by the creative use of a mix of local and international resources.

The state

In the case of Cambodia, analysis of collective action may also be applied to the analysis of the state itself. Following Sorpong Peou, this study views the Cambodian postcolonial state as weak in terms of its ability to maintain the allegiances of its employees, to maintain its coherence and project its power vis-à-vis society. In its current form, the state emerged only recently as a hastily constructed edifice of the incoming Vietnamese-backed People's Republic of Kampuchea regime of the 1980s, following the overthrow of the destructive Democratic Kampuchea. Built from the ground up in the 1980s, the new state emerged, intertwined with a much smaller political party, the Kampuchean People's Revolutionary Party, later renamed the Cambodian People's Party, and supervised by foreign advisors from Vietnam as a result of strategies of more or less forced co-optation at a time when Cambodian society lay in ruins following the disastrous policies of the DK era.

The challenges facing the state in recruiting members after much of the pre-existing elite had been killed, sustaining their allegiances in a context of war and material dearth, and promoting their ideological adherence to party tenets at a time when communism had been comprehensively discredited in Cambodia, constituted an ambitious exercise in collective mobilization and organization. The weakness of the state that emerged from these endeavours is important in understanding the policies of Cambodia's leaders in the 1990s, for whom state formation remains a key goal, in the context of continued insurgency, until 1998, and perception of threat from Cambodia's more powerful neighbours, Thailand and Vietnam. These factors have significantly affected the state's response to international pressures to democratize, and its response to collective action within society.

This study suggests that Cambodia's transition in the 1990s has been based upon a transformation in the structure of economic incentives and opportunities, which has had profound implications for the organization of state power. The emergence of an unregulated free market at the end of the 1980s prompted the emergence of a decentralized and entrepreneurial state, which uses coercion to retain a competitive edge over civilian entrepreneurs. At the same time, international intervention has promoted new forms of political activity, in the realm of the state, political society and 'civil society'. Internationally promoted constitutional structures, a multi-party sphere and a flourishing sector of non-governmental organizations have interacted with the power structures of the transforming state in pursuit of internationally sponsored goals, such as human rights and democracy.

In the struggle to promote their contending conceptions of the future of Cambodia, both state and non-state actors have competed to monopolize political terrain, constructed from opportunistic use of economic and cultural resources, and social and political institutions. In doing so, they have been forced to adapt themselves to the contours of the terrain they construct, while at the same time coping with its highly fragmented and unstable nature. A particular concern of actors attempting to promote liberal democracy has been the constitution of a public sphere in which non-state agents can confront, debate and challenge state policies, in the security of civil liberties and in the knowledge that the state is forced to respond. However, this has proved to be a tall order given the skewed distribution of international resources, which have by and large failed to significantly disrupt power relations in rural Cambodia, and the reluctance of local non-state actors to engage directly with the state in a contest over resources.

By contrast, the state, which has attempted to shore up its own cohesion through the development of exploitative networks of entrepreneurial activity, has sought to resist the constitution of such public terrain, and to maintain personal and hierarchical relationships with non-state actors. It has supported this effort with an appeal to particular conceptions of a traditional 'Khmer culture'. Yet this distinction between a universalist non-state sector and a particularist state is blurred. International sponsorship of democratic processes has entailed that the state has also developed a public face. Meanwhile, the non-state sector includes actors who have been co-opted into state networks of power and privilege. Even those non-state actors who specifically pursue the goal of democracy have found it expedient to focus on private networking in areas where the economic resources to support autonomous public action were lacking. In flowing across both public and private terrains of power, both state and non-state actors have oscillated between a modernizing concern for the constitution of a national politics, and the defence of a more particularistic conception of political relations, in pursuit of resources to bolster their position.

Crucially, for the expansion of democracy beyond periodic electoral exercises characterized by an impoverished level of political debate and towards a more substantive and participatory set of state-society relations on an everyday level, the absolute level of poverty in rural areas has rendered resistance to state monopolization of political control in rural political arenas extremely difficult. Neither central government, reformist political parties, pro-democracy NGOs, nor international intervenors have been able to break this monopoly, in large part because the dearth of resources in the rural economy renders monopolization of them relatively easy, and because of the high level of militarization in Cambodia, which renders confrontation of the state, particularly in rural areas, dangerous and difficult. In the cities, by contrast, such terrain has developed, with significant international input, and is being used to support the emergence of a healthy, diverse and spontaneous grassroots mobilization in pursuit of democratic accountability.

In deploying this model, this study takes a significantly different starting point from that of much of the recent literature on Cambodia's transition. Firstly, the model of state–society relations often employed in the context of Cambodia, in which society is portrayed as lacking in any form of resistance, is explicitly rejected. Both habituation and political culture theses are frequently deployed to explain the internal political struggles of elites and their success and failure in forging the kind of intra-elite pact that can support the institutionalization of democratic processes. This view of the state has been particularly powerful in the context of the literature on Cambodia, arguably for three reasons: firstly, because of discourses of Cambodian political and cultural 'passivity' that emerged from the colonial era; secondly, because of the concern to exempt ordinary Cambodians for responsibility for the disastrous Democratic Kampuchea era; and, thirdly, because of the rapidity with which certain groups in the UNTAC era and after occupied Western-sponsored terrain for political activism. It is argued that government policy since 1989 has rendered open resistance very difficult in rural Cambodia in the 1990s. However, these assumptions fail to acknowledge both the significant resistance to state formation that occurred in rural Cambodia in the 1980s, and the imaginative uses to which public terrain has been put by urban social movements in Cambodia in the 1990s.

Furthermore, in making these arguments, this study will challenge the orthodox view that democracy has been nipped in the bud in Cambodia. Many commentators have suggested that UNTAC's brand of democracy was a Western construct, bound to undergo radical changes in the Cambodian context. However, many commentators have also underestimated the extent to which a new form of modern, hybridized resistance has emerged from the efforts of Cambodians to turn the resources, discourses and opportunities of intervention to their own advantage. These efforts have not been unproblematic and, where they have confronted certain state-making trajectories, they have been assaulted. But nevertheless a marked change in the state–society relationship has emerged which, while it does not conform to the Western parliamentary tradition, continues to develop along fairly radical lines. It represents neither habituation to Western models nor submission to cultural imperatives, but the manipulation of both, by contending political actors. Creativity in drawing upon both newly available international resources and new interpretations of local traditions has altered the repertoire of Cambodian resistance, to the advantage of some groups and the disadvantage of others.

These concerns dictate that the chapters of this study are structured according to terrains of action, rather than around a chronology of events. Chapter 2 begins with an examination of the development of the state in Cambodia, in particular since the mid-1980s. It suggests that, perceiving the essential problem to be the weakness of state cohesion, the Cambodian government in the late 1980s used the transition from command economy to free market as a means to consolidate allegiances among state employees. In doing so, the state co-opted and transformed patron–client relations portrayed as 'traditional' in an attempt to claim customary legitimacy for newly exploitative practices.

The consequence of this for the emerging nature of the state and for state–society relations through the 1990s is investigated in Chapter 3. It is argued that, by decentralizing economic policy, the central government made a virtue of necessity in recognizing the private production that had been ongoing in the villages with the collusion of local authorities since the early 1980s. Profiteering from this production was no longer in breach of central government policy – indeed, the central government acted to protect operations by entrepreneurial local authorities and military units, even where these entailed the use of violence and breach of the law.

At the same time, the opening of the economy of international investment and aid permitted a new infusion of economic resources which was channeled through the state apparatus, enriching and empowering local political and military authorities. These changes significantly strengthened ties of allegiance and loyalty between central government and local civil and military authorities. The abandonment of attempts at collectivization removed the rudimentary safety net available to the rural poor in the 1980s, rendering the poorest families both vulnerable to exploitation and dependent upon the goodwill of local authorities. The net effect was heightened insecurity in rural areas, increased ability by local power holders to dominate through monopolization of resources, and decreased capacities for local level resistance beyond that of flight.

At the same time, however, international intervention in the shape of the United Nations Transitional Authority in Cambodia awarded every Cambodian a vote in general elections that could, in theory, be used to oust abusive power holders. Chapter 4 examines the ways in which the party which oversaw the state reforms described – the Cambodian People's Party – has attempted to win electoral legitimacy for economic reforms that intensified exploitation of the farmer by the state and marginalized the poor. The CPP has been transformed since the 1980s into a mass organization that presents itself as based upon traditional relations of patronage and gift exchange, but which is more accurately viewed as a mass mechanism for surveillance and mobilization. The CPP today has departed significantly from the semblance of socialist ideology propagated by its forerunner, the Kampuchean People's Revolutionary Party (KPRP) of the 1980s, emphasizing personal charisma and benevolence in political campaigning, and combining these with a nationwide surveillance apparatus, invoked at election time, which seeks to co-opt the ordinary citizen who has been excluded from economic gains during Cambodia's boom years.

This claim is examined with particular reference to rural Cambodia, where this strategy has been highly successful in delivering votes during national and local elections in the 1990s. In particular, it is argued that the ways in which state and party have operated in the 1990s are possible primarily because the economy of rural Cambodia remains at a level of precarious subsistence. Inclusion in networks of protection and donation are essential for impoverished families following the demise of collectivization. Arguably, this economic imperative has led to a tendency towards political conformity in rural villages, at least in public. The provision of a new covert form of resistance, in the form of the vote, prompts reverberations in Cambodian elite politics, but has not as yet significantly altered the terms of state–society relations in the village.

After delineating the mechanisms of power that have emerged to preserve the dominance of the CPP over the state apparatus and rural politics, the study then moves on to examine spheres of politics in Cambodia in the 1990s in which this dominance has been contested. Chapter 5 investigates the idea of an 'international community' as a forum in which Cambodian politics has been conducted in the 1990s, and the ways in which both the CPP and its domestic rivals have gained access to this sphere of political activity and exploited its resources. The limits to the ability of international intervention to reach into rural villages to disrupt the monopoly of resources held by local authorities are posited as a significant limit to the efficacy of any international effort to promote democracy.

Chapters 6 and 7 investigate this further with respect to the internationally promoted and supported spheres of Cambodian political and civil society, both of which, it is argued, have expanded at the expense of the state-dominated sphere only in urban areas, where economic power is more diffuse, and where there is greater overlap between domestic and international political activity. In rural areas, attempts to create a new public and institutionalized form of politics have been largely thwarted, in large part due to the dearth of material resources in rural Cambodia for independent political action.

Finally Chapter 8 contrasts the situation of rural Cambodia with the political economy of the city of Phnom Penh, examining the emergence of a variety of grassroots urban protest movements in the late 1990s. It is argued that these protest movements, which have emerged from popular concerns, reflect the major example of attempts at popular participation in political agenda-setting, which can imbue Cambodia's 'follower democracy' with a significant degree of democratic substance. Although benefiting from the political terrain established in Phnom Penh by the activities of political parties, non-governmental organizations and the 'international community', these protest movements have stepped onto this terrain in order to pursue agendas of their own, emerging from personal experience and interest. The democratic significance of these movements in manipulating and co-opting international and local resources and using them to demonstrate a new form of autonomous and public grassroots political participation in Cambodia is profound.

2 Economy and state–society relations

Economic and political transitions

Georg Sørensen writes that 'in weak states, political power is also economic power'.[1] The state dominates through its ability to monopolize, distribute and extract economic resources. This contention goes to the heart of the problems of state formation, particularly in a context of formalized popular sanctions over the state by means of periodic national elections.

The political economy approach to democratization suggests that democratization is spurred by a process of economic development, in which organized social groups emerge with wealth held independently of the state, and that the possession of this wealth both alters the structure of opportunities for mobilizing to contest state action, alters the ideational resources that permit the imaging of such a contest and helps to determine the strategies selected. In a situation of severe underdevelopment and exogenously sponsored democratization, the relationship between economic production and the political power of social forces is quite different. Where economic production occurs mainly for subsistence, the unit of production is the family, which operates largely autonomously, and thus is relatively immune to state action short of coercion, but which lacks the surplus to fund its own political activities. In this circumstance, both the ability of the state to extract resources for the consolidation of power and the ability of non-state actors to mobilize as a collective to promote political goals is significantly constrained, and state–society attachments, rather than representing thick bonds of mutual interdependence, rest upon rather slender threads.

State–society relations in such a context are highly dependent upon the ability of power-holders to find alternative means of consolidating both partisan support and broader notions of citizenship among farmers, and upon the ability of farmers to find means of resisting and regulating state intervention. Across Asia, great attention has been paid to the practices of patron-clientism, defined by James Scott as

> a special case of dyadic ties involving a largely instrumental friendship in which an individual of higher socio-economic status (patron) uses his

> own influence and resources to provide protection and/or benefits for a person of lower status (client) who, for his part, reciprocates by offering general support and assistance, including personal service, to the patron.[2]

These ties linked the elite to the labourer in pre-modern times, and have transformed in conditions of modernization and electoral democracy into practices of corruption, rent-seeking and vote-buying, on the part of elites, and diffuse processes of negotiation, co-optation, passive resistance and periodic rebellion on the part of the peasantry.[3]

These trends have been present in Cambodia since independence, albeit in forms that have been heavily influenced by ongoing foreign intervention and the contingent opportunities for political action that this has offered. The ability of the state, in turn, to implement managed programmes of political and economic change have been severely constrained by the thin nature of state–society relations, and the opportunities for resistance awarded by external intervention. In investigating this proposition, the period of the 1980s and 1990s are particularly significant in offering an insight into the various ways in which the state has attempted to mobilize for state-making, in a context in which countervailing pressures have been strong. This insight is crucial for understanding Cambodia's current political trajectory and, in particular, the obstacles problematizing attempts to promote participatory democracy as a new basis for state–society engagement.

The 1980s and 1990s saw a transition taking place in the Cambodian economy in which failed attempts at state-sponsored socialist transformation were replaced by an embrace of the free market. The move to the free market took place only four years prior to the first milestones of political change in the form of the UNTAC election and the promulgation of the new constitution. Significantly, for Western writings of Cambodia's history, the process of economic change began before the arrival of the UN and its cohorts of foreign workers, at a time when access to the Cambodian countryside was much more restricted and when sources of information were relatively limited. The rapid process of political change following the economic reforms has tended to obscure the impact of the reforms themselves. Because of this, Cambodia's current economic practices, and state engagement with them, have largely been viewed in the literature as a function of the country's political trajectory, rather than as propelling it.

However, the 1989 reforms were crucial in transforming the field of opportunities for action available to the Cambodian state, and to the population for influencing and resisting state action, thus determining the trajectory of political reforms. The economic liberalization that took place within Cambodia swiftly came to be viewed by power-holders as offering a matrix of resources that could shore up exclusionary loyalties within the weak state apparatus, and reducing the field of action for resistance in rural villages, as a means to strengthen the state militarily and politically. In this, the economy of the 1990s differed sharply from the economy of the 1980s, which had offered few such opportunities. However, this view of economic reform was a view sharply at odds with the agenda of international intervenors, who saw a decrease in the exclusionary politicization of the state apparatus, and broader political participation, including by former insurgents, as the prerequisites for peace and stability in Cambodia.

State-building in the 1980s

Sorpong Peou is one of the few analysts writing on Cambodia to have explicitly connected the goal of state formation with the contingencies of elite politics. For Peou, Cambodian politics is marked by continual attempts by a variety of regimes to achieve 'hegemony' based upon theories of modernization. Peou also points out that the support of Cambodian society is necessary to this project.[4] Given this starting point, the changes that took place in the Cambodian economy are best viewed, not as a means to a goal, as implicit in terms such as 'development' and 'rehabilitation', but as a determining strand in the ongoing negotiation of political power in Cambodia.

The present Cambodian state apparatus was formed in the wake of the destruction of the DK era by incoming Vietnamese advisors and the National Front for the Salvation of Kampuchea. That destruction has been graphically described by many observers. Eva Mysliwiec, an American aid worker present in Cambodia in the 1980s, offered the following characterization:

> Of 450 doctors before 1975, only 45 remained in the country in 1979. The rest had been murdered or had escaped abroad. Of the 20,000 teachers in the early 1970s, only 7,000 remained. Very few trained administrators survived, so those who found jobs in the Heng Samrin government were generally very young and inexperienced and often rejected by their friends as 'working for the Vietnamese'. The fishing industry was hampered by the lack of boats and nets. Few archives and books were left so that at first books, school, and training curricula had to be restructured from memory. Only a handful of lawyers were left in the country to write a new constitution and rebuild an entire judicial system. The country, by 1979, had no currency, no markets, no financial institutions and virtually no industry. There was no public transport system; no trains ran and the roads were damaged and unrepaired. There was no postal system, no telephones and virtually no electricity, clean water, sanitation or education.[5]

Taking control of this situation was the task of the National Front for the Salvation of Kampuchea (NFSK), and its Vietnamese backers. Sorpong Peou argues that while the People's Republic of Kampuchea (PRK), which was set up by the NFSK in the 1980s, was perhaps less vulnerable than some of its detractors have suggested, it was nevertheless a 'weak state'. He bases this evaluation on a number of grounds. Firstly, the new leadership did not have the capacity to impose a low level of collectivization effectively. Secondly, the population distrusted both the Vietnamese and communist orientation of the new regime. Thirdly, membership of the party was small, less than 30,000 in 1991. Peou suggests that this reflects not only the party's distrust of the people, but the people's distrust of the party. Fourthly, the party, while highly militarized, was unable to score decisive victories against the resistance forces.[6]

In the following discussion, these problems are examined in detail with particular regard to identifying key questions which have continued to pose problems for the Cambodian state into the 1990s. The ability of the state to recruit officials, control the economy, and to deal with insurgency speak to the core aspects of state formation. The limits to state abilities, and the force of a diffuse resistance to state policies, are examined. The ways in which the transformation of the economy from 1989 then contributed to a strengthening of the hand of the state at the expense of the rural villager is discussed. It will be argued that it was the economic reforms of 1989 which provided the key to the strengthening of the state's power to mobilize and administer, that has continued through the 1990s.

Recruitment of state officials

The National Front for the Salvation of Kampuchea, which putatively 'led' the Vietnamese invasion of 1979 that overthrew the DK regime, was a small-scale operation. Nicolas Regaud suggests that the conference of 12 December 1978 that created the Front comprised 200 members, while in 1980 the new Kampuchean People's Revolutionary Party numbered no more than 800. In 1981, according to Regaud, a congress of the Central Committee of the party comprised 19 permanent members. These included 11 veterans of the *Khmer Issarak* communist army that had fought in the independence struggles in the early 1950s, and who had spent the intervening years in Vietnam. They also included 7 former cadres of the ousted Democratic Kampuchea regime. Regaud comments that this extensive use of former DK cadres was unsurprising given the extreme lack of competent officials in Cambodia at the time.[7]

Nayan Chanda offers a similar characterization of the incoming regime, describing it as 'hastily organized' and only 'nominally' in control. He argues,

> the party's two hundred members and the inexperienced bunch of Khmer exiles and defectors that formed the Revolutionary Council were not up to the job of reviving a nation and restoring a modicum of normalcy to a population emerging from a nightmare. Most important,

> they could not hope to defend the new regime against armed opposition from the Khmer Rouge.[8]

This incoming government, with the significant input of Vietnamese 'advisors', faced the task of building almost from scratch a state capable of governing the country in the context of, firstly, famine, and later, war, as the remnants of the DK regime regrouped on the border with Thailand and began to attract international support from Thailand, China and, indirectly, the West. The first task was to recruit state officials to staff the newly forming state structures.

State employees of the 1990s recalled how they were first recruited to their positions in the aftermath of the Vietnamese invasion. One judge, appointed in the early 1980s, recalled that 'after the revolution there were not enough people to serve, so [the incoming regime] just appointed people with a general education'. A Kampot court official, asked in 1996 how he had felt about his appointment to the judiciary, commented, 'In the old days you just agreed with the appointment. You had no choice'.[9] A former teacher recruited as a journalist to serve on the Salvation Front's newspaper described the circumstances of his new appointment, and his less-than-enthusiastic reaction:

> After the liberation and occupation, many staff and officials had been killed. There was a shortage of officials. I came back from Battambang in July and I wanted to join the Ministry of Education. But the Vietnamese said I must study politics ... I had to study the history of the friendship between the Communist parties in Indochina. I didn't agree, but I just kept quiet, voiced no opinion. Then I was asked to write out my CV, and told I could work on the newspaper. I couldn't refuse ... I didn't want to work for the newspaper, because it was political work and I wanted to go back into technical work. But they put pressure on me. They said, 'if you want to be a journalist, you have to die with your journalism'. And it was mistranslated – I thought it was a threat and I was scared. Because if you lose the trust of the Vietnamese expert, then it is a risk for you.[10]

A similar story is told in the memoir of Bunheang Ung, who worked as a cartoonist in the Ministry of Information and Propaganda after 1979. On returning to Phnom Penh, and being allocated a job in the Ministry, Bun was required to attend political seminars focusing on Vietnam–Cambodia relations and the atrocities of the Pol Pot regime. His memoir states:

> Bun was not happy with the new constraints under which he worked. He disliked the ubiquitous presence of the Vietnamese. In every ministry and office, ultimate authority rested with the Vietnamese 'experts' attached to it. Life was still very hard and food supplies still meagre.

> Public servants received a monthly ration of 13 kilograms of rice and maize per person. A black market had sprung up and bribery was commonplace. To get a job working in a government-run factory, a man had to give the manager a third of a damlung of gold. Payment was demanded to pass government checkpoints, to obtain interviews, to process documents. Official morality was lax'.[11]

These accounts reflect the problems faced by the new regime in building new state organs in 1979. The new regime lacked pools of educated supporters who could be appointed willingly to fill official posts in the new state. Brief re-education programmes were implemented, and individuals with education were coerced into new tasks, whether or not they had experience or a political commitment to the new regime. Many complied out of fear of the Vietnamese who at that time 'took all power into their own hands'.[12]

Political re-education programmes notwithstanding, the new regime must have been aware of the fragile technical and ideological basis upon which they were rebuilding. While Vickery holds that the Vietnamese invasion was welcomed by exhausted farmers in 1979, and that subsequently the impact of the Vietnamese presence on the Khmer population declined rapidly, there remained a reluctance to 'work for the Vietnamese', as Mysliwiec suggests. Vickery's own interviews with educated individuals who fled to the border in the early 1980s, rather than serve the new regime, bear out this suggestion. Ideological, as well as nationalist, sentiments also intruded. Mysliwiec comments:

> While compulsory political education at all levels attempts to win civil servants over to the current political system, one can detect fear and cynicism among intellectuals over what socialism can do for Kampuchea.[13]

In the 1980s, external analysts, both sympathetic and hostile to the new regime, agreed broadly on three points: that there existed a perception within Cambodia that Vietnamese dominance was widespread and oppressive; that ideological allegiance to Vietnamese-style communism among state employees and the wider population alike was extremely weak; and that coercion played a central role in the building of the new state apparatus. Furthermore, the administrative capacities and cohesion of the newly formed state, in a context of severe material dearth, was called into question. State officials in the provinces enjoyed 'considerable autonomy, including financial autonomy (within budgets received from the centre). This autonomy extends to control over a number of industrial enterprises, as well as the actual implementation of national-level priorities and programmes'.[14] Such autonomy reduced the information available to central planners whose 'capacity ... to compile accurate statistics, or to verify the statistical claims of local authorities, [was] very low'.[15] Attempts to rectify the situation by promoting greater integration of central and provincial staff reportedly failed:

> Efforts by PRK ministries to improve communications with local officials by means of sending civil servants out to rural areas for three months look like having the undesired effect of demoralizing the central functionaries.[16]

Such analyses suggest strongly the centrifugal forces at work in Cambodian politics in the 1980s in which the local authorities on the ground were significantly empowered through their close proximity to resources, while the central authorities, distanced by paucity of infrastructure and lack of enthusiastic personnel, operated blindly.

While limits to the enthusiasm of Cambodian civil servants in the 1980s were thus widely reported, there were nevertheless economic incentives favouring employment with the state at this time. During the early 1980s, state salaries ranged from 100 riel/month for low-ranking civil servants (approx. $15 at 1983 exchange rates) to 500 riel/month for high state officials. While this represented rather a poor level of cash remuneration, it was supplemented by rations of subsidized rice, cloth sugar, cigarettes, detergent and soap, petrol and paraffin.[17] These supplies could not be extracted from the population, but were flown in from supportive countries in the Eastern Bloc. The state also offered civil servants cheap rates for electricity and allocated them housing and land within the city of Phnom Penh. Curtis suggests that:

> Each family attempted to have one member work for the State so as to receive the subsidized goods (some of which were subsequently sold on the free market for cash) with other family members involved in private enterprise including trading activities.[18]

From 1987, in response to difficulties in mobilizing sufficient rice supplies to feed the urban population, the Party encouraged state employees to engage in secondary economic activities such as growing vegetables at home, raising animals and making handicrafts. Small-scale agricultural production could also be undertaken on land allocated by the state in the city, including public land along the top of Phnom Penh's dykes, by the sides of railway lines and in former parks. These perquisites of state attachment were significant in a context where surpluses could be traded on a black market tolerated by the state. However, throughout the 1980s, the state remained heavily dependent upon support from CMEA countries to provide goods for state employees. As the position of the Eastern Bloc declined towards the end of the decade, worsening exchange rates, rocketing inflation and severe shortages of goods began to threaten the slender attachments developed between the state and its employees.

Beyond the state apparatus itself, one effort to increase the legitimacy of the new regime was made through the creation of mass organizations, which Regaud describes as a 'bridge' between state and population. The three major mass organizations, the Association of Kampuchean Trade Unions, the Women's Association and the Youth Association, enjoyed a higher level of membership than the party, numbering 200,000, 900,000 and 40,000 members respectively. Mysliwiec suggests that these organizations were significant in promoting modernizing programmes:

> at first politically oriented and motivated, [they] played a significant role in civic, health and sanitation education, in literacy campaigns, vaccination campaigns, and in assisting the families of soldiers lost in battle.[19]

However, given the enormous tasks confronting the incoming regime, the lack of material resources to assist in these endeavours, the contribution of these organizations was constrained, and the modernizing capacity of the state, consequently, was limited also. The mass organizations were the most important structures of the Solidarity Front for the Reconstruction and Defence of the Kampuchean Motherland which replaced the National Front for the Salvation of Kampuchea formed during the invasion. The official role of this organization was to 'mobilize the entire people to implement the political tasks of the party and the state'. In 1986 it contained around 120,000 members. Regaud comments, 'like the communist party itself, it appears that it remained numerically very feeble'.[20]

That the state remained feeble also emerges from the picture of policy failures in crucial areas offered by analysts of Cambodia in the 1980s. The extent of these policy failures has been subject to much less emphasis by recent commentators, who have tended to view the Cambodian population as oppressed by a powerful and overbearing state. Frequently, the resistance of the Cambodian population to a range of ideological projects of the 1980s is erased from contemporary Western accounts of Cambodia's political development. David Roberts, for example, wrote in 2001 that the PRK ruled 'in a political vacuum' during the 1980s.[21] While there were few organized social forces that openly opposed the constitution or policy making of the 1980s state or party from within the territory under Phnom Penh's control, nevertheless contemporaneous reports suggest that the PRK faced considerable, if diffuse, resistance, sufficient to derail economic policies and to perpetuate state vulnerability to external attack.

State control of economic resources

Aside from the ideological fragility of the new party–state apparatus, the technical capacity of this state to project power across the Cambodian heartland in a context of instability, economic disaster and war was also limited. In the early years of the regime, in particular, society itself was in chaos. David Chandler suggests that 'over the [first] year or so, the Vietnamese and the PRK bureaucracy were cautious about imposing stringent political and economic controls', in an environment where thousands were on the move. With the lifting of the draconian constraints of the Democratic Kampuchea period, people struggled to return to former homes, to track down missing family members, to exploit the new situation for economic gain, or simply to flee the country altogether. With regard to this last goal, Chandler reports that famine conditions emerging following the neglect of the harvest constituted a 'push' factor during the years 1979 and 1980, and were exacerbated by the 'pull' factor of relief agencies along the Thai–Cambodian border providing food and, after 1980, the opportunity (for some) to be resettled abroad.[22]

The response of society to the events of the late 1970s emerges from this account, not as a passive and traumatized awaiting of deliverance from abroad, but an active effort to relocate surviving family members, and to find a new place to live where basic needs could be met most effectively. Cambodians today recall the horror of journeys to the Thai border and back along heavily-mined mountain roads, during which many died from exhaustion or explosions. These journeys were undertaken in pursuit of economic and personal security in a context in which agricultural practices had been severely ruptured, resulting in famine, and in which the incoming Vietnamese army were an unknown quantity. For the incoming regime, taking control over this situation in a context where few material or human resources were available was extremely difficult.

Michael Vickery, who visited the north-west border in 1980 and Phnom Penh in 1981, described the situation as characterized by 'laissez-faire market and general social indiscipline' and viewed the policy of tolerance for this on the part of the new regime as 'emergency first aid for a basket case'.[23] Serge Thion similarly commented in a contemporaneous account,

> we must note another side to the Pol Pot legacy. Because of the oppressive character of that regime, the imposition of even minimal discipline and organization is more difficult than before. Any kind of regulations may be interpreted as a return to Pol Potism ... Since the present government has been installed and maintained with Vietnamese support, any unpopular measure it takes may be interpreted as Vietnamese domination; and it is likely that the extreme freedom which has been allowed people in their choice of work (or non-work) and place of residence has been to gain popular support and avoid any hint of Vietnamese interference in everyday life.[24]

Furthermore, Thion noted, the presence of an alternative for Cambodians on the Thai border made it difficult for the regime to 'take some of the organizational measures which are necessary' including the imposition of tax.[25] PRK attempts at mobilizing revenues from the farming population, including purchases of agricultural output as well as taxes in cash and kind, were documented by the Economist Intelligence Unit (EIU) throughout the 1980s and little success was noted. Partly, this is because food security in rural Cambodia was poor throughout the period from 1979 to 1987. From 1979–81, the dislocations attendant upon the collapse of the DK agricultural collectives engendered massive food shortages, only ameliorated by a UN sponsored emergency relief operation costing $213 million. While harvests improved in 1982, poor weather conditions limited production in 1983 and 1985.

However, weather conditions exacerbated two pre-existing problems – poor organization on the part of the state and resistance on the part of the farming sector to state interference and policies of extraction. It was reported in 1984 that the government procurement targets for rice and other agricultural products were 'not met' and that, because local collective production teams were 'failing to retain collective control over some local produce, local redistribution of food on the basis of need or in payment for state inputs or local services has broken down'. Agricultural taxes were introduced 'to gain greater control over available surpluses', but the difficulty of collecting such taxes led to an abandonment of the scheme in 1985.[26] Instead, in November 1984, the Party held an emergency national cadres conference to address the rice crisis, at which it was decided to form a committee to supervise increased training of managers of local production teams *(krom samaki)*. This was intended to 'promote political, ideological and organizational stability' within the communes, as well as improving deliveries of produce to the state.[27] However, in 1985, only 33 per cent of the target for domestic rice purchases was achieved,[28] and external economic analysts noted that 'while this year's rice shortage is much larger than last year's, peasants have produced much larger stocks of secondary, uncontrolled food crops than last year, an indication of where family labour has been silently invested'.[29]

The Five Year Plan for 1986–90, formulated in 1985, called for a consolidation in state control of farm products. It was proposed that the relationship between the state and the farming community should be consolidated by means of the slogan, 'selling rice to the state is a patriotic act and selling goods to the peasants is a manifestation of the state's responsibility toward the people'.[30] Stirring sentiments notwithstanding, the procurement crisis continued in 1986, when the Phnom Penh municipality managed to purchase only 24 per cent of its paddy requirement from the rural sector. This was seen as linked to poor management of the state economy and insecurities as the civil war intensified, as well as farmers' complaints that procurement prices were too low, and there were few goods in state-run stores available to buy with the cash.[31]

The situation eased in 1987, but only after increases in April 1986 in government procurement prices of more than 50 per cent for rice, and more for other goods. In all, farmers' recalcitrance forced the price of state rice purchases up from 1 riel per kilogram in 1980 to 2.5 riel per kilogram in 1986, and up to 7 riel per kilogram in 1989.[32] In 1989, the EIU attributed the consistent failure in state procurement and taxation of agricultural produce to 'aristocratic and paternalist expectations about the state'.[33] The practice of state rice purchase was finally ended in 1992. New taxes on land were introduced in 1989, but these were abandoned again in 1992, and by 1998 all the major Cambodian political parties included a commitment to refrain from taxing farmers in their election manifestos.

Just as the state found it difficult to exercise control over farming products, it also faced problems in controlling the mode of production. Viviane Frings comments that attempts to re-collectivize the economy in Cambodia took place between 1982 and 1987, particularly through the introduction of *krom samaki*, or solidarity units. These represented a limited form of political, administrative and economic collectivization, significantly looser than those imposed by the DK regime, but reflecting the emphasis upon socialist ideology of the KPRP. Frings suggests that the importance of the *krom samaki* to the KPRP was not only ideological but also administrative. She comments

> The 'solidarity groups' were not only aimed at organizing the people in order to increase production, but also at indoctrinating them to serve the political objectives of the Government and to fight its enemies.[34]

However, the ability to implement collectivization was severely constrained. While the form of the *krom samaki* was projected across Cambodia's agricultural sector in the 1980s, there was a significant loosening over time of the extent to which collective activity actually went on within them.

Krom samaki were divided into three categories. Level one groups were fully collectivized. No private property was permitted and distribution of food and other goods was according to work capacity. According to World Bank estimates, approximately one-third of all *krom samaki* fell into this category in the early 1980s, but by 1989 they had 'all but vanished'. Level two groups divided land and equipment among member families who worked their patch and kept the output, joining together as a collective unit only for important tasks such as harvesting. Around one-half of all *krom samaki* fell into this category in the early 1980s, but by 1987 the proportion had risen to two-thirds. Level three *krom samaki* were little more than loose associations of independent, land-tenured family farms. They comprised 10 per cent of groups in the mid-1980s, but 90 per cent by the end of the decade.[35]

From 1987, private sector and family economic activities were encouraged – a response to the failures of collectivization, which also reflected the impact of concurrent changes throughout the Soviet Bloc under the influence of Mikhail Gorbachev's reform programme in the Soviet Union. Throughout this period, the government failed to meet procurement targets to supply the urban markets with agricultural products, relying heavily upon aid from Vietnam to feed the urban population. This reliance was increasingly threatened by changes in the Soviet bloc as the decade of the 1980s drew to a close.

However, a number of sources indicate that the loosening of collectivization policies was also prompted by internal resistance. The EIU country profile of Cambodia presents the erosion of the *krom samaki* system over the course of the 1980s in these terms. Team leaders were reported to be allocating collective land informally to individual families. The report noted:

> Although efforts were made by the government to promote greater collectivization in some regions, leading to the creation of a few 'model' villages, the drift back to private and family based production within the framework of a war economy (making official heavy handedness unwise) was irreversible.[36]

Using information gathered during his own visits to Cambodia, and analysing more extensive fieldwork undertaken by Stephen Heder at the same time, Vickery also agrees that the collectivization programme was poorly implemented by local officials. He argues that the 'socialist content [of the programmes] was increasingly ignored, and in the inevitable difficulties in deciding who should be the owners of private property, the tendencies of the village committees were very important, which must have meant that pre-1975 owners were favored and the maximum amount of equipment distributed as private property'.[37]

Thion, also, noted as early as 1981 that:

> it is quite possible that the old society pattern will covertly subdue the *samaki* system, if not cause it to disintegrate completely. In those countries which have attempted to collectivize agriculture, such a trend is usually offset by government pressures and even harsh measures to promote higher level cooperatives, in which local peasants have a lesser say and party cadres and administrators have a bigger role. But in Cambodia the party is very far from having enough personnel to go down to the village level, and administrators are totally unprepared for this kind of task. Thus a race is set between the State's ability to work downward to manipulate the rural society and the upward trend to restore growing inequality and private control.[38]

Chanda and Thion both note the importance of smuggling across the borders of Cambodia between Thailand and Vietnam to the economy of Cambodia under the PRK.[39] The willingness of the regime to permit this trade underlines the weakness of the state in economic terms. Furthermore, the private trade that flourished in the cities and on the borders represented a failure of the state in its key socialist role of commanding the economy.

Developments in economic practices over the course of the 1980s suggest that any socialist ambitions nurtured by the new regime were quickly thwarted by the lack of co-operation of members of society in any ideological project, and by the inability of the state to project power sufficiently to enforce them. Control over the *krom samaki* was limited by the resistance and non-co-operation of farmers, and consequently policies for state control of the economy could not be implemented.

Limits to security

The PRK state was undoubtedly a repressive entity, if not to anything like the degree of its predecessor, the DK. PRK repression was primarily defensive, aimed at preserving a tenuously constituted state from external attack, rather than at imposing ambitious and intrusive state policies upon the population. Despite the banning of non-state organizations within society, and the imprisonment of many dissidents, the state did not achieve the power to enforce even its key policies of economic development and socialist transformation. Similarly, the state never achieved the defeat of insurgents, operating both on the border and within the country.

The military stalemate that continued throughout the 1980s reflected this. Analysts of the security situation in Cambodia drew explicit connections between the legitimacy of the state and the ongoing insurgency. Chang Pao-min, for example, commented in the late 1980s:

> what is remarkable is not that the heinous atrocities the Khmer Rouge once committed against their fellow countrymen are clearly abhorred and still remembered by the people, but rather the fact of the resilience and cohesiveness this unpopular group has been able to display and sustain since the invasion. The only possible explanation is that the Kampuchean people's common hatred of the Vietnamese has turned out to be greater than their disgust with and distrust of the ruthless Khmer Rouge.[40]

Attempts to conscript young men to defend Cambodia from the 'Khmer Rouge', both through service in the army and through forced labour on defensive projects, such as the 'K-5' bamboo fence along the border with Thailand, met with an unenthusiastic response. The EIU reported in 1986, a year of 'insecurity in all regions of the country', including the outskirts of the capital, Phnom Penh,[41] that

> in spite of strenuous government propaganda efforts to mobilize public support for the war, resistance to participation in civilian labour projects and to conscription into the PRK armed forces appears to be increasing.[42]

The same report questioned the effectiveness of civil defence projects such as K-5, but concluded that these were partly political in intent, aimed at 'forcibly eliciting a spirit of urgency, solidarity and sacrifice from the Cambodian public' – a strategy that was considered to be 'backfiring'.[43]

Conscription was arbitrary and conducted with a significant degree of force as army teams swooped down upon villages, seizing young men and carrying them away. This was resisted by Cambodian men, who frequently hid in the fields when rumours of an impending sweep reached them. The way in which conscription was conducted, and the resistance to it by the population, suggested the inability of the state to evoke much of a sense within the population that defence of the PRK from the resistance armies, including the 'Khmer Rouge', was significantly in their interests. Today, memories of conscription, and particularly the K-5 project, are used in opposition party rhetoric to indicate the oppressive nature of the 1980s regime.

Reluctance on the part of Cambodian troops offered a significant military advantage to the resistance forces. The *EIU Quarterly* reported in 1985 that,

> The targeting of the most vulnerable, least trained and most politically unreliable of the PRK armed forces has forced Vietnamese and PRK military leaders to form special mixed Khmer–Vietnamese militia units, known as 770 units to protect transport and food distribution in vulnerable areas.[44]

The EIU also reported in 1986 accounts by refugees arriving in Thailand that suggested infighting between Khmer and Vietnamese units within the KPRAF, sparked by alleged Vietnamese mistreatment of Khmer labourers. Diplomatic sources were also cited in support of claims of mutinies in two provinces.[45]

Given the unwillingness of the population to transfer any kind of resources – whether labour, 'patriotic contribution' or even minimal co-operation in implementing policies – to the state, the PRK remained heavily available upon Soviet Bloc support for its functioning. Until 1990, CMEA aid to Cambodia amounted to 80 per cent of the Phnom Penh government's budget.[46] However, from January 1991, CMEA countries, as applicants for IMF means, were no longer allowed to provide aid to third parties, and a new economic mode of production was urgently required.[47]

Economic reform

In 1989, a raft of reform measures were introduced, some of which merely recognized the de facto creeping privatization of land ongoing since the early 1980s, and others of which unleashed new forces in Cambodia's political economy. The 1989 reforms consisted of a change in land tenure policy and farm-level structure of production, improvements in pricing, tax and marketing policies, and a disengagement of the state from production through the reduction of subsidies and the privatization of state-owned enterprises. The constitution was changed to permit three forms of private ownership: transferable private land titles for houses or home lots for market gardening and small-scale animal rearing; inheritable possession or usufruct rights to state-owned land; ten- to fifteen-year concessions for surplus land, conditional upon demonstrating the ability to cultivate it. Cambodian citizens were permitted to launch private enterprises and joint ventures with the state. A Department of Land Reform and Titles was established to provide support for provincial governors charged with issuing land titles, and for district authorities charged with issuing usufruct rights and concessions. Between the announcement of the reforms and June 1991, applications for property rights to home lots covering 3.7 million hectares were issued, along with usufruct rights to 0.23 hectares of land.[48]

In terms of agriculture, the reforms of 1989 largely authorized an incremental privatization of land that had been ongoing since the very start of the PRK's collectivization programme. The liberalization of the economy was not initially envisaged as going hand in hand with political liberalization, in line with the concern to strengthen the state in a context of insurgency. Rather, the abandonment of the *krom samaki*, and the related reforms, were an attempt to promote a greater legitimacy that could render ideological drives more effective. Viviane Frings writes that the initial plan was to replace production groups with political education groups: 'an organized form of people's groups to manage administratively the political and ideological life [of their members] and to implement the task of fighting the enemies and defending the motherland'.[49] These would strengthen the administrative ties between state and society, even while economic liberalization promoted their acceptability in the eyes of the farming community.

Other measures aimed at boosting the popularity of the state included the reduction and eventual elimination of state controls on prices, imports and movement of goods to create a unified and market-determined price structure and to legalize the black market in foreign goods. Agricultural taxes and forced state purchases were officially abandoned. At the same time, state-owned enterprises were awarded autonomy and privatization processes were set up. Carlyle Thayer described the immediate impact of economic reform in 1989 as having prompted 'a dramatic increase in economic activity'. [50]

Economic reform and the poor

This dramatic increase did not offer benefits equally throughout society, however. Rather the move to the free market significantly increased social stratification, enriching those in positions of power, particularly those with power over the privatization of land and resources, and created large groups of marginalized and property-less poor. Frings reports that the policy of awarding land rights to farmers was very popular, but that it was also open to abuse in certain areas. Although usufruct rights were, in theory, not able to be sold on the open market, in practice land transactions 'occur frequently and are condoned by the cadastral officials who agree to disguise land sales as "gifts" '.[51] Particularly in the areas immediately around Phnom Penh, land prices increased rapidly and complaints emerged about 'misappropriation' and 'requisitioning' of land. Gavin Shatkin, in a 1996 survey of land use in Phnom Penh, reports that

> in the chaos of the UNTAC era, due to the lack of clarity regarding land tenure in many areas and the lack of a clear regulatory framework for land use, village, commune and district officials frequently sold lands which had belonged to the state, often for personal profit.[52]

Appropriation and sale of land in Phnom Penh took two forms: recognized and unrecognized. Shatkin suggests that the ability to have acquisition of land officially recognized was a function of economic, military and political power. Families without such power frequently found themselves excluded from land they had occupied legally until 1989, and Shatkin remarks that there was significant displacement of the urban poor from newly valuable properties in the Daun Penh and Chamkar Morn districts in the centre and south of the city from 1990. Furthermore, families without such power were frequently unable to gain recognition of their purchase, often from moonlighting officials or military, of new land. Shatkin reports that the illegal squatter settlements that mushroomed in Phnom Penh from 1990 were often established when displaced families bought plots illegally appropriated by soldiers and officials.[53] This report was confirmed in interviews with squatters displaced from an illegal settlement in the centre of Phnom Penh that burned down in 2001. Of fifteen families interviewed, nine gave details of having purchased either land or house in the illegal site, some from soldiers. Some had paid local authorities to issue family books which recognized their residence in the area and only found later, when they were evicted, that recognition of residence did not translate into recognition of ownership in these cases.[54]

The inability of the poor to gain equal recognition of property rights as compared to those with wealth and power also applied to the resolution of disputes over property. During the period of United Nations administration of Cambodia, from 1992–3, a complaints committee was set up that was intended to hear grievances relating to abuses of human rights. However, the most common complaints submitted to the committee were complaints over land administration arising from disputed boundaries, appropriation of land by officials and disputes over multiple occupancy. With regard to the latter, Shatkin found that almost a quarter of squatters in illegal settlements in 1996 had been forced out of their previous residences by other occupants.[55]

Frings's evaluation of the impact on rural households and Shatkin's evaluation of the impact on the urban poor both found that reform was attendant upon an increasing stratification as the relatively disadvantaged of the 1980s became the marginalized and excluded of the 1990s. Frings argues that, while the *krom samaki* functioned poorly, they nevertheless offered some utility to 'the most disadvantaged population groups' – namely, widows, old people, disabled people and farmers lacking implements and draught animals.[56] With the demise of the pretence of collectivization, these groups often found themselves not only without assistance from their neighbours, but also excluded from the land distribution exercise altogether.

Similarly, the practice of granting concessions of land to foreign companies for the extraction of natural resources imposed a cost upon farmers who had previously had free access to these resources. Economist Sik Boreak found in the year 2000 that:

> Although common property in Cambodia is not clearly defined by existing regulations, it has been observed to have been diverted to private ownership at an alarming rate. Considerable areas of common property resources, such as forests, rivers, lakes and agricultural land which were not redistributed in 1989, have become privately controlled. Millions of hectares of forests have been granted to private companies as concession forests. Many large plantations have been developed. Many private fishing lots have been created along the banks of major rivers and lakes; and a considerable amount of unallocated agricultural land has been illegally encroached upon, and has dubiously become private property. As a result of privatization, common property is becoming less accessible to other people, and hence, benefits to the majority have been reduced.[57]

The importance of this issue to the ability of farmers to make a living was borne out by questions asked by villagers at a campaign rally in Kompong Thom province before the 1998 elections. Asked by the candidate to raise grievances, three villagers commented:

> Our Cambodian people remain impoverished. Now the ponds and the rivers all belong to somebody else. People have no water to use.

> The ponds and lakes that our ancestors have given to us, from the past – we cannot use them any more. We cannot bring our cows and raise chickens – cannot use that water. When we take the cows to drink the water, the owner of the pond arrests us and extorts money with threats. Please help us.

> About forestry – the farmer goes to cut trees for firewood and to make ploughs. He has to pay 500 riel ... The place where we used to go to cut

> trees for making ploughs and firewood, we can no longer go there. So now if we have a lot of democracy, what are you going to do when your representatives are elected? How will you help us?[58]

Similarly, in 1998, villagers in Prek Prasath District, Kraceh Province, complained to an election candidate at a party rally that a lake in the area had been sold to a private company and could no longer be used by villagers as a water resource.[59] These issues arose again in the 1998 post-electoral demonstrations. A medical student from Kampot province, participating in a demonstration against alleged electoral irregularities outside the European Union headquarters in Phnom Penh after the elections, stated his major grievances as follows:

> In my district, six mountains were sold to foreign companies. Before Cambodian people used to go there to get soil for fertilizer but now they cannot. They could make cement and now they cannot.[60]

The privatization of previously free goods and the imposition of a cash fee for use of them was burdensome for subsistence farmers.

It is important to note, also, the very marginal nature of Cambodian subsistence agriculture. Frings suggested that one motivation for land reform was the observable failure of farmers to invest in upgrading their land through the application of fertilizers and other capital investments.[61] This lack of investment in the productivity of farmland is both a legacy of war, a reflection of the ongoing paucity of surplus production in family farms, and the cause of extreme vulnerability to natural disasters such as drought and flood. The reforms have not, in fact, significantly addressed this situation. Cambodia continues to produce low rice yields at 1.3 metric tons a hectare, compared to an average 3.2 metric tons per hectare in Vietnam and 2.1 in Thailand. The government's draft socio-economic development plan puts the low level of productivity down to the fact that most land in Cambodia is single- rather than double-cropped, and that only 23 per cent of agricultural land is irrigated – a reflection of a lack of investment.[62] A non-governmental organization's case study of needs in three villages in the south-eastern border province of Svay Rieng in 1996 found members of all three villages viewed low agricultural productivity due to lack of irrigation and capital inputs such as draft animals and fertilizers as their greatest problem. In one village in Svay Teap District, villagers described 98 per cent of the village as experiencing difficulties in feeding their families as a result of this lack of investment in agriculture, with many trapped in a cycle of poverty whereby the need to hire out their labour to raise cash for food in the rainy season prevented them from reaping an adequate harvest from their own land.[63]

Figures for overall food security in Cambodia underline the problem. In 1997 an estimated 36 per cent of the population continued to enjoy a per capita consumption level below a poverty line set at the equivalent of 2,100 calories per day. The United Nations reported chronic food shortage, or the continual inability to meet basic food needs, as a problem in 261 – one in seven – communes in Cambodia in 1996/7. Periodic food shortages caused by contingencies such as flood, pests and droughts were reported in a further sixty-four.[64] In the election year of 1998, the problem of hunger was particularly acute. In July, the United Nations World Food Program provided emergency food aid to 650,000 people throughout the country.[65] The late arrival of the 1998 rains increased the number to more than a million by October of that year.[66] The year 2000 brought further suffering in the shape of massive flooding of the Mekong river, which killed more than 300 and displaced around 84,000 families, rendering half-a-million Cambodians dependent upon emergency food aid from international agencies.[67]

The increasing impact of state activity on rural areas in the 1990s, observable in the successful implementation of policies such as the privatization of free resources, has offered few compensations in the form of increased access to services or utilities. In the mid-1990s, only 1 per cent of rural households enjoyed electricity, sanitation and a regular water supply.[68] More than 70 per cent had no access to clean water.[69] Accommodation remained poor, with almost 60 per cent of rural houses constructed of thatch or bamboo.[70] The United Nations Population Fund reported in 1998 that only half of the Cambodian population had access to a functioning health facility.[71] Most medical facilities imposed some official or unofficial fee for services, which often put them out of reach of poor families.

The net effect of the reforms was only a marginal increase in standards of living for the poorest in society. According to Cambodian government statistics:

> While the poorest 20 per cent of the population increased their real consumption expenditure per capita by 1.7 per cent between 1993–94 and 1997, the corresponding increase for the richest 20 per cent of the Cambodian population was 17.9 per cent.[72]

Inward investment was heavily oriented towards the urban areas, while aid projects were also largely urban in scope. Sectoral growth figures for the 1990s suggested that, aside from the years 1997 and 1998 when a military battle in Phnom Penh significantly affected urban service industries, there were consistently higher growth rates in the industrial and service industries clustered tightly around the capital city than there were in agriculture (see Table 2.1 and Figure 2.1).[73] Agricultural production grew slowly throughout the decade, representing only a slow income increase for 'the vast majority of the people', according to the Cambodian government's analysis – indeed, the rate of value-added in the agricultural sector grew below the rate of population growth in the rural areas.[74] The difference between strong rates of growth in urban areas and weak growth in rural areas contributed to a

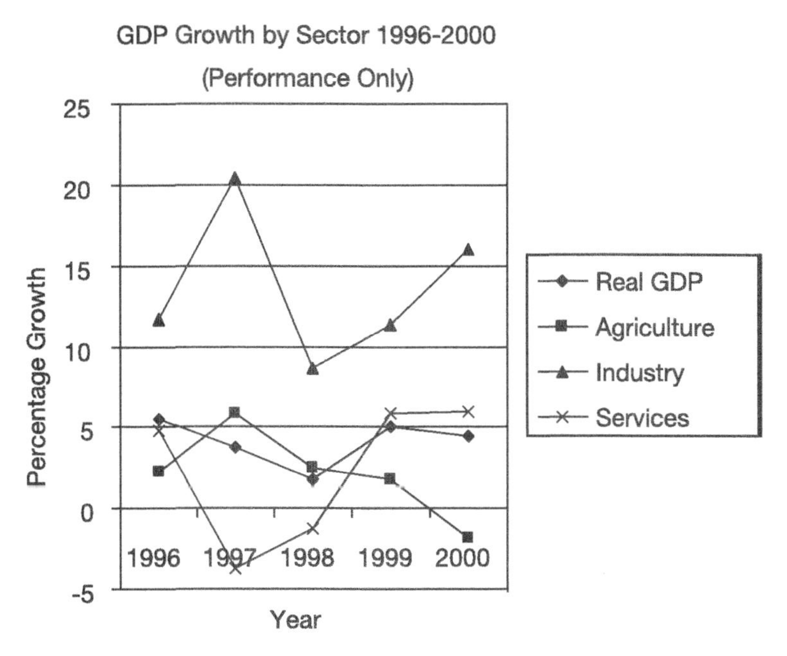

Figure 2.1 GDP growth by sector 1996–2000 (performance only)
Source: Royal Government of Cambodia (2001)

Table 2.1 Real growth rates, targets and performance

	1996	*1997*	*1998 (est)*	*1999 (est)*	*2000 (est)*
Real GDP					
Target	7.5	7.5	7.5	7.5	7.5
Performance	5.5	3.7	1.8	5.0	4.5
Agriculture					
Target	5.2	5.2	5.2	5.2	5.2
Performance	2.2	5.8	2.5	1.8	1.8
Industry					
Target	11.8	9.8	9.8	9.8	9.8
Performance	11.7	20.4	8.6	11.4	16.0
Services					
Target	8.2	9.0	9.0	9.0	9.0
Performance	4.8	-3.7	-1.3	5.8	6.0

Source: RGC 2000

high rate of rural–urban migration, which 'increased the pressure on over-burdened urban facilities and contributed to rising urban problems'.[75]

Similarly, the government reported in 2001 that the public investment programme of the first Socio-Economic Development Plan, covering the years 1996–2001, had initially been formulated to award 65 per cent of public investment to the rural sector and 35 per cent to the urban sector. However, with respect to 45 projects completed by 2001, actual expenditure in urban areas amounted to 47 per cent of the total, in rural areas to 17 per cent of the total, with 36 per cent of the total financial expenditure invested in projects spanning both rural and urban areas. On the assumption that projects spanning the rural–urban divide were split evenly, this represented a final split of 65 per cent of public investment concentrated in urban areas, and only 35 per cent in rural areas, despite the fact that 90 per cent of Cambodia's poor live in the countryside.[76] It was noted that most of the completed projects were in the fields of transport, communications and electricity. No public investment projects for improving health or education services had been completed in either urban or rural areas.[77]

Yet even within the urban areas, including Phnom Penh, absolute poverty was widespread throughout the 1990s, estimated at just under 30 per cent of the urban population at the close of the decade.[78] While this represents a relative decline in the poverty headcount from the start of the 1990s, in absolute terms the subsistence of the urban poor remained highly precarious. In 1998, an international aid organization reported a 'severe food insecurity situation in at least nine villages in Russei Keo District in Phnom Penh', indicating that hunger is not confined to the countryside, but is present in urban areas also. Urban unemployment is also a problem, standing at 9.2 per cent overall in 1998, and more than 12 per cent for urban women.[79]

In what sense, then, has the economic change of the 1990s contributed to securing the position of the Cambodian state? These changes have had a profound impact on the nature of the state and its relation with society, the major outcome of which has been an internal consolidation of state cohesion at the expense of increased inequality between rich and poor and an increasingly exploitative relationship between state and society at large. The ways in which these changes have promoted the consolidation of the state and have undermined the capacity of society to resist intensified state exploitation are discussed in the next chapter.

3 Economic reform and state-making in the 1990s

The economic reforms of 1989 transformed the relationship between central and local government, and between local government and society. In the 1980s, central government policy had run up against resistance at the local level, including difficulties in obtaining information and co-operation from local authorities, and, consequently, problems in extracting economic resources from society. In the 1990s, the situation was transformed. New and more generous sources of international aid were available following the arrival of the United Nations Transitional Authority in Cambodia (UNTAC), which funded up to 50 per cent of the central government's budget. Furthermore, the inflow of foreign investment in Phnom Penh and Sihanoukville offered a new source of revenue for government officials, decreasing the dependence of the centre upon the periphery. Rather than attempting to gain the co-operation of local authorities in extracting resources from the population, the central government was now more concerned to strengthen the political attachment of local authorities, to deliver the electoral victories necessary to qualify for further international recognition and aid. Consequently, central government now assumed the role of protecting civil servants and military units in their entrepreneurial activities vis-à-vis the local population and locally available resources. This strengthened the ties between central and local government, even while it prompted the marginalization of those who were dispossessed or exploited by the profiteering of local and military authorities.

Economic reforms and state allegiances

Laura Summers, at the start of the 1990s, suggests that while the PRK had enjoyed only limited success in securing its legitimacy, it had nevertheless built the state into a cohesive and loyal apparatus:

> To the extent that the KPRP has secured a national political base, bearing in mind that the party was hastily organized following the Vietnamese invasion at a time when communism had virtually ceased to

> be an acceptable national ideology, that base is none other than the SoC state apparatus.[1]

The emergence of a cohesive and loyal state apparatus in the 1990s, given its weakness in the 1980s as documented in Chapter 2, may be traced to the reforms of 1989. These made a virtue of necessity in significantly altering the role of central government vis-à-vis local government. In the 1980s, the major central government policies had been the imposition of socialist planning on the economy and the defeat of opponents in the civil war. In the 1990s, central government's role was reconceptualized; the job of central government was now to provide an umbrella of protection to entrepreneurial local authorities and military divisions, particularly against the perceived threat from former civil war opponents now brought into Phnom Penh under a UN-sponsored peace plan.

This limited the central government's role, particularly in relation to the economy which was now left in the hands of an entrepreneurial local government and military apparatus. In permitting local power-holders to enrich themselves at the expense of the poor, the central government placed the incentive for extracting resources from a recalcitrant population at the level where the task was most readily fulfilled – the level of local authorities and military. The incentives for resource extraction were heightened in the new consumer society, which, particularly once UN peacekeepers were deployed in their thousands, offered new opportunities for the amassing and spending of money. Furthermore, in offering protection to the authorities engaged in this resource extraction, and in diverting new resources of international aid to them, the central government strengthened the loyalty of local power-holders to the centre. Rather than conspiring with local villagers to avoid the levies of the central government, local power-holders now conspired with central government and the armed forces to extract resources from villagers. From the late 1980s, and certainly from August 1989, the renamed State of Cambodia achieved a transformation not only of ideology, but also of structure. The weak ties of coercion and mutual attachment in the context of external threat that formed the shaky basis of the state in the early 1980s was transformed into much more powerful ties of protection and facilitation of practices to amass individual wealth after 1989.

The change in relations between central government, civil servants and society is illustrated by the changing level of public salaries from the 1980s to the 1990s. The demise of Eastern bloc aid led to a public expenditure financing crisis, that left 60 per cent of the government budget unfunded prompted soaring inflation between 1988 and 1992. Consequently, employees of the Phnom Penh administration, including the military, saw their state salaries becoming ever more worthless in an increasingly, from 1991, consumerist economy. Prices rose 90 per cent in 1989, and more than 150 per cent in 1990, and inflation reached a peak of 180 per cent during 1992. At the same time, the value of the riel weakened against the dollar, leading to extensive dollarization in response to a collapse in public confidence.[2] UNTAC's Office of Rehabilitation and Economic Affairs reported in June 1993 that:

> In real terms ... civil service remuneration has fallen dramatically and an early measure the new government may need to take will be to restore salaries to some previous historical level. In effect it will probably be necessary to at least double nominal public sector wages in order to make good some of the serious erosion of purchasing power that has taken place over the past year.[3]

The decline in public salaries, coincident with an increase in economic opportunity, led to the expansion of profit-making activities by public employees. This was, to a large degree, facilitated by the government. Just as the Phnom Penh administration had turned a blind eye to smuggling and black marketeering as a necessary evil in the 1980s, it now overlooked the looting of the state by its employees and the transformation of the bureaucracy into a network for private enterprise, often based upon the protection of powers that could be used to elicit resources from the wider population.

Of course, to a great extent this had already been going on in the 1980s, when local officials had great discretion in the implementation of central government policies due to the inability of the central government to exercise effective oversight. However, the abandonment of even a pretence of collective farming and the granting of land-ownership rights created new opportunities in permitting individuals to amass more land than they could use and rent it out to tenants. The development of a market for land also prompted a new drive to the speculative acquisition of land, particularly along roads and around the city of Phnom Penh. The legitimation of private property and the increasing uses of cash in an economy opening up internationally increased the opportunities and rewards available, and the protection by central government of local exploitation of these opportunities integrated state employees more closely into the state structure.

An early analysis suggested that the 'pattern of overemployment and underpayment expanded' from 1993, as more individuals were cemented into the state structure. This analyst commented:

> Public employment continues to be the main means through which ordinary Cambodians tap into the state apparatus to guarantee a personal social safety net.[4]

Similarly, the World Bank noted that the award of greater autonomy to state-owned enterprises from 1989 did not lead to a rationalization of staff. Limits to the autonomy awarded included pressure to avoid mass lay-offs of workers because of 'security, social and political considerations'. The bank noted that even enterprises that had ceased production retained their employees on leave with reduced pay.[5] The rations of basic goods that had supplemented civil service salaries were phased out, even as the value of those salaries fell, but this loss was compensated by new opportunities to use civil service positions to monopolize not the merely the use of goods and resources, but their appropriation.

A group of inter-governmental organizations prepared a statement for donors in 1993 in which the dangers of continuing shortfalls in the public budget in 1993 were highlighted. Delays in the pay of civil service salaries, it was argued,

> demoralized the civil service and led to excessive absenteeism ... There are clear indications that a number of departments both at the central and at the provincial levels are ceasing to perform even some basic functions.[6]

The agencies suggested that 'without further external assistance, administrative structures will almost certainly crumble', and feared that 'this situation is likely to result in instability, and indeed an unravelling of the very fabric of Government'.[7] However, on the contrary, the increased dependence of civil servants on sources of income other than their derisory government salaries did not, over the course of the 1990s, result in a crumbling or unravelling of government structures, but rather in an increased personal ties among state employees engaging jointly or individually in economic activities in which the abuse of their position constituted the profitable element.

Simultaneously, for the state employee, the pressure to express allegiance to a political ideology and a 'foreign' administration was replaced by the less onerous expression of personal allegiance to a political boss within a state structure whose foreign backers had withdrawn. Within both the national and the local arena, these changes had the effect of transforming the divide between the powerful and the powerless into a divide between the increasingly wealthy and exploitative rich and the increasingly impoverished and excluded poor. As the divide widened so did the need for coercion and protection to underpin exploitative activities, and so, in consequence, did the cohesion of the state increase.

In the central government in Phnom Penh, the transition to the free market entailed an immediate sale of government resources, by those who controlled them. In a review of private transactions in the land market conducted in the year 2000, economist Sik Boreak discovered that

> it is not just private property that has been transferred: in the course of privatization of state-owned property, buildings, land, cinemas, factories, hotels etc. have also been sold or leased for long term investment. All these assets are now privately owned or leased for the long term (up to 99 years) ... The official figure for transactions of state property has never been made available to the public.[8]

Similarly, the privatization of state-operated enterprises enriched individual civil servants rather than the Treasury as a whole. The World Bank noted that the privatization that occurred was enacted by an inter-ministerial National Committee on Foreign Investment comprising the vice-chairman of the Office of the Council of Ministers, several other ministers and the governor of Phnom Penh. The Ministry of Finance – the ministry with responsibility for guarding the national treasury – was not involved. The bank commented on the privatization process generally:

> The National Committee and Phnom Penh have focused on the speedy execution rather than the transparency and equity of their deals. Most transactions have been negotiated directly with one or a few interested investors. Tenders have been rare.[9]

Similarly, the award of contracts and licences by the government to foreign firms led to rumours of fabulous amounts of money changing hands. Sam Rainsy, former Minister of Economics and Finance, implicated the two prime ministers themselves in this when he criticized the acceptance of 'gifts' and 'tips' by the two prime ministers from private companies when governmental contracts were signed, including a tip from the Malaysian firm Ariston of $108 million.

The central government has also played a significant role in the transformation of the state apparatus insofar as it has provided protection for entrepreneurial activities at the level of local officials and authorities. For example, a controversial article in the Civil Servants Law, passed in 1994, declared that state officials and members of the military could not be prosecuted for any crime unless the court first gained the permission of their immediate superiors in the civil service or armed forces. This had the effect of exempting state officials from prosecution for crimes conducted in connection with networks of profiteering within the state apparatus. The efficacy of such provisions was described by judges interviewed in 1996, who remarked that letters written to gain permission from heads of departments in the civil service or in the military frequently went unanswered. After six months, according to the law, the suspects, who could not be tried, had to be released.

The judiciary themselves were also implicated in networks of protection. According to a human rights lawyer interviewed in 1996:

> [Verdicts are dictated by the Ministry of Justice in] all the cases that are related to political members. For example – you are working in one political group – for the CPP. And the judge asks you to do something that is not in favour of you. So you will go to any person who you know and then that person will ask the Ministry of Justice to provide anything like that. To support you.[10]

This support from the centre underwrote the use of violence in pursuit of competitive advantage in entrepreneurial activities in the regions. In the 1990s, the Cambodian economy outside Phnom Penh remained largely dependent upon the exploitation of natural resources – primarily land, timber, rubber, fisheries and gems. Control of these resources, or of access to them, became a key source of revenue for entrepreneurial military and civil authorities in rural Cambodia. To the extent that these resources were exploited for the local market, raising revenue entailed the demand for payment from foreign companies. Insofar as these resources were used locally, claims of ownership over them, or control of access to them, permitted the extraction of resources from the local population, often by force of arms.

Commercial exploitation: timber and fish

The timber industry offers an example of how central, local and military authorities cashed in on the demand by foreign companies for local resources. Aside from ownership rights and inheritable usufruct, the reforms of 1989 also permitted the purchase of 'concessions' by farmers, which awarded them the right to cultivate publicly owned land. This was presented as a move to promote productivity by increasing the land available to farmers with excess labour, but the World Bank noted that 'in practice, concessions are issued mainly to large investors for the planting of agro-industrial raw materials such as rubber, pepper, soybean and sugar cane'.[11]

The concession system led in the early 1990s to an unbridled bonanza of unsustainable stripping of resources, which was criticized internationally. This policy has been attributed directly to the process of state-building, as political leaders both participated in and turned a blind eye to the sale of concessions by political and military power-holders in the provinces as a means to bind their loyalties in a situation of continued counter-insurgency in the countryside and political struggle between the coalition partners in Phnom Penh. International pressure resulted in the imposition of periodic bans, quotas and moratoriums on logging, but were widely viewed as having been ineffective for most of the 1990s. The World Bank estimates that between 1973 and 1993 the rate of deforestation in Cambodia amounted to approximately 70,000 hectares per year, but between 1993 and 1997 this increased to more than 180,000 hectares per year.[12]

In the 1990s, concerned observers, including international environmentalists, the World Bank and IMF, and opposition politicians in Cambodia, alleged that the timber industry was important in sustaining the state apparatus from top to bottom. The 1990s saw a number of legislative efforts at limiting the timber trade, frequently prompted by international pressure, which nevertheless failed to halt this rapid depletion of resources. Sam Rainsy, former Minister of Economics and Finance and later president of the opposition Sam Rainsy Party, charged in 1995 that both prime ministers had reneged on commitments to limit timber exports. Rainsy argued that the prime ministers were involved in secret exports carried out by the military under the Ministry of National Defence, thus avoiding scrutiny by customs officers and by all other organs of state.[13] Rainsy suggested that vast sums were being lost to the national budget from this unscrutinized and untaxed trade; the same was true in the rubber industry, which was largely controlled by 'armed gangs', 'provincial governors' and 'warlords'.[14]

The World Bank documented the practice of unofficial payments to various state agencies by loggers operating legally in Cambodia. According to the bank, to ship logs from the forest to processing plants in Phnom Penh costs US$14 per cubic metre of timber in unofficial fees. These are paid out to a variety of actors including the provincial authorities (who receive approximately $7/m^3$), the local military (who receive approximately $1.7/m^3$) and forestry personnel (who receive approximately $5.6/m^3$). Additional 'facilitation fees' amount to US$50 per cubic metre of timber felled.[15] Illegal logging offered an even more lucrative source of fees to local state personnel.

This view is supported by Global Witness, which claimed in 1997 that

> illegal logging is fuelling a parallel budget to equip and feed .... 'private armies' which de-stabilize the country and hinder economic development .... The effects of the situation run counter to development, plunder the country's resource base and result in increased human rights abuses. 'Forestry officials can't do their job anywhere .... Independent RCAF groups are popping up because of the income .... There are well-armed and financed groups all over the place'.[16]

Global Witness pursued a policy of international lobbying of organizations such as the IMF and the US State Department as a means to pressure the Cambodian government over the issue. This international campaign resulted in a suspension by the International Monetary Fund of Cambodia's Enhanced Structural Adjustment Facility in May 1996 following reports that the Cambodian co-prime ministers had signed a deal with Thai loggers authorizing the export of 1.1 million cubic metres of timber to Thailand. The deal was the target of international outrage for three reasons: its scale at a time when the sustainability of forest exploitation had been called into question; the fact that many of the logs to be exported were in areas held by the insurgent National Army of Democratic Kampuchea, and would thus benefit the outlawed PDK; and the fact that the Cambodian government failed to offer convincing explanations of where the money generated from the deal – expected to amount to US$35 million – would go.[17]

Even where government monitoring agencies were set up, they invariably proved lacking in the power to act decisively against high-ranking officials and businessmen with control of military power. Global Witness reported on a Forest Crime Monitoring Unit established in 1999 in response to World Bank pressure over forestry issues:

> Illegal logging is still primarily in the hands of elites, and it is beyond the power of civil servants, even though they have a powerful mandate and Hun Sen's personal backing to confront such people. Illegal activities are often not reported by provincial officials, either because to do so they would be at risk from physical intimidation, threats to their careers, or because they are involved in illegal activities themselves. The Department of Forestry and Wildlife has reported once incident in Koh Kong Province when the military denied them access to a logging site.[18]

Global Witness documents meetings attended by the group, which has the status of the IMF's official watchdog on the Cambodian logging industry in various Cambodian provinces, in which local power-holders asserted personal power to issue licences and permits in defiance of the law and benefited financially from doing so. One example, from Ratanakiri province in January 2000, reads as follows:

> Global Witness was invited by the Governor of Ratanakiri, Kem Khoeun, to take part in a provincial meeting to review the logging crackdown on 21 January 2000. At this meeting, it was evident that the governor's office, the provincial offices of the Ministry of Agriculture, Forestry and Fisheries and the Department of Forestry and Wildlife, and all provincial Royal Cambodian Armed Forces units including the Police, Military Police and Border Police were colluding in the perpetuation of illegal logging activities that were 'legitimized' by locally issued permits. The local office of the Ministry of the Environment was alone in identifying specific incidents of illegal activity, the veracity of which Global Witness confirmed on its subsequent investigation. At the meeting, virtually every other departmental head publicly rubbished the Environment Director's findings; not surprisingly, as many of those present were responsible for carrying out the activities that he cited.[19]

The wholesale incorporation of local, provincial and military authorities in profiteering from resource extraction entailed that attempts at independent governmental oversight was impossible, and all levels of the state cashed in on the inflow of resources from foreign companies.

The collaboration of state, military and foreign investors in the stripping of Cambodia's natural resources had a profound impact upon the poor, who were denied access to resources previously taken for granted as a result. A similar situation was reported in the fishing industry, and the importance of fish as a source of protein in the Cambodian diet entailed that these activities had a major impact on the rural poor. The involvement of the military in the over-exploitation of private fishery concessions was also noted in a report released in 2000 by the Environment Working Group of the NGO Forum of Cambodia. The group reviewed declining fishery catches in the remote north-eastern province of Stung Treng, and found that the award of fishery concessions included the sale by the provincial authorities of streams, and the denial of access for fishing to local people. These practices were illegal for a number of reasons: namely, the 1987 Fishery Law awards jurisdiction over fishing and fishery resources to the national Department of Fisheries, and not to the provincial authorities; furthermore, Stung Treng has been declared a protected fishing area because of the importance, variety and rarity of fish species in the Mekong River in this province. The province is also covered by international treaties for the preservation of wetlands, to which Cambodia is acceded. Finally, a 1999 declaration signed by Prime Minister Hun Sen calls upon all levels of authorities to co-operate with fishery officials to crack down upon illegal sale of fishery concessions.[20]

In violation of this legal framework, the report described the use by private companies of ecologically destructive fishing practices, such as the deployment of finely meshed drift nets to block the river passage, and the suspected use of pesticides, explosives and electrocuted fishing gear. The forcible exclusion of subsistence fishermen from the concession areas was also documented. The report noted:

> The current fishing lot owners ... are supported by military and police. Armed men from the military and police have threatened villagers who have tried to complain to high ranking provincial authorities.[21]

Following the presentation of a petition to the provincial authorities, a meeting of provincial and district authorities was held to discuss the conflict in which 'the authorities at all levels in the province accepted the fact that the concessions are illegal, but suggested that all in the province should help to keep this a secret'. When a group of NGOs assisted villagers to protest this issue, they were 'intimidated' by 'armed men'.[22]

The importance of violence in privileging local authorities, the military and their business associates vis-à-vis the rural poor cannot be overstated. Resistance to these activities was rendered extremely difficult by the ongoing militarization and insecurity of the Cambodian countryside, which put armed local authorities and soldiers in a privileged position compared to civilian competitors and local activists. A Cambodian human rights lawyer commented on this situation:

> Most Cambodian officials ... just use their power for their own interests and it starts from there. Because if you are a policeman, you have a gun and because you have this you are able to get any interest that you need.[23] That's the problem.[24]

The invulnerability of military entrepreneurs in particular was characterized by human rights activists in 1996. A human rights activist in Kampot commented, 'Many cases of human rights abuse involve the military, but no one can intervene when they are involved'. Human rights activists in

Kompong Cham described the eastern rubber-producing districts of the province as effectively no-go areas for human rights organizations, under the de facto control of armed gangs:

> There are places that have a lot of human rights abuse on the other side of the Mekong ... This organization and other organizations cannot reach there. When we go there, they just point guns at us, and ask for money. They are armed men – we don't know who they are. They just come from the jungle.[25]
>
> The unstable areas in this province are the economic areas, for example the rubber areas. And the border areas, because they are far from the town and close to the Vietnamese border. There is often fighting there because soldiers accompany goods that are being exported to Vietnam and there may be fighting between local militia forces and the people who are exporting the goods.[26]

Human rights activists in Kompong Cham regarded violence against civilians as occurring as a result of land expropriation by the military and provincial authorities 'for development',[27] indicating the strong link between violence, militarization and the entrepreneurial activities of the military, which were bolstered by the transition to the free market.

Local authorities and expropriation of land

While the exclusion of the poor from the use of natural resources was burdensome for rural Cambodians, exclusion of them from the use of land was disastrous. The mass privatization of land in 1989 placed great power in the hands of local officials charged with issuing land titles. Officials frequently used such power for personal profit in a climate of economic and political uncertainty in which their salaries were declining at a dramatic rate. Gavin Shatkin reports:

> In the chaos of the UNTAC era, due to the lack of clarity regarding land tenure in many areas and the lack of a clear regulatory framework for land use, village, commune and district officials frequently sold lands which had belonged to the state, often for personal profit.[28]

Land disputes comprised the single largest category of complaints received by UNTAC's Human Rights Component between 1992 and 1993, and by governmental and non-governmental rights organizations from 1993 to the late 1990s. Two human rights activists characterized the situation as follows:

> Land disputes are very important. After the liberalization of the economy, the price of land increased and the powerful people or the

> authorities – some of them violate the rights of the people. They occupy the land using the military, by force, or by other means, tricks ... For example in Kompong Speu town, we helped the people to remain in the same place after they arrested some people and put them in jail; or after they trick the people, we assist the people ... But sometimes we fail also.[29]

> Some property of the people has been confiscated by the authorities to sell to the rich, to businessmen ... [T]he land issue in Cambodia is a very, very big question right now. Because land attracts a high price. So people who have a plot of land near the city have been victims of land confiscation. Sometimes in the provinces.[30]

A letter to an opposition newspaper in 1996 argued that the demolition of 'hundreds of illegal buildings and small houses', which took place before the 1993 election under the slogan 'Improving the Beauty of Phnom Penh', was in fact used to clear plots of land which were

> sold by the CPP to investors under the slogan of free market economics. Not only this, but factories, undertakings, public buildings, village halls, houses, hundreds more places that belong to the state were sold.[31]

Early reports from Amnesty International investigators visiting Cambodia in early 1992 suggested that evictions by security forces of families from land in and around Phnom Penh led to the fatal shooting of two villagers in four months, and the injury of more.[32] More than a decade after the economic reforms began, stories of expropriation continued, and increasingly the victims of expropriation made their way to Phnom Penh to protest their treatment. A group of 272 protesters from the border town of Poipet, who camped in a park opposite the National Assembly building in Phnom Penh for nine months in 2001, claimed to have been the victims of unjust forcible eviction by local authorities acting on behalf of businessmen who wanted to build a casino on the land. One protester commented that when the protesters had filed complaints with the local authorities, officials had 'responded by pushing us around. I am scared to go back'.[33]

Land disputes are complicated by a paucity of land ownership records following the upheavals of the last twenty-five years, and by the lack of effective and meaningful judicial oversight. The pressing nature of land rights questions has arisen from the widespread practice of arbitrary confiscation of land by officials or the military, and the lack of avenues for complaint and redress. Recourse to the courts over land questions often leads to demands for bribes which bias judgements in favour of the rich. Interviews with human rights workers who deal with many such cases suggest that land confiscation may or may not involve violence; evictors are often armed and threats often used. The current land situation in Cambodia may thus be characterized as a swift concentration of land in the hands of the rich and powerful at the expense of the tillers, who were awarded ownership in 1989.

A 1998 Oxfam study of access to land in Cambodia found that some cases were indicative of 'legal dysfunction', but that, equally, cases where villagers were dispossessed of their rice fields or houses by armed militias, or sections of the military, with the connivance of local government officials are common. The Oxfam study suggests that these situations emerge from the incomplete nature of Cambodia's transition – from a lack of institutions to regulate the land market; and from the weakness of such institutions that do exist, and their failure to penetrate the decentralized power bases of rural district and commune chiefs. The Oxfam report remarked upon the emergence of large landowners in Cambodia, many of whom are 'high government officials, police or military officers, or important businessmen'.[34] However, land dispossession exemplifies the diversification of power-holders in the former one-party state – officials, police and military – into other sectors of power, following the liberalization of the economy, and their attempts to establish an economic base to support continued political power in the new environment. Oxfam's view that this trend reflects the failure to promote the independence of regulatory institutions of the state, such as the judiciary, does not recognize the fact that the drive to economic inequality was itself intended to facilitate the strengthening of a weak and incapacitated state.

Whereas attempts to promote institutional structures capable of sustaining the rule of law across Cambodia as a means to regulate local authority behaviour would have been as problematic as attempts to promote socialist transformation in the 1980s, if not more so, the policy of protecting and facilitating the ad hoc local privatization of resources was extremely successful. Not only did it transform local authorities into willing political servants of those Phnom Penh leaders who protected them, but it also encouraged the defection of NADK units to Phnom Penh. The lure of international legitimation of local-level economic and political structures, with the access to resources of aid and trade, as well as the protection of the Phnom Penh leadership from further military attack, proved sufficiently powerful to overcome the long-standing ideological antipathies of the Cold War years.

Limits to state power

The depiction of a state empowered at the expense of civilians must be qualified by two further points. Firstly, different state employees were empowered to a different extent by this transformation, and officials of weaker state agencies might find themselves significantly exploited or threatened by more powerful colleagues. While most public servants are forced, due to their poor salaries, to engage in some form of entrepreneurship, ranging from the forced expropriation of land to the charging of informal fees for services, the scale of benefit accrued varies enormously. For some state agents, the benefits do not outweigh the disadvantages of being similarly exploited by other arms of the state in their own everyday lives.

Teachers in rural areas, for example, struggle to make a living because the impoverishment of rural families means that attempts to supplement their meagre incomes through charging fees for education is likely to result in children leaving school, rather than in families paying up. A letter to a newspaper from a former teacher outlined the poor salary and working conditions faced by teachers:

> A teacher's salary is $20 a month and never lasts long enough ... Tell us, who wants to be a teacher in the countryside with a salary like that? ... [P]eople from Phnom Penh who go to work as teachers in the countryside always suffer from surroundings that are not good, like the buildings of the state schools, that are like ruins, smashed, crushed in all ways.[35]

Similarly a university professor in 1996 bemoaned the lack of action among teachers in demanding a better salary from the government:

> The teachers' salary is low, about $20, it can't support life. Why doesn't the teachers' association say anything about this? They always discuss at home, or in the street, or at the table in a restaurant. They know about democracy and liberty but they don't know how to apply liberty on this issue. The problem influences society – schools, university departments. That's why teachers are always writing to the newspapers about it – but they write under a false name.[36]

Similarly, while provincial judges have found themselves in a position to make money from bribes, they have also found themselves under threat from the armed forces. Two judges, interviewed in 1996, described the problem:

> Since the recent [1993] election, we have become independent [but] ... in reality, we have pressure from the military, local authorities, other departments. Sometimes there is violence, sometimes oral threats. To deal with these cases we depend on the local authority. Sometimes they can protect us. But sometimes it's a big leader of the Armed Forces and they cannot ... Most of the time we have got to be careful. Our safety is not guaranteed. People who violate the law are normally people with arms. Weapons are spread everywhere.[37]

> One difficulty is that ... Cambodia doesn't have enough peace in the community ... People who lose cases come to the court with guns. They bring armed people to threaten the court. They don't obey the ordinance of the court.[38]

Limited support to judges under threat was offered by the then Minister of Justice Chem Snguon, who protested over two incidents of violence against court personnel in January 1996, but judges interviewed reported no specific policies implemented to suppress these violations.[39]

It is also notable that, amongst state employees, the promotion of a liberal democratic agenda by international donors, and the promulgation of a liberal democratic constitution by the elected Constitutional Assembly in 1993, has created a degree of ambivalence towards this type of state action. This is particularly notable amongst those state employees who benefit little from entrepreneurial activities, but are nevertheless obliged to conduct rent-seeking activities in order to supplement their salaries. A number of such individuals, interviewed in 1996, bemoaned the fact that their poor salaries prevented them from using their position to participate in the reform agenda that has been promoted internationally for Cambodia. For example, a provincial court official, interviewed in 1996, commented:

> A really serious difficulty is the standard of living of the court personnel. We can only just exist ... If our living standard was good enough, we could be honest. But if we don't have enough money, even honest people have difficulties.[40]

Similarly a university staff member at the Faculty of Law, interviewed also in 1996, noted:

> Teachers have very low salaries – they cannot live on their salary. The teacher has to take cakes to sell to the students, or give a private course at lunchtime. You can't expect the pedagogical standards to improve. And the dignity of the teacher – the teacher has to both teach the student and sell cakes to the student, so it affects the relationship between the teacher and the student. The student is not respectful to the teacher. This has a very big influence on the education system and on society, because if the education system is low, society cannot go far.[41]

Secondly, the transformation of the state in this way in effect only recognized the limited ability of the central government to control local authorities. Recognition of this, and facilitation of the pursuit of locally based entrepreneurial interests by local officials has strengthened the power of the entrepreneurial and militarized regions vis-à-vis the centre. This makes the dissemination of policy from the centre potentially as difficult in the 1990s as it was in the 1980s if local power-holders view particular policies as operating against their local interests.

At the end of the 1990s, pressure was brought to bear upon central government by international donors to promote policies of reform. The May 2000 meeting of the Consultative Group of international donors generated a working group for public administration reform, with a remit to promote good governance in Cambodia. This included judicial and legal reform, anti-corruption, natural resource management and military demobilization.[42] State reforms advocated by international interveners reflect a concern to rationalize and legalize the extractive and repressive activities of the state, and to leaven them with ideas of free market sustainable development, which will generate profits that can trickle down to the poor.

At present, international aid constitutes up to half the Cambodian state budget. However, Cambodia's economic destiny ultimately depends, not upon aid, but upon free market trade. To facilitate this, Cambodia's donors have called for the state to reform, shedding workers, demobilizing soldiers, promoting the judiciary as a guarantor of property rights and contractual obligations, extracting higher levels of tax, and putting more of the revenue from extractive industries through the books of the Ministry of Finance and Economics. These policies amount to an institutionalization of the repressive and extractive capacities of the state – capacities that are at present mediated through personal self-interest in a context of patrimonial protection. Such an institutionalization would improve efficiency, accountability and transparency in the name of good governance. This is a reform agenda strongly advocated by Cambodia's opposition party, the Sam Rainsy Party.

However, root and branch reform of the state apparatus is likely to encounter significant local resistance, perhaps sufficient to unseat any government that attempted it. The concerted efforts of local authorities to exclude the SRP from rural Cambodia, described in more detail in the next chapter, are an indication of this. While the present government, led by Hun Sen, cannot afford to reject outright the donors' reform package, there is unlikely to be significant movement on it, because of the political economy of state cohesion.

Developments in Cambodian governance since the formation of the new government at the end of the 1998 reflect significant rhetoric, more tentative implementation, and, equally, steps back when reform appeared to become too threatening to loyalty structures. Examples of tentative implementation include the demotion of generals involved in logging in Kompong Cham, implementation of Value Added Tax, the initiation of demobilization programmes for the military and rationalization programmes for the civil service, and the holding of local elections.

However, at the same time, there are signs that the CPP leadership is attempting to reassure, if not protect, both the civil service and the military from the impact of this agenda. In early 2000, the *Phnom Penh Post* reported that foreign investors were disappointed with the progress made in an anti-corruption drive announced in late 1999.[43] Several months later Prime Minister Hun Sen defended the military against accusations of illegal expropriation of land and human rights abuse. He stated that such accusations 'affect the dignity of the military and I can't accept it'.[44]

International observers have noted that government efforts to address the crucial problem for good governance – the lack of a credible commitment to the rule of law which would restrain powerful actors such as the military – have been cursory at best. A report by the Special Representative for Human Rights in Cambodia, Peter Leuprecht, in December 2001, referred to 'mixed signals' from the Cambodian government on the question and commented:

> Despite numerous, and in some cases, voluminous plans, reports and strategies, as well as institutions, dealing with judicial reform in Cambodia, there is little to report in terms of implementation or progress in this area. At last year's meeting of the Consultative Group in Tokyo, donor countries expressed their concern about the lack of action in the area of judicial reform.[45]

Dylan Hendrickson, investigating reform in the Cambodian military in the 1990s, suggested in 2001 that the political role of the military continued to represent a significant barrier to these reforms. He argues that military spending has not declined significantly, despite heavy pressure from donors urging the government to divert public spending into social sectors such as health and education, and that downsizing of the military is similarly problematic as 'the security forces remain the power base of the CPP'.[46] He concludes that the Cambodian government is in a Catch-22 situation – while it does not have the freedom to reject the donors' reform agenda, by the same token, 'if it were to follow through with all of the reforms that donors are asking for it would have no more power'.[47]

Prospects for local resistance

In the 1980s, resistance to state policies was possible because of different interests between central and local authorities. Whereas central authorities were closely answerable to Vietnamese experts who promoted the policies of a socialist command economy, the ability to obtain the co-operation of local authorities in these was minimal. Contemporary accounts suggest that even the basic level of collectivization achieved, and the policy of state ownership of land and other natural resources, provided some semblance of a subsistence safety net for farmers – at least when the weather was good – even though this was severely compromised by the insecurity of warfare, including central government conscription policies.

In the 1990s, insecurity attendant upon warfare receded. However, economic insecurity was heightened in a situation where access to local resources – including land, timber, water and fish, and inflowing resources such as development aid and government services – were increasingly restricted by force of arms and subject to demands for cash. Furthermore, continuing militarization, even as the civil war died down, entailed a continuing level of physical insecurity.

In this situation, opportunities for resistance on the part of local farmers were severely reduced. The extraction of resources was now enthusiastically pursued by local authorities, backed by armed force, under the sanction of the central government, and could extend to the loss of land and protection, leaving families without any means of attempting to secure their subsistence. Furthermore, the paltry level of civil service salaries had reverberations beyond the immediate circle of civil and military power-holders, and also affected the provision of services such as health and education. Demands for cash from patients and schoolchildren entailed the restriction of access to such services, and imposed a great burden on the poor.

The very marginality of existence, in this context, entailed that farming families had very few resources to devote to resistance. Even the possession of assets such as land was contingent upon the recognition of ownership rights by local authorities. Access to development aid was also concentrated in a relatively few hands. John Vijghen describes how mechanisms for infusing development aid from international NGOs through various local authorities – for example, Village Development Councils, District Agricultural Offices – rather than through commune chiefs and village chiefs, altered local power balances between these different organs.[48] However, Vijghen notes that these power shifts within the authorities did not alter the fact that aid was distributed along lines of clientelism and favour, implying the exclusion of certain families. The fact that control over economic resources altered between arms of the local authorities as different aid agencies infused aid by different means did not significantly affect the position of the poor, who tended to be excluded in any case unless they could ingratiate themselves somehow with those who controlled the funds. This significantly reduced possibilities for resistance on the part of subsistence farmers in a condition where food security was marginal.

The broadening of access to economic resources, precisely as a means of promoting democratization of rural life was a concern of the *Seila* (Foundation Stone) programme, implemented by the Royal Government of Cambodia and funded by UNDP and other donors under the Cambodia Areas Rehabilitation and Regeneration Project (CARERE) in the 1990s. The major feature of the *Seila* programme was the creation of Village Development Committees, which were intended to offer forums for village-level participation in setting development initiatives. The VDCs were to be elected from village inhabitants, and thus provide village-level control over the spending of resources entering the villages, undermining the power of the administrative authorities.

Again, Ledgerwood and Vijghen's research suggests that this has caused a shift in relations among an insider group of local authorities, but has not addressed the gulf between local authorities – still viewed as a undifferentiated group – and marginalized families and groups in the village. They report:

> Without resources to aid people in need no patronage links could be maintained. This became the issue when humanitarian aid began to be channeled through VDCs. Suddenly a new power source could be tapped to maintain a 'clientele'. The power of distributing development aid in this village became the sole power from which patronage derived, although other actors could maintain some influence. It will be no surprise that former 'patrons' took over the new power positions. Village chiefs or their deputies or their relatives became chairmen, or at least members of the VDC, and thus re-established their power base.[49]

Access to physical security was similarly contingent upon connections to powerbrokers who were viewed as interchangeable by the marginalized and by non-state actors such as NGOs. For example, a human rights NGO activist in Kampot province commented:

> Before we provided training to [the local people] there was a very serious incident in one family. The daughter was raped by the local authorities, and they just did not know where to make a complaint. They thought that if they went to the Commune, or to the District, it's useless because all those guys are friends with each other.[50]

For families who fell foul of the local authorities, or who lost their means of subsistence – for example, through land expropriation or forced sale in the event of illness and the need to raise money for treatment – the only option was flight from the village into a condition of vagrancy in Phnom Penh. The need to avoid this by cultivating ties with local authority figures significantly impeded the ability of villagers to develop public or collective strategies of resistance in the 1990s.

This situation contrasts sharply with the situation described by Girling, in which economic development prompts a proliferation of economic resources – of education, information, and employment – which renders monopolization by political power holders difficult.[51] The growing industry in the trafficking of women and children for prostitution in 1990s Cambodia offers an example of the ways in which exploitation of the poor is possible in these circumstances. Human rights activists characterized human traffickers as 'gangs' or 'mafia', suggesting a view of the industry as operating in the realm of organized crime, rather than in the realm of the state. This view is supported by the cross-border aspects of the trade in which Cambodian women and children are sold to brothels in Thailand. However, alleged police and military involvement in prostitution and associated 'protection' of brothels – significant in keeping women and children in the industry against their will, and in insulating protected brothels from occasional government- and NGO-sponsored drives to release captive sex workers – suggests the burgeoning of decentralized links between state employees and private sector brothel owners.[52]

It appears that the enslavement of women and children in the sex industry frequently begins with their sale, either deliberately or inadvertently, by heads of households in rural areas. Deliberate sale of individuals into sex slavery arises from poverty, while inadvertent sale is the result of a lack of education and the dream of the consumer society entered by those who gain employment in Phnom Penh. Human rights activists report that parents are frequently tricked into handing children over to traffickers posing as legitimate employers in return for a lump sum, initially characterized as an advance on wages. The children are then told that they have been sold and now 'belong' to the brothel owner. Parents are frequently unaware of avenues for complaint and remedy, while children, once they have entered the violent world of the brothel, have no access to any external assistance. The distinction created by the move to the free market between the greater impoverishment of marginalized families, a consequent lack of access to education and information, and the rapid urbanization which offers them a vision of wealth, on the one hand, and the ability of state functionaries and their business associates to extract profit from society through connections with the military, and with organized and transnational crime syndicates, constitutes the problem.

It is also the case, however, that the militarization of the state has been accompanied by a militarization of society, and the power awarded to those with connections to the state apparatus allows the use of coercion within villages, between neighbours, and even within families. Weapons ownership is widespread in Cambodia, and abuse within and between families, with the complicity of state agents, is well-documented.[53] Domestic violence is believed to be particularly widespread. A recent survey of women and children's experiences of violence in Banteay Meanchey and Kampong Chhnang provinces found that 'access to weapons of male family members due to connections with police or high-ranking government officials' was a 'key factor predisposing women and children to [small arms]-related incidents' of abuse.[54]

Equally, revenge attacks continue to be a common means of dealing with private conflict in the absence of an effective state apparatus maintaining public law and order. A recent survey found that a common chain of events was as follows: 'jealousy over [the] changing socio-economic condition of another family' could lead to 'deception' or 'verbal abuse' followed by the 'inciting of male family members to help solve conflict' and the 'use of weapons to solve [the] problem and/or intimidate the powerless'.[55] Frequently, personal connections with the military or police are invoked in such situations.

In these circumstances, the marginalization of those lacking personal connections with power-holders results in extreme poverty and insecurity. The fact that state officials extend their protection and assistance into society through personal networks also entrenches the authorities more firmly into the village, making open alliances of solidarity against the local authorities difficult to forge. This renders resistance difficult. Furthermore, the record of foreign investment in Cambodia in the 1990s made significant change in the availability of economic resources at the village level unlikely in the near future.

Between 1994 and 1999, 836 projects worth a total of $5.8 billion in fixed assets were approved. Almost 40 per cent of these were in industry, notably wood-processing, cement-making and garments, while 55.6 per cent were in services, particularly tourism and construction. Only 5 per cent were in agriculture. Figure 3.1 shows the proportion of private investment emerging from different regions. It is indicative of the highly personalized and specialized Cambodian business environment that from 1994–9 more than one-quarter of private investment was local. In 1999, following the domestic political turmoil of 1997/8 and the regional financial crisis, more than half of all private investment was Cambodian.

Thus Cambodia's low level of economic development and high level of militarization entailed difficulties from the outset in engaging Cambodia's farmers in open support of democratizing policies, at least insofar as local authorities viewed these as threatening to their power and their entrepreneurial activities. This represented a significant barrier to the implementation of pro-democratic reforms in the 1990s, such as the promotion of multi-party political competition and civil society. In particular, the transformed state of the 1990s operated to promote the ubiquitous presence of the party of state, the Cambodian People's Party, as a barrier to the entry into rural political arenas of independent political actors that could use their own resources to organize resistance.

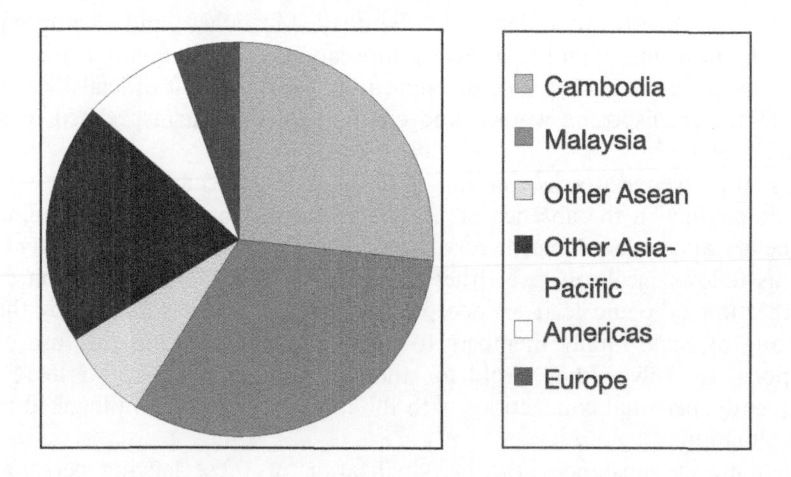

Figure 3.1 Private investment in Cambodia: 1994–9
Source: RGC First Draft 19

4 State and party in the 1990s

The successful use of the state apparatus to consolidate the loyalties of local authorities and military across Cambodia by co-opting these in the exploitation and marginalization of the poor occurred in the context of an impending United Nations intervention in Cambodia aimed at ending the civil war. The State of Cambodia needed to engage positively with this intervention in order to gain the inflows of international aid, trade and investment that were necessary to the new political economy of the state. However, the United Nations' plan incorporated general elections, which would award every citizen of Cambodia – including the newly dispossessed and marginalized poor – a vote that could, in theory, be used to oust the CPP and put resistance leaders, many of whom espoused a liberal reformist ideology – particularly vis-à-vis the economy – in charge of the state apparatus.

The elections created a new role for the party that had emerged alongside the state apparatus in the 1980s – the Kampuchean People's Revolutionary Party, now renamed the Cambodian People's Party. The KPRP had been a numerically small organization, comprising a political elite closely associated with the Vietnamese Communist Party. However, the CPP swiftly became a mass organization, drafting millions of voters into its ranks. Furthermore, whereas the KPRP had espoused, at least rhetorically, a socialist ideology, the CPP in the 1990s turned to a new rhetoric which continued to emphasize the role of the party in ousting the DK regime in 1979, but which termed this victory and subsequent achievements in nationalist, rather than socialist, terms. Indeed, the CPP sought to reinvent itself as a party associated with a re-emergence of Khmer culture and nationhood, distancing itself from the rhetoric of socialist fraternity with Vietnam that had characterized it in the 1980s.

This has been viewed by a number of commentators as the genuine reassertion of Khmer political culture, long buried by warfare and invasion but at last allowed free expression following the demise of alien ideologies. However, it is argued here that the CPP's rhetorical emphasis upon re-emerging traditions was used in an attempt to legitimize a reinvention of the state in the context of the move to the free market, which is more accurately viewed as an effort at modernization rather than a reversion to tradition. Much emphasis was placed, both within the party and between the party and the electorate, upon ideas of patronage and benevolence portrayed as traditional in Khmer society. Arguably, however, in the context of free market reforms, the substance of patron clientism as an economic practice was radically altered, engendering a far more exploitative relationship with the poor. Traditional forms were used to disguise a very modern operation of mass surveillance which had the explicit purpose of marginalizing opposition.

The campaigns of the CPP in the 1990s, while they make self-conscious reference to culture and tradition, were not merely a product of these. Rather they represented the co-optation of such references – a co-optation that went hand in hand with attempts to also co-opt new, international ideas and resources. The activities of the CPP over the course of the 1990s comprised efforts to use a whole range of contradictory rhetorical tropes – of reform, tradition, culture, modernization, nationalism and internationalism – in different ways to legitimize an effective monopolization of the material resources for political action in the countryside. In doing so they sought to protect and legitimize the exploitative activities of the transformed state apparatus, while at the same time marginalizing and stifling dissent in the villages.

Transformed patronage

The transition to the free market from 1989 entailed an abandonment of the justificatory framework of socialist ideology with its promise of liberation based upon equality and solidarity. It is likely that most of these ideals were abandoned with some relief by the Cambodian People's Party as the discrediting of socialist language, noted by observers entering Cambodia shortly after the demise of Democratic Kampuchea, had entailed that socialism operated as a burden rather than as a source of legitimacy for the 1980s regime. However, some new legitimizing myth for describing state–society relations was required in the 1990s to disguise, partially at least, the naked exploitation of the poor by the state that was unleashed by economic liberalization. This was achieved by the adoption of political iconography that was propagated as somehow essentially Khmer.

This tactic is familiar in Cambodian politics. John Girling and Milton Osborne documented Sihanouk's use of similar imagery in the post-independence regime of the 1950s and 1960s, while also noting the lack of any observable connection between Sihanouk's policies or style of rule and precolonial practices that could be evidenced.[1] The similarity between the strategies of Hun Sen, as the prime ministerial contender on behalf of the Cambodian People's Party in the 1990s, and those of Sihanouk in the 1960s have been widely noted by observers. For Hun Sen, as for Sihanouk in the 1960s, the rhetoric of Khmer cultural revival, and the rationale for the apparent resurrection of traditional patronage practices, was distinctly modern.

By embracing the free market in 1989, the SoC could free up resources that could then be used to bolster legitimacy through the award of gifts and positions in a manner that evoked memories of earlier and better times while, in fact, shoring up a system of government that was modern, anti-royalist and oriented towards economic development. In particular, the introduction of a modified patron–clientism could bridge the gap between modernizers within the state and the conservatism of farmers in the countryside, long-since disillusioned with the ideological drives of successive regimes. This could allow the exploitative practices of rent-seekers in the military and state to be dressed up with a customary legitimacy that might render them more, rather than less, palatable to the broader population than a discredited ideology of socialist modernity.

There are important ways, however, in which the current form of what have been viewed as 'patronage links' are significantly different from those existing in Southeast Asia in earlier times. Traditional forms of clientelism, as described by Scott, contributed to the broad legitimation of hierarchy and privilege within society. The patron extracted resources from the client by virtue of his landholdings or other privileges, but in return guaranteed the social and spiritual fabric of village life. This was achieved through the building of temples, the sponsorship of religious festivals and the provision of contributions to funerals and weddings. In this sense, pre-colonial patron–client relations, in so far as they functioned in preserving the stability of rural hierarchies, operated to ameliorate the consequences of unequal local distributions of land ownership among members of a same community, entangled in a common set of social relations and cemented by adherence to the same ritual calendar. For Scott, patron–clientism eroded as a means of elite legitimation in the colonial era. This was because the bargaining power of clients diminished, and the relationship consequently became more exploitative, due to the increased social differentiation, the expansion of the state's ability to support property rights through coercion and the concentration of landholdings, often in the hands of absentee landlords, under conditions of increased capitalist penetration.[2]

The modified patron–clientist relationships that have emerged within and around the state since economic reform in Cambodia at the end of the 1990s are significantly different in their mode of operation, even though they may have prompted the re-emergence of social languages and etiquettes submerged by the socialist rhetoric of equality. Firstly, the employment of modified patron–clientism within and around the state has consisted of a grouping of clients around a patron based within a ministry or military command. This bureaucratized patronage entails that the resources offered by the patron comprise access to posts, perquisites, opportunities for rent-seeking and protection of these rather than the provision of emergency welfare subsidies in hard times and the sponsorship of a legitimizing cultural and religious life.

This distinction has two effects on the set of social relations instituted by these practices. Firstly, the modified patron provides opportunities for clients to enrich themselves at the expense of outsiders. The police who extort protection money from small traders, or the soldiers who demand payments from taxi-drivers at checkpoints along the road enrich themselves at the expense of third parties, who are not included in the dyadic patron–client relationship. These third parties provide the resources that represent the clients' 'rewards', yet they benefit little, if at all, from any patronage or protection in return. Even while strengthening bonds between patrons and clients, such practices alienate a significant group of exploited outsiders. Secondly, the bureaucratic orientation of the mechanism entails that this patronage does not preserve a holistic conception of order in the lived community, but rather preserves the privilege of both patron and client vis-à-vis the outsider.

The modified form of clientelism is purely extractive in relation to wider society. It does not provide any legitimized social or cultural rationale for the privileging of state employees and their connections over non-state actors, who receive little or nothing from the deal. It is a form of extraction whereby patrons bolster the privilege of state employees by means of offering them the opportunity to form coercive and exploitative one-way relations with the third party to the relationship – the outsider. While it sustains a mirage of customary legitimacy for insiders, it is ultimately dependent upon coercion and is unlikely to be recognized by the outsiders, who are only exploited by the arrangement as a practice that operates to their benefit.

While the use of transformed patronage relations to cement the allegiances of state officials went some way to resolving the problems of state weakness in the 1980s, the 1990s brought new challenges. Foremost among these was the impending arrival of the United Nations Transitional Authority in Cambodia, the creation of the Paris Conference of 1991 at which the Cambodian parties had signed up to one of the UN's first complex peacekeeping operations. The broader attempts by UNTAC and the international agencies that succeeded it in Cambodia to transform Cambodian political structures are examined in detail in later chapters. However, in understanding the interplay of political and economic power in determining the evolving relationship between state and party in the 1990s, UNTAC's implementation of elections is highly significant.

The introduction of elections in Cambodia in the 1990s entailed a new problem for both the State of Cambodia and the associated Cambodian People's Party. The state could no longer rule by coercion and co-optation alone – ultimate political protection of personal networks required a victory in the election for leaders sympathetic to the new mode of state organization. The party consequently acquired the function of eliciting these. In particular, the secrecy of the ballot introduced by UNTAC as a key aspect of the 1993 elections, and affirmed by international monitors in the 1998 elections, rendered problematic common tactics of heavy-handed and partisan state supervision as a means of securing popular acquiescence. In the 1990s, the party was required to deliver bonds of allegiance sufficiently powerful to ensure that the subservience of the population in public would translate into private expressions of loyalty in the polling booth.

In part, the move to the free market, the commodification of the state and the operation of transformed patron–client relations that preyed upon a significant pool of outsiders caused extra problems in attempting to ensure public allegiance to the party. Even within the state, the policies of economic reform, and the ways in which they were used to cement allegiances at the expense of broader constituencies, caused early dissent. Early episodes of privatization sparked rare public demonstrations in 1991, indicating a potentially threatening pool of resentment against the State of Cambodia and its party. According to Amnesty International observers, the demonstrations 'were led by and organized primarily among workers and staff of SoC state enterprises who accused their superiors of pocketing money made from selling off or leasing factories and official residences to private entrepreneurs, particularly foreign firms'.[3] Demonstrators also included employees from a variety of ministries, and university students. One demonstration, in December 1991, led to the ransacking and burning of a house 'said to have been misappropriated by Ros Chhun, the Minister of Communications, Transport and Posts'.[4]

The emergence of demonstrations in which civil servants and state workers participated suggests a significant degree of ambivalence on the part of state employees with regard to post-reform mechanisms of state control. Clearly, a significant constituency existed which viewed the shift from an inclusive socialist ideology to exclusive personal ties devoted to exploitation and rent-seeking as a retrograde step. This constituency has frequently been associated with a 'traditionalist' wing of the CPP, said to be led by party president Chea Sim, and which is believed to oppose the reformism of the party's prime ministerial candidate Hun Sen.

Yet, given the extraordinarily widespread nature of rent-seeking in the Cambodian state, it is unlikely that the demonstrations of 1991 and the sporadic public denunciations of 'corrupt' senior officials, which have continued throughout the decade, represent a struggle between corrupt insiders and honest outsiders working side by side in the ministries. Rather, they suggest that the transformed patronage system established in the early 1990s is not monolithic, but contains its own tensions and contradictions that can cause outbreaks of discontent. They also strongly suggest that there is a dual and ambivalent recognition of the apparently 'traditional' discourse of hierarchy and patronage by civil servants participating in these networks, and the alternative discourse of 'corruption' aggressively promoted by urban opposition parties such as the Sam Rainsy Party. This dilemma is captured by the ambivalence of the judge cited in Chapter 3:

> A really serious difficulty is the standard of living of the court personnel. We can only just exist ... If our living standard was good enough, we could be honest. But if we don't have enough money, even honest people have difficulties.[5]

Such comments belie the contention that rent-seeking and patronage by state officials represents the reassertion of 'traditional' values; rather, it is a response to a modern system of control and expropriation, and has been received with ambivalence even by those who have no choice but to participate in it and gain from it in their everyday working lives. This ambivalence also indicates that, while the state could expect its employees to remain engaged in these practices, this would not necessarily translate into expressions of support in the private context of the polling booth. In both 1993 and 1998, the electoral strategies of the CPP vis-à-vis the state have been highly effective in promoting public allegiance by civil servants to the party, even to the extent of mobilizing the state apparatus in support of CPP campaigning, but have been much less successful in actually eliciting votes in areas where there are high proportions of state employees.

The CPP's narrow defeat in the 1993 elections is a clear sign that the transformed patronage model of party relations was not immediately successful in promoting unequivocal private allegiances even while it laid a sound foundation for a gradual consolidation of the public power of party and state over the course of the years from 1989 to 1997. In the first instance, the sudden separation of outsiders from insiders, consequent upon the aftermath of economic reform, distanced the party from the electorate, particularly in the capital, where speculation over land was most frenzied and where sections of the civil service, who were less well placed to cash in on the bonanza, suffered hardships consequent on the decline in salaries. In 1993, the CPP secured only 30 per cent of the vote and four constituency seats out of twelve in Phnom Penh, as compared to FUNCINPEC's 54 per cent and seven constituency seats. In 1998, the CPP again won four constituency seats in Phnom Penh compared to four each for the FUNCINPEC and Sam Rainsy Parties.

At the same time, the pressure placed upon public employees to exhibit public allegiances to the party was highly successful in promoting an image of intertwined and inexorable SoC and CPP power. In the lead up to the UNTAC-organized elections of 1993, activities carried out to shore up this image included apparent politically motivated shootings of state officials seeking to found new political parties. The abduction and murder of state official Tea Bun Long on 22 January 1992, and the attempted assassination of former Transport Minister, Ung Phan, represented the most high-profile cases, and were regarded by observers as successful in promoting a climate of intimidation within the state apparatus.[6] Equally, Amnesty International reported that civil servants and students were warned against attending congresses held by opposition parties.[7] UNTAC's Information and

Education Division summed up the situation in Phnom Penh in a September 1992 report as follows:

> There is no sense, especially among students and other educated people who might be likely to do so, that it is now possible to be active in other political parties. Students say flatly that if they were known to have joined a political party that they would be thrown out of school. State employees similarly say that if they are known to have participated in the meetings of a political party, they will lose their jobs. If you suggest to them that they now have freedom of speech, of assembly and so on, they would find your suggestions absurd.[8]

Such fears were accompanied by pressures to campaign actively for the CPP. Michael Doyle noted, 'the State of Cambodia clearly enjoyed unfair advantages with its ownership of the Cambodian media, and mobilization of public officials for CPP campaigning'.[9] UN human rights monitors commented upon the coercive means used to prompt the SoC apparatus into campaigning and voting for the CPP. Similarly, the US State Department noted,

> CPP party membership swelled to over three million, substantially more than the CPP vote tally at the polls. SoC civil servants, students and soldiers were regularly coerced into joining the CPP and campaigning for it.[10]

Similarly, the *Phnom Penh Post* reported in December 1992 that in Siem Reap province:

> Local SoC authorities are requiring all state employees to register as party members, local residents report, and dismissals are threatened if they don't cast their votes correctly. While these might constitute human rights violations, UNTAC investigators are bogged down by the lack of anyone willing to go on record to object. For most civil servants, just the request from SoC officials is enough to get compliance.[11]

The consensus among international observers that pressure was exerted upon SoC officials to gain their public allegiance to the party, and the belief that considerable numbers of officials must have voted against the party in the polls, is consonant with the view of state employees as ambivalent in their response to the changing orientation of the state in the 1990s. Clearly, attachment to the state continued to offer opportunities to make a living, despite falling salaries, in an economy that offered few alternatives aside from agriculture. Attachment in this way necessitated participation in networks of exploitative practices, and, although these may have been distasteful to civil servants in the view of contending opposition discourses denouncing 'corruption', many officials no doubt rationalized their activities with reference to survival imperatives. Similarly, public membership of and campaigning for the CPP was a fact of life for the state employee, but did not necessarily translate into a loyalty that would hold firm in the private context of the polling booth. Thus, the paradoxical situation arose in which there may well have been state officials who mobilized villagers, exhorted them to vote CPP and threatened defectors with violence, but who did not themselves vote for the party.

This control over public allegiance was effective in 1993 in limiting the ability of other parties to campaign. A FUNCINPEC provincial chief in Kompong Speu told the *Phnom Penh Post*, 'We are afraid to travel from one village to the next because SOC people may harm us'. Similarly, the provincial chief of the smaller Republic Democracy Khmer Party claimed, 'People are intimidated by the SoC, and UNTAC is afraid to get involved'.[12]

While pressure was exerted, in particular, upon state employees in urban areas, in particular to support the CPP, in rural areas these kinds of sanctions were replaced by more direct 'harassment', including assassination of political activists, drive-by shootings and grenade attacks on party offices. This was complemented by PDK campaigns to prevent elections from going ahead, including, in particular, massacres of ethnic Vietnamese. Amnesty International reported in early 1993 that a 'general climate of fear and intimidation' existed, which was more severe in rural areas, and which constituted real restrictions on freedom of expression and association.[13] Similarly Boutros-Ghali reported in November 1992 that 'there has recently been a disturbing number of what seem to be politically motivated acts of harassment, intimidation and violence, as well as an increasing banditry and urban crime'.[14]

During 1992, according to UNTAC's Human Rights Component, complaints from opposition party activists included arrest, dismissal from employment and threats of violence. The most serious allegations came from the KPNLF and BLDP, who claimed that several of their members were the victims of political assassinations in the run-up to the BLDP party congress in Phnom Penh in May 1992. Significantly, the Human Rights Component of UNTAC was unable to investigate these complaints due to delays in deploying personnel into the countryside.

If the response of state employees to the twin campaign of transformed patronage and violence was equivocal once safe within the polling booth, the response of the broader voting public could be expected to be even more so, and this can account for the narrow defeat of the CPP by the royalist FUNCINPEC party in 1993. Yet the maintenance of a powerful veneer of public allegiances, the control, through acts and threats of violence, of public space, and the promotion of a network of private economic interests, permitted the rapid regrouping of the party once again after the elections on the public terrain of the state. The marginalization of FUNCINPEC appointees who attempted to enter the ministries during the period from

1993 to 1997 has been widely documented. At the same time, the party, and more specifically, the individual personality of Hun Sen, were used in an attempt to promote an attachment to the party that went beyond a pragmatic accommodation in everyday life, to a deeper allegiance constituted from a haphazard mixture of personal charisma, socialist ideal, cultural revival and scaremongering.

Surveillance and the thumbprint campaign

An interesting example of the mixture of styles and references found in CPP campaigning was the thumbprint campaign launched in 1998. This campaign illustrates the harnessing together of 'Khmer cultural practices' with more modern bureaucratic methods of surveillance and intimidation. Throughout the 1990s, senior party officials considered that their most reliable officials were those in the local commune and district administrations, who had been elected in 1982 and permitted to run their localities with little interference from the centre every since. One official characterized the position of the party as follows:

> Our party organization runs from central to provincial to district to commune level and within each commune we have cell leaders. Now the total number of these activists we cannot tell. But we have a good organizational structure ... from Liberation Day, 7 January 1979, we have rebuilt and reorganized our party. Since 1979 we have some experience of leadership ... The principle of our party is that the grass roots is very important – the commune or district. The voter is in the commune, not in the centre. Therefore we pay very great attention to education, to educate and improve the knowledge or principle of the party for the grass roots members.[15]

The Cambodian People's Party is indeed ubiquitous at the village level, with the party's logo – an angel scattering flowers – along with the personal monogram of Prime Minister Hun Sen appearing not only on party offices and signposts, but also on schools, temples and roads built or rebuilt by senior members of the party. The entwining of the party with the structures of local state power and the strategy of personal provision of collective goods to village communities formed the twin prongs of the Cambodian People's Party's campaign strategies in 1993 and 1998.

In 1998, as in 1993, the CPP's electoral strategy was based to a great extent on the advantages of incumbency and politicization of local administration to launch a programme of voter surveillance.[16] From 1992, the CPP's first strategy was to employ its position as key power broker in government and monopolist of local politics to dominate the political environment in the villages, thus displaying to voters the effectiveness of their control.

Consequently, the CPP extended its political presence in the villages by implementing a massive membership drive, in which millions of people were dragooned into the party by the simple expedient of issuing all voters with party cards. In 1998, this was organized by means of a ten-person cell structure. Hundreds of thousands of 'group leaders' collected millions of voters' thumbprints in special booklets allocated by the party. Each 'group leader', often a member of the local authorities or a villager appointed by them, was required to collect ten thumbprints of 'group members', thus forging a relationship which remained in place throughout the electoral period. The thumbprints were made in a booklet retained by the group leader. The booklet also listed four responsibilities of group leaders:

1 Know the exact number of members in the group. The group leader and the members must know each other.
2 Teach the members in the group to love and support the CPP.
3 Direct all members in the group to register to vote.
4 Make sure that all members of the group cast their votes, know how to cast their vote and vote for the CPP.[17]

The relationships formed via this membership drive provided the organizational base for mass mobilization for the elections.

The United Nations Cambodia Office of the High Commissioner for Human Rights (COHCHR) reported that the collection of thumbprints was often accompanied by threats, including:

- if a person refuses to cooperate, his or her 'security cannot be assured';
- if a person claims to be neutral, he or she will 'be ineligible to register and vote';
- if a village shows its support in sufficient numbers, it will receive develop ment and humanitarian aid after the election, while if they refuse they will receive nothing;
- if they do not join the CPP they will be accused of belonging to the Khmer Rouge.[18]

The giving of the thumbprint, often allegedly accompanied by a pledge to vote for the CPP in the elections, sometimes made in a temple before a statue of a Buddha, and sometimes accompanied by the ritual of drinking a glass of water containing a bullet, represented the agreement to join the party and the surrendering of the voter to the party's surveillance. Viewed in these terms, the campaign was pronounced a form of 'intimidation':

> They intimidated people to be members of the party, to make them swear and they give a donation in exchange for their promise. Then they collect the registration card and take a record of the number. The state

> power treats very well the people who belong to the party, but they treat badly the people who do not belong.[19]

Following his or her absorption into the system, the voter would then be periodically contacted by the group leader to receive a party membership card, to have their voter registration number taken down and to attend rallies for the regular distribution of gifts of cash, packets of monosodium glutamate (a vital ingredient in Khmer cuisine), traditional skirts and scarves. The voter would also attend education sessions and mock ballots in which villagers were required to go through the exercise of ticking the CPP's box on a mock ballot paper, which often did not show the names of any of the other parties. Group leaders led their groups to register during the month-long voter registration campaign, and, it was claimed by the opposition, led their voters to the polls also.

Shortly after the election, a candidate for the opposition Grandfather Son Sann Party, Keat Sokhun, claimed that his party had found a copy of instructions to CPP village chiefs in Kompong Speu province which read as follows:

- Gather all members of the CPP and ask them to go and vote for the CPP. Check the number whether they all go or not.
- Give the logo of the CPP with number 35 on it to all members of the CPP who go to vote. The six names who are responsible for groups have to stay at a point close to the polling station and order voters to vote for number 35. Some members should be in the polling station where their duty is to arrange with the CEC to bring all members of the CPP together and whisper to the members to remind them. Do tell them the number of the station.
- Opinion leaders take all members of the CPP and others to vote for CPP and tell them to tick at the right place, outside close to the polling station, and inside the polling station.[20]

Many of these activities had no coercive power in themselves. For example, the taking of a thumbprint or the noting down of the number of a voter registration card, both widespread practices, could not be used to connect a voter to any particular ballot paper. Voters may or may not have known this, and in some cases they were misled. The main purpose of the system was to combine the carrot of gifts with the stick of exclusion to those villagers who refused to co-operate with the CPP's mobilization. This comprised an exercise of power which acted by constituting a set of political relationships which ran counter to those engendered by the politics of the secret ballot.

It is significant that the CPP's membership drive in 1998, like its drive to economic liberalization in 1989, was closely tied to an apparent revival of 'traditional' values. The membership drive, like the economic liberalization process, led to the apparent re-emergence of indigenous practices of patron–clientism; yet, like the ties of economic protection and exploitation that constituted the new patron–clientism within the state, this wider patronage on the part of the party significantly rewrote understandings of patron–client relations to fit the needs of a mass-based, participatory political process.

An important aspect of the party membership drive in 1998 was the rationalism of the scheme, which sought to be as inclusive and all-encompassing as possible. In this respect, it differed from the ad hoc and personal nature of patron–clientism as defined by Scott, and as analysed by Hanks in his analysis of patronage in Thai society. Hanks, in particular, emphasizes the shifting and open nature of patron–client relations in which individuals may form relationships with as many patrons as they please, and may sever relations if they are not meeting an individual's needs.[21] The personalized nature of patron–client relations suggests their limited nature – a client may resist, downgrade the relationship, or decamp entirely to a position from which he is beyond the limits of the patron's power. Scott's account of the hardship of peasant farmers in Vietnam and Burma in the 1930s emphasizes that the rationalization of power under the colonial state entailed significantly greater hardship for peasants. This was because landlord–tenant relationships became an issue of contract law, backed by state power, rather than an issue of patron–client relations, backed only by the personal resources of the individuals concerned.

This distinction between particularistic and rationalized power relations is significant in explaining a decisive alteration of the nature of patron–client relations between parties and voters in the Cambodian case also. A senior CPP official claimed that such activities had nothing to do with intimidation; that the thumbprint campaign was a membership drive and the donation of gifts represented the Cambodian custom of giving presents during visits, and the traditional 'sentiment between old and young, high and low, official and people'.[22] Yet the universal scale of the thumbprint campaign altered the terms on which individual voters engaged with it, transforming exchange practices used to cement dyadic ties into an exercise in mass surveillance, softened by the provision of incentives for compliance and by the framing of coercion in terms of acceptable cultural practices. The thumbprint campaign was less an exercise in shoring up particularistic local support bases than a rationalization of party support backed by coercive power.

In two districts of Kandal province studied during the 1998 elections, villagers who were not members of a CPP group and who remained outside the mobilization were few in number, limited to known activists of opposition parties only. Although these villagers were not asked to participate in CPP activities, their special status made them conspicuous and this, in turn, led to feelings of fear. For example, one commune activist said:

> I joined FUNCINPEC since 1993, so they didn't come to ask me [for a thumbprint]. I don't receive donations and neither does my family. Nothing has happened but I am still afraid.[23]

The bases for such fear are instructive, emerging from the inculcation of a sense of exclusion and vulnerability rather than from the employment of direct threats or coercion. During studies undertaken during the 1998 election campaign, eleven accounts of 'intimidation' were collected. Of these, only two comprised a directly stated threat by a CPP member to a FUNCINPEC supporter that FUNCINPEC supporters or activists would be physically harmed as punishment for their support of the opposition.[24]

Five accounts of intimidation consisted of threats that opposition supporters would have CPP membership cards and gifts donated by the CPP confiscated.[25] One family, who had been recruited into a CPP group, but had subsequently erected a FUNCINPEC party signboard in front of their home, said that their CPP membership cards had already been confiscated by CPP group leaders. They were afraid that they would be asked to return donations later, although this had not been stated as a threat. The mother of the family was unable to sleep at night because of these fears.

Demonstrators from rural villages, who came to Phnom Penh to protest about the conduct of the elections in 1998, reaffirmed the view that within the village an individual's political allegiances were well known by his or her neighbours, and that support for an opposition party could entail danger. For example, two demonstrators commented:

> If you support Sam Rainsy or Funcinpec party they will find a problem for you. *How do they know who you support? Are you an active member?* I'm not a member, but people know who supports who. For example, I have always supported the King, and I have told people that I love the King.[26]

> [On polling day] they used soldiers in civilian clothes standing all around the polling building and watching the people. *Could the soldiers see who the people voted for?* They couldn't see who the people voted for, but they are communists so they already know. For example, if you catch one kind of fish and you recognize this species of fish, then you know what this kind of fish will do.[27]

In this context, patron–client relations, which in an idealized traditional form, were used in an inclusive manner to promote vertical attachments, were transformed into primarily exclusionary tools. The value of gifts offered was small, and their quality, according to many villagers encountered in 1998, was poor. Their purpose was not primarily to promote the voluntary attachment of the recipient, but to symbolize their inclusion in the dominant system of power, as opposed to the exclusion of a vulnerable minority. The withdrawal of such gifts thus represented a removal of protection also in a political, social and economic climate of widespread violence and uncertainty. This far-reaching effort to establish divisions between the co-opted and the excluded in every Cambodian village arguably constituted a systematic climate of fear – that is, a situation in which rumours and indirect threats reverberated widely and encouraged villagers to act within self-imposed constraint with regard to the political process.

The climate of fear was used explicitly to prevent villagers not only from voting and campaigning for other parties, but from receiving information about other parties. FUNCINPEC activists reported that villagers who were CPP group members were afraid to talk to them. In one Lvea Aem village, a FUNCINPEC supporter said that villagers could be excluded from donations for listening to Voice of America radio's daily Khmer-language broadcasts. Asked whether violence was threatened against these villagers, the supporter said:

> There is no violence, but they will just come to take it back. And whatever gifts haven't been distributed yet, you won't get.[28]

Other accounts of 'intimidation' were in fact rumours, rather than direct threats, that donations would be confiscated and dissidents would 'face problems later' or, sometimes, be killed. For example, in one account the issue of death threats and donations were combined in village rumours:

> *What are people afraid of?* They may ask for their donation back. But they are mostly afraid of getting killed. If they get the donation and then don't vote then they might get killed. That's a rumour.[29]

A FUNCINPEC commune activist related belief in such rumours to the long-standing condition of insecurity in Cambodian villages:

> People who don't belong to any party – they give a donation and a card to them and if they accept another party's card they will have their donation taken back. *Do you know anyone who had their donation taken back?* No. But people are afraid to meet the other parties' members, and are afraid to break their promises, because they were under oppression for a long time.[30]

Rumours were an important aspect of the climate of fear which pervaded the villages, and observations of villagers talking among themselves suggested that these rumours were considered highly credible. The difficulty of separating accounts of first-hand experience from the recounting of rumours heard in villagers' descriptions of intimidation causes problems in establishing the exact nature of villagers' fears. The fear that donations might be taken back was a real and immediate fear, partly because villagers said they could not afford to repay. Yet a deeper significance to the withholding of donations and the confiscation of party cards was evident in the light of the nationwide system of inclusion and exclusion from protection and patronage that the gifts and cards symbolized.

Judy Ledgerwood and John Vijghen, studying power relations in a rural village in Takeo province in the run up to the elections, found similar dynamics at work. They reported that following a visit of FUNCINPEC politicians to the village, a meeting was called by the most powerful person in the village – a CPP supporter, whose wealth and position put him in a position to exert influence by, for example, extending loans and employing other villagers to work in his fields. Ledgerwood and Vijghen describe the meeting as follows:

> After a long speech blaming those who attended the campaign meeting, the 'sinners' were forced publicly to confess their misconduct. As one respondent later said to researchers, it was 'like during the Pol Pot regime'.[31]

All the villagers confessed, except for one *achar* who denied any wrongdoing. Ledgerwood and Vijghen reported that 'during the following days, the Powerman and other notables visited the old man repeatedly to convince him to repent, but without success. The old man was consequently isolated, including by his former peer group'.[32]

Such isolation has far-reaching implications in the context of villages in which economic resources are frequently distributed by power-holders in accordance with concepts of loyalty. John Vijghen describes how traditions established in the 1980s led to local authorities possessing 'the power to decide who would receive land and relief aid'.[33] Vijghen notes that decision-makers invariably distributed such resources amongst their own 'clientele'.[34] The marginal subsistence of many villages in Cambodia, and their dependence upon external aid in case of disasters such as drought and flood, as well as for participating in development initiatives, entails that political exclusion entails economic marginalization also. This combines with fears of outright violence to render public political dissent risky.

The sense of vulnerability produced by the kinds of events noted in Kandal and by Ledgerwood and Vijghen in Takeo, was heightened further by the occasional perpetration of politically motivated violence. UN human rights monitors reported that a Sam Rainsy Party activist named Lith Pras, murdered ten days before the 1998 election in Siem Reap, had been told by officials after she joined the party that 'now you live outside of society'.[35] Such warnings were doubly threatening in an economic environment in which establishing supportive relationships with neighbours and patrons has long been a matter of life and death.

Equally, shortly before the commune elections of 2002, Sam Rainsy wrote that an SRP agent, who had been the victim of a shooting and robbery,

> remembered a famous rumour generally known in his home town that: nobody is responsible of any difficulty facing to people who believe on Sam Rainsy Party.

Rainsy commented: 'A status of social exclusion is confirmed by such an armed robbery'.[36] The SRP also reported in January 2002 that an SRP candidate in Oddar Meanchey province was told by the CPP chief of his village: 'Once Sam Rainsy does not win the election, you will be chased from the village'.[37]

Two opposition candidates in 1998 similarly summed up the climate of fear in the villages as it was perceived by opposition supporters on the outside of the CPP network. Oeur Hunly, candidate for FUNCINPEC in Kandal, commented:

> the way they intimidate – in the first stage they do it in a nice way. They say, 'if you join we'll support you, support your family'. And those who don't join know they are a target. And the standard of living – everyone is looking for support. If you have no support, how can you live? So they feel isolated – if you two are in the CPP and I am not, I don't know when you might hurt me. And then the second stage: they say, 'I'm going to kill you'. And they are already scared so they run.[38]

SRP secretary-general Yim Sokha said:

> The CPP has formed cell heads to force voters to promise and swear to vote for the party … The CPP knows very well the psychological effect this has on the voters, because ever since the Pol Pot time the people have been afraid.[39]

In setting up the group system in which the giving of donations was formally connected by means of the pledge and the thumbprint to the performance of a political service, the CPP transformed the familiar patronage system into something much more threatening, while at the same time extending the mobilizational power of their district and commune chiefs. These practices were justified, and perhaps rendered palatable to those who went along with them, by the mobilization of ideas of Khmer traditions of mutual exchange. Rumours and threats aimed at those outside the system would have been familiar to villagers who were well aware of the insecurity in normal times of those who are outside the protection of the village authorities. Outright coercion, in these circumstances, is not necessary as villagers make the connection for themselves and instead pursue a policy of anticipatory surrender.

The importance of the thumbprint campaign also reflected the importance of the village authorities and the need for ordinary Cambodians to maintain relationships with local officials as a means to stave off insecurity, whether economic or physical. The level of fear experienced by opposition voters varied from province to province and from district to district, and may well have been connected to broader issues of insecurity and isolation from the protective umbrella of international monitors based in Phnom Penh or in the provincial capitals. In Kompong Cham, for example, opposition supporters frequently slept in the provincial headquarters in Kompong Cham town, close to the offices of United Nations monitors and international NGOs, rather than returning to their districts where they felt under threat.[40] This may be explained by the greater degree of militarization in Kompong Cham province, particularly in the isolated eastern districts among the rubber plantations and forests controlled by the military and illegal loggers. A number of interviewees, including Cambodian electoral monitors, claimed special military forces were being prepared in secret in the rubber plantations of Kompong Cham:

> Right now Hun Sen has sent a lot of killing forces to hide in Memot, to make a reserve force for when he loses the election. Right now the people related to Hun Sen, the Mafia guys like Mr Soeun, have set up their own forces. They have cut down a lot of forest and killed a lot of people. Maybe there will be fighting.[41]

In these areas, where communications are poor and villages isolated, the dependence of villagers on the goodwill of local chiefs is more pronounced than, for example, in districts in Kandal, close to the capital city of Phnom Penh.

Following the 1998 elections, the opposition parties claimed that the percentage of votes counted for the CPP was consistently higher in remote communes than in those that were well connected to the major towns. While the opposition alleged that this was evidence of electoral fraud in distant areas less well served by election monitors, it may equally be evidence of the greater impact of the thumbprint campaign in these areas. The connection between remoteness, general insecurity and the vulnerability of opposition supporters was emphasized by one 'witness' from Kampot province, who was produced by the Sam Rainsy Party after the election to testify to intimidation:

> People are very fearful, they know about the situation but they are fearful and they stay silent. I live in a place with a lot of jungle. If they say they'll shoot you they will shoot you … I dare not question, the situation is very dangerous. A few nights before a lot of robberies of motorcycles took place in the village, a lot of people were very scared.[42]

Distinctions between the security situation in urban areas such as Phnom Penh and rural political arenas were drawn by election monitors also. One commented:

> In Phnom Penh [parties could travel freely in 1998], there were many international observers so [the authorities] could not do anything illegal, but in the remote areas it was easy for them, especially for the local authorities. Sometimes people were shot dead if they didn't do something.[43]

In fact, the 1998 election campaign as a whole saw less electoral violence than the 1993 campaign. Reports by the Special Representative of the United Nations Secretary General for Human Rights in Cambodia suggested that five murders with clear political motives took place between 20 May and 25 July in Kompong Cham, Kompong Thom, Kandal and Siem Reap, and another eleven in a single attack by 'Khmer Rouge' soldiers in Anlong Veng on polling day. A further five killings, three in Siem Reap and two in Pursat, before the election, were judged to have mixed political and personal motives.[44] This compares to more than 200 politically motivated killings during the 1993 election period,[45] plus grenade or shooting attacks on party offices which numbered 89 in one month alone.[46]

Yet intimidation and protection played a major role in the election campaign because voters anticipated economic sanction or violence, if not immediately, then at some unspecified time in the future. The history of atrocities in Cambodia, the extreme economic insecurity of voters and the concomitant prevalence of suffering and death in rural Cambodia complement policies designed to inculcate a fear of violence. The experience of 1993, and the more recent memory of between 40 and 60 extra-judicial executions in July 1997,[47] combined with the thumbprint campaign to promote a climate of fear which imposed limits to public political action.

The three planks of CPP support resemble traditional patronage relations in their organization around hierarchical relationships in which protection is awarded in return for political support. However, in the context of processes of modernization, state formation and capitalist penetration, these relations have altered in their functioning and effect. They are no longer ad hoc particularistic mechanisms for promoting harmonious relations between rich and poor within the village. Nor do they ensure the reinvestment in the economic, social and cultural of life of village resources. In the context of the free market and mass election campaigning, these relationships have been extended and rationalized across the country. Flows of resources are used not to temper and legitimate local inequalities, but to promote a systematic co-optation and exploitation backed by coercion, which rationalizes the power of surveillance and thus renders exclusion not merely unprofitable but physically threatening.

Donations and development

At the same time as the CPP used individual gifts to transform the particularistic relations considered part of Khmer 'tradition' into a nation-wide network of surveillance, they also adopted a broader strategy in which a similar discourse of gifts was used to signify CPP dominance over public amenities.

Complementing the CPP's tight control of rural power structures was the party's rural development programme, pursued energetically since 1993 and intensified following the July fighting. A CPP campaign leaflet describing the 'eight achievements of the Cambodian People's Party', claimed the party had implemented 'social and economic development, rural development, building of 2000 schools with 9900 buildings, roads, bridges, irrigation canals, hospitals, temples, development zones'.[48] The condition of Cambodia's war-torn and inadequate infrastructure gave this strategy extra impact in that intelligent investment in a road, bridge or school building could win a party or individual the gratitude of an entire commune.

During its period in government from 1993 to 1997, FUNCINPEC also had participated in this effort; the *Reastr Niyum* party of Ung Huot also advertised development activities sponsored by the party between 1997 and 1998. Yet CPP dominance in this area of activity is immediately visible in the course of travels through Cambodia's provinces a decade after the peace agreements.

In S'aang District, Kandal, FUNCINPEC activists compared the local development efforts of Hun Sen, whose residence was in nearby Ta Khmau, to those of the late FUNCINPEC Minister of State for the Interior, Ho Sok, who had lived in the district before his extra-judicial execution in July 1997. In the year after Ho Sok's death, villagers claimed that in some places local CPP authorities prevented villagers from using infrastructure donated by Ho Sok, such as pumping equipment, and took down plaques commemorating his donations in others.[49]

Attempts to erase the name of Ho Sok from the S'aang landscape suggest concern on the part of the CPP not only to remove the memory of a benefactor who might come to be considered a FUNCINPEC martyr, but also to dominate rural infrastructure. According to FUNCINPEC activists, the people of S'aang had lost a generous patron and powerful advocate when Ho Sok was killed:

> Before he died, when villagers made a complaint, Ho Sok came to help, but after he died there was no more intervention. Ho Sok planned a lot of projects around the countryside but they are still not finished.[50]

The abandonment of Ho Sok's projects half way through illustrates the limits to FUNCINPEC's ability to make a substantive impact on the lives of the poor in rural communities, and contrasts sharply with the flourishing nature of Hun Sen's Kraingyov Development Centre, also in S'aang District. The centre is located in a commune which has benefited from millions of dollars donated personally by Hun Sen.

Within Kraingyov commune, almost every road, bridge and public building bears Hun Sen's name. Although individual houses appear poor, higher than usual quality of planning, construction and maintenance is immediately evident in the public infrastructure. In July 1998, the thickly growing and well-advanced rice crop that was irrigated by water pumped from clear roadside channels, in which flocks of ducks dabbled, also formed a clear contrast with the poorer, drier fields with their choked and stagnant irrigation canals outside the commune.[51]

In 1995, Kraingyov villagers achieved notoriety after ransacking the office of a pro-SRP newspaper which had criticized the Development Centre, beating staff members and destroying equipment. At that time, the commune was considered to be almost fanatically loyal to Hun Sen, who visited the area regularly to make emotional speeches and to denounce political rivals.

Reports in 1998, in contrast, suggested that relations between commune dwellers and the Second Prime Minister had soured following a mock election held by the CPP in the area, which the CPP lost.[52] It was suggested by demonstrators from Kraingyov, who joined opposition post-electoral demonstrations in Phnom Penh, that the control of local CPP authorities over disbursements of development money had heavily benefited certain groups within the commune at the expense of others, and that this had caused tension within the commune.[53] These demonstrators took advantage of the protest space established by the opposition parties to protest their own perceived exclusion from the spoils of the Kraingyov development project. Two protesters from Kraingyov Commune, one of whom described herself as a servant and the other as a farmer and a campaigner for FUNCINPEC, commented:

> Hun Sen just helped the commune chief and the military chief. The people were not allowed to use the things that Hun Sen gave.[54]

> The authorities in Kraingyov [are] the ones who oppress us. They are the dogs of Hun Sen. I want you to put their names in the newspaper. [Hun Sen] helps only the heads of the village, but he didn't give anything to the people.[55]

While personal programmes of rural investment created a pool of loyal supporters that could be brought to the city for political purposes, it equally created a pool of excluded rural outsiders who in 1998 came to the city to protest their exclusion.

Similar construction efforts on the outskirts of Phnom Penh had an apparently positive influence on CPP popularity. A CPP parade of trucks which wound its way through the Phnom Penh streets from the central 7 January District to the outlying district of Dangkao, saw a marked change in its reception by voters as it approached its destination. While city centre voters saw their economic circumstances decline drastically following the July fighting, villagers in Dangkao benefited greatly from the construction of the first built road to be constructed through the district, donated by Phnom Penh CPP deputy governor Chea Sophara.

According to CPP activists, the road considerably eased the journey by farmers in this district to markets in the centre of the capital.[56] The parade had been met largely by indifference with occasional muted expressions of either support or hostility in the centre of Phnom Penh. Yet it found hundreds of people, gathered in enthusiastically cheering and flag-waving crowds, waiting in Dangkao District.[57]

The connection between development activities and the election campaign was clearly illustrated in a radio news report concerning a donation made by Hun Sen to a skills training centre in Meanchey District, Phnom Penh. The report said that Hun Sen had personally donated half the funds for the construction of a new building in the centre, and when asked why he had not donated the full amount, answered:

> that he wants to wait for the election results in August 1998. If he wins the elections he will pay again for other half of the cost of the building construction. If he loses the elections, the building will stay half-completed forever. The Second Prime Minister said, 'I don't want to start electoral propaganda, but surely this [aid] will link up with the election results'.[58]

For the CPP, dissemination of ideological propaganda in electoral campaigning was subordinate to a strategy of establishing an inflexible bottom line throughout Cambodia. The key message of the CPP was that attachment to the party pays. Given the control over aid money retained by CPP officials in central and local government, the ability of villagers to participate in an empowered discussion of development needs and priorities was diminished by strategies which rendered development assistance contingent on loyal political support. Equally, in a situation of marginal subsistence, villagers could not afford to be seen to defect from the CPP's agenda.

Security and the 'strongman'

The inscription of Hun Sen's monogram on public space was mirrored by a strategy designed to promote him as the foundation of security in the Cambodian state. For the state, the newly constituted basis of state–society relations has proved successful in terms of ending insurgency and consolidating power across the country. This reflects both the ending of significant international funding of insurgency, and also the ability of the state to offer attractive deals, including material benefits and protection to defectors in the insurgent movement. The closure of refugee camps and return of refugees to Cambodia placed these individuals also under the purview of the state.

However, in the process of this consolidation, new tensions were created along with new conceptions of power and leadership in society. The use of recast patronage relations to achieve greater cohesion within the state and, indeed, to secure the defection of insurgents to the government, had a marked effect on the nature of political power in Cambodia. State–society relations became decentralized and particularistic, based upon the proliferation of multiple inter-personal power relationships in which those with wealth, arms or political protection were privileged.

Election results suggest that in fact the state was most effectively strengthened by this means in rural areas – indeed, an opposition party claimed in 1998 that commune-level voting patterns indicated a direct and positive relationship between the level of CPP votes and the remoteness of the commune. In both 1993 and 1998, the CPP lost most heavily in the most populated areas, particularly Phnom Penh, Kandal and Kompong Cham. Similarly, in the commune elections of 2002, the CPP achieved its lowest share of the vote (50 per cent) in Phnom Penh, while in the remote provinces of Preah Vihear, Ratanakiri and Mondulkiri, the CPP gained 67 per cent, 74 per cent and 78 per cent of the vote respectively.

These outcomes suggests that the power of the strengthened state to turn out votes for the CPP does not depend directly on the votes of state employees but upon the cohesiveness of the state as an institution capable of marginalizing other forms of collective action. This has not been achieved within urban areas where the influx of foreigners in the shape of UNTAC, international aid donors, and international NGOs has entailed a greater flux and diversity that has nurtured non-state political action. In rural areas, where the impact of such alternative sources of power, money and protection is much less marked – where, indeed, obtaining access to such resources is difficult – the CPP has successfully strengthened both state and party, entwining the two in a matrix of power that has yet to be significantly ruptured.

The successful recasting of patron–client relations, and the linking of these relations into economic practices, entailed a swift exacerbation of pre-existing economic inequalities from 1989. It also prompted a new self-portrayal by the man presumed to be at the top of the patronage heap – Prime Minister Hun Sen. For Hun Sen, the emergence of inequalities of wealth closely tied to new configurations of political power engendered a transformation of his own role as the dominant party's dominant figure. The increasingly charismatic nature of Hun Sen's leadership is frequently viewed as evidence for a retrenchment of Cambodian political culture into the norms of the 1950s and 1960s. However, Hun Sen is not Sihanouk, and cannot capitalize on the electability of the aura of royalty. Rather, Hun Sen's ascendancy is attributable to the new secularity of Cambodian politics in the 1990s and the reorientation and rationalization of clientelism that has been attempted.

The reordered patronage that underpins the state in the 1990s is dependent, less upon distribution of wealth, than upon distribution of protection. The changing role of Hun Sen reflects this transformation in the SoC since the 1980s, from a state ostensibly based upon ideological loyalties, to a state based upon mutual ties of self-interest. The pyramid of protection offered to state employees requires a lynchpin, and it is this requirement that has fed the personal image of Hun Sen as Cambodia's 'strongman'.

The elevation of Hun Sen in this fashion has caused concern within the Cambodian People's Party, where attempts by Hun Sen to insert key supporters into positions of party power have on occasion been thwarted by discontented congress delegates. Yet in terms of the state, and in particular the military, Hun Sen's power is pre-eminent, as indicated by his successful ousting of Prince Ranariddh in July 1997. Underpinned by a judicious policy of support and non-intervention, and an aggressive strategy to win the loyalty of defectors, Hun Sen has consolidated the necessary military power to make his claim to provide protection credible. This is a claim that Hun Sen has made publicly time and again, particularly in the mid 1990s when his relations with FUNCINPEC were declining.

For example, in a speech delivered by Hun Sen to CPP Ministry of Transport workers in 1996, he emphasized his own strength, emerging from the support and loyalty of state workers. He explicitly compared this to the weakness of his rival, First Prime Minister Prince Ranariddh. For example:

> The first and second Prime Ministers have the same rights, but perhaps my effectiveness is more than [Ranariddh's] because I have a mechanism. [Ranariddh] can order but our people won't listen if [he] give[s] the wrong order. But if I command these people will act. That is the difference.[59]

The distinction between 'right' and 'effectiveness' is significant in this context. It promotes a view of state power that exists outside the law or constitution – power is not viewed as a legal entity but a matter of force, located particularly in the cohesiveness of individual members of the state. The 'mechanism' to which Hun Sen refers can only be the links of patronage established within the state and party in the context of the emergence of the free market from 1989. This is a conception of power that has been consistently promoted within the Cambodian state throughout the 1990s.

This speech was made at a time when tensions between FUNCINPEC and the CPP were running high, and throughout the speech the effectiveness and cohesion of the CPP is compared favourably to the weakness and fearfulness of FUNCINPEC. The speech also underlines the ways in which the state has consolidated vis-à-vis the strategies of covert resistance common in Cambodian society in the 1980s. For example, the distinction depicted here by Hun Sen between the power of the First Prime Minister, drawn from a democratic mandate, and the power of the Second Prime Minister, drawn from effective chains of command within the state, underlines the difficulty of translating conceptual resources such as democratic legitimacy into the practical ability to govern. CPP strategies throughout the 1990s were primarily designed to maximize capacity to govern, and elections which awarded power to society were viewed as a threat to ongoing efforts, which began in the 1980s, to promote the military and bureaucratic cohesion that was the source of that effectiveness.

In this speech, Hun Sen characterized his opponents within FUNCINPEC as 'dogs' who are 'as scared as anything, off they flee, off to France out of here'.[60] While the immediate inference is that FUNCINPEC are 'scared' of the CPP, Hun Sen's speeches also carry intimations of broader, more anarchic powers at work in society, including 'Pol Pots',[61] 'worms that destroy society',[62] and 'gangs of thieves and gangs of criminals who were released from jail in the UNTAC era'.[63] While there is often a strong implication in these statements that these destructive forces emerge from or are supported by FUNCINPEC, this rhetoric is effective in that it speaks to a wider unease over the instability of Cambodian society. Consequently, Hun Sen's emphasis on the strength of the CPP as opposed to FUNCINPEC can be read as not only implying a threat to the opposition parties, but also as offering a rationale for continuing CPP dominance of the state, given the importance of party, as well as state, relationships in sustaining the patronage relationships formed as the bulwark against chaos.

A later confrontation with First Prime Minister, Prince Norodom Ranariddh, following threats by Ranariddh to withdraw from the governing coalition of a deal to share administrative power at local level were not implemented, elicited a similar response. Hun Sen decried Ranariddh's threat as a threat to the Constitution, and once again mobilized threats of effective, rather than legal, force to exhibit his superior power:

> Power is based on reality – what you dare to say you must dare to do … When they listen to what you say, this is power, and when no-one listens to you, this is no power. If [they] demand the dissolution of the National Assembly or the Royal Government or to affect the Constitution, Hun Sen would like to declare to use armed forces to suppress [them] … I have the strength to do … I have the power to order troops, armed forces, that power entitles me to protect the Constitution.[64]

While the 'Constitution' is clearly used as a rhetorical device in this speech – particularly given the consistent failure of both FUNCINPEC and the CPP from 1993 to 1998 to pay any attention to constitutional provisions – the characterization of power in defence of a conception of the political community is significant. Once again, power is portrayed here as a function of individual attributes and loyalties, which in turn award entitlements.

This portrayal of power as an individual attribute is essential to the emergence of a mass of secular, personal patronage links throughout the Cambodian state in the 1990s. Moreover, it suggests that the state is itself a function of those links which can mobilize for collective action as well as extracting resources for the enrichment of individuals. During this period, FUNCINPEC, winners of the 1993 elections, failed to consolidate power and failed to achieve a similar level of loyalty within the most crucial arm of the state – that of the military.

The assertion of operational administrative power as prior to and separate from any authority awarded by the electoral mandate was particularly evident in Hun Sen's rhetorical identification of himself with the security of elections in Cambodia in 1998. In doing so, Hun Sen established not only his control over the electoral process, and the dependence of other parties on his tolerance and good will, but also reiterated the subordination of democratic processes and the emerging mandate to a framework of power sustained by the personal relationships within the state which culminated in the person of the 'strongman' – i.e. Hun Sen himself. Thus, interviewed by foreign journalists about allegations of impartiality in the Cambodian electoral organizing committee, Hun Sen commented ambiguously:

> They call Hun Sen strongman, but now I think if the (National Electoral) committee is pro-Hun Sen he is no longer just a strongman but a superman from now on.[65]

Hun Sen further portrayed himself throughout the electoral period as elevated above the fray of political competition, but rather in control of the process:

> If I campaign, it would look no different from a football player who also blows the whistle. And it would not look good even if I win.[66]

In particular, he emphasized the discretionary nature of electoral security. He told an English language magazine shortly before the start of the election campaign that he had 'personally guaranteed' the security of the elections in his capacity as Commander in Chief of the Royal Cambodian Armed Forces, and commented that the situation had been enhanced particularly by the suppression of 'all anarchic forces' in July 1997.[67] After the elections, Hun Sen emphasized the importance of his personal 'victory' in organizing a peaceful election, and commented that the CPP's defeat of FUNCINPEC was 'only the icing on the cake'.[68] By emphasizing his facilitation of the election and exploiting the twin themes of security and democracy, Hun Sen was able to use his great political strengths – control of the armed forces, usually associated with anti-democratic rule – to support his claim for international legitimacy as a democrat, while simultaneously rendering the democratic process contingent upon his own continued power as the overseer of state security.

Subordination of the election to the power of Hun Sen exposed the weaknesses of other parties, who relied on the electoral mandate as their major resource of power. A question frequently asked by voters during the 1998 election campaign was that of how security would be assured and power transferred following the election should the CPP lose.[69] From the July fighting of 1997, Hun Sen identified himself personally with the security of Cambodia and of the election, and his ouster was perceived as engendering a power vacuum which the other parties were widely viewed as too weak to fill.

Conclusion

The combination of these techniques allowed the party to both build upon and offset the exploitative and threatening relations that underpinned the cohesion of the state. The particular methods used allowed the CPP further to claim a role as guardians of an 'authentic Khmer' tradition – an important discursive resource for a party formed by the invading Vietnamese, and still tainted by that association, in election campaigns whose rhetorics largely revolved around the definition of the 'real Khmer'.

In addition to forming an ideational edifice in which the CPP were portrayed as close to the people, the dual structure of exploitative and transformed patrimonial relations which the CPP employed were significant in distancing the opposition from the rural arena. Consequently, the CPP were not only able to build upon their dominance of the state to discipline society, while promoting a party-based ideology for allegiance, but also, and at the same time, use the resulting nexus between insecurity, control and cooptation/exclusion to marginalize other parties in the multi-party arena of the 1990s.

5 International intervention and 'international community'

The changing interaction between state, economy and party, described in previous chapters, occurred in a context in which international intervention sought to open up significant new terrain for political and civil action in Cambodia in the 1990s. The strategies of state- and party-building described can be understood only in the context of a polity which has been heavily influenced by the presence, discourse and practice of a variety of powerful international actors, whose activities press beyond the bounds of Cambodia's foreign relations to shape the contours of the domestic polity itself.

An important strand of political analysis of Cambodia's transition has focused upon international intervention as the key explanatory variable for interpreting the successes and failures of Cambodian democratization. The actions and inactions of international interveners has been seen as a crucial determinant to the forging and breaking of elite pacts, and the emergence or collapse of new political structures and processes in the Cambodian polity. In consequence, analyses of international intervention have frequently focused on the strategies, mistakes and normative attitudes of various international actors, as determining the trajectory of political change in Cambodia. This approach to the understanding of Cambodia's transition has been promoted, in particular, by the opposition leader Sam Rainsy, who has consistently campaigned for greater intervention by the 'international community' under the terms of the Paris Agreements. Rainsy regards a tightening of international supervision of the Cambodian government, particularly through aid conditionality, as crucial for the deepening of democracy in Cambodia. For example, he stated in 2002:

> My message to the world is ... quite simple: 'Hold Cambodia to international standards'. Cambodians want it and deserve it. I'd like to highlight three areas where the international community can help achieve the goal of international standards in Cambodia: Justice, Elections and Governance.[1]

This chapter examines the nature of ongoing international intervention, arguing that this has been significant in stitching Cambodian political activity at home into a variety of networks and realms of political action which extend beyond the borders of Cambodia itself. International intervention has created new arenas of political struggle both within and without Cambodia, and the different characteristics of these various political arenas offer different opportunities and resources to different political actors. Consequently, the forms of political struggle, domination and opposition have multiplied in post-war Cambodia, as they have colonized different arenas at home and abroad.

However, international intervention has also been limited, particularly in its impact beyond the urban centres. Rainsy's view that international intervention can transform Cambodian politics fails to suggest the mechanism by which the impact of international scrutiny at the centre could overcome significant resistance from the state in the rural areas. Like other political actors, international interveners face manipulation of, and resistance to, their efforts. Even so, the interaction between these different forms of political activity, and the different arenas in which they resonate, is as significant for understanding the multifaceted nature of Cambodia's political trajectory since 1991, as Cold War and regional influences were for understanding the nature of Cambodia's internationalized civil war in the 1980s.

Analysis of new, internationally influenced political arenas is complicated by the shifting relations between international and local actors. Shifts over time cause new arenas to appear temporarily, only to collapse later as the focus of political activity moves elsewhere. Here, some of the major arenas that have opened up for political activity are characterized, and the chapter concludes by suggesting that a key strategy of political actors outside the state in the 1990s has been attempts to stabilize and render permanent access to international channels of influence or arenas for struggle, which are, arguably, more complex and fluid in the 1990s than they were in the 1980s. The state, in turn, has attempted to monopolize or close down international connections.

Analysis of the impact of international intervention on Cambodian politics over the course of the 1990s requires an examination, initially, of its various formations. The unusual importance awarded to Cambodia by the superpowers, as a result of its propinquity to the conflict in Vietnam during the Cold War, entails that Cambodia has long been the target of intensive international attention. The current 'international community of Cambodia watchers' replaces the bipolar blocs of the 1970s and 80s, which supported different sides in the civil war years. In the 1980s, these bipolar blocs comprised China and Thailand, broadly supported by ASEAN, the Western powers and the United Nations, on the one hand, and the Soviet Union, the Socialist Republic of Vietnam and the rest of the Soviet Bloc, on the other hand. Interventionary policies on both sides during this decade varied from diplomatic to economic to military support for the contending armies.

The power of these contending interventionary drives and their devastating impact on Cambodia in the 1980s is well-known, and has been blamed for trapping Cambodia in a bloody but internationally and regionally convenient, stalemate for a decade.[2] The focus of international actors on maintaining the control of contending armed forces over separate territories, and supporting this with the provision of military aid, to a great extent facilitated the dominance of warfare as the primary form of political struggle. From the beginning of the US secret bombing campaign in 1969 to the reorientation of relations in Communist Asia marked by Gorbachev's Vladivostock speech in 1986, Cambodia had been regarded as a 'sideshow' into which the malignant effects of East–West and East–East confrontations were displaced through the cynical operations of *realpolitik*.[3]

From 1986, however, when the utility of this policy began to wane, Cambodia achieved a new status as the target of, and testing ground for, interventionary policies of multilateral conflict management, peacebuilding, democratic enlargement, good governance and poverty alleviation. These have been widely portrayed as benevolent and restorative, and have prompted a change in the focus of political struggle, away from warfare and towards various kinds of political interaction between the parties.

Interventionary practices since the decline in the importance of the war as the arbiter of political power can be divided broadly into four time periods demarcated by events in Cambodia. The first period is the era stretching from the emergence of international interest in a peace process in the late 1980s to the end of United Nations authority and the promulgation of the new constitution in 1993. There then followed four years, from 1993 to 1997, of less direct international engagement with the coalition government, primarily mediated by means of aid and trade policies, but with significant monitoring of political developments The military battle between the coalition partners in Phnom Penh in July 1997 marked the start of a period of more direct intervention in the form of diplomacy, conditionality and intensive monitoring between 1997 and 1998. The final period of intervention began at the end of 1998 with the return of Prime Minister Hun Sen as elected prime minister and the formation of a new coalition government.

The presuppositions legitimizing international intervention have been diverse, both within and between time periods, and this has had a profound impact upon the trajectories of local actors, including the state, the CPP, other political parties and civil actors. However, two broad strands can be identified as underlying international interventionary policies. The first is an 'idealist' strand, predicated upon the presupposed efficacy of international intervention in promoting a liberal framework for domestic politics – an efficacy marred only by diplomatic cynicism and a lack of 'political will' internationally. This strand is exemplified by the stance of Amnesty International which stated in 1997:

> the international community has invested heavily in Cambodia, both politically and financially and therefore has a position of special leverage as well as a special responsibility. Governments involved in this process should send a clear and unequivocal signal to the Cambodian authorities about their human rights record.[4]

The second strand is an 'economist' strand in which economic interaction is viewed as the important goal of intervention. The promotion of specifically liberal policies is subordinate to policies for stability and economic growth, although frequently helpful in promoting these goals. The interplay between these two strands of thinking has been complex, particularly because of a tendency, on the part of international interveners and their local partners, to play to different audiences in articulating their concerns. However these related sets of motivations have had an important impact on the ways in which international intervention has been formulated and implemented, with profound implications for the nature of Cambodian politics in the 1990s.

International community in the post-Cold War era

Before exploring international interventionary policies and their local impact in more detail, further clarification of the concept of 'international community' itself is required. The term is problematic in that it is used in two different ways: firstly, it is used simply to designate the array of international actors interacting in some way with Cambodian politics; secondly, it is used to imply a certain unity of purpose and systematicity of conduct amongst those actors. The first usage is largely descriptive, but the second has a rhetorical impact in that it is frequently used to imply the existence of a scrutinizing international public committed to particular norms and values.

The second usage of the term 'international community' is a corollary of liberal internationalist ideas of post-Cold War global governance, and, as such, is connected with interventionary policies that are formulated – or at least promulgated – within liberal internationalist frameworks. For liberal internationalists, the 'international community' has been conceptualized as a realm of legitimacy providing the foundation for the pursuit of normative goals. Within Cambodia, the term *samakum intraciet* is common in local political discourse, although mobilized to different effect by different political actors. Significantly, it is often used by Western interveners to legitimize their activities, and is frequently treated by these as a unified actor with a variously conceptualized but ordered set of preferences and manifest repertoire of powers.

Ideas regarding an international community emerged powerfully at the end of the Cold War in the context of visions of a newly united world, as captured in George Bush's vision of a 'new world order',[5] Francis

Fukuyama's declaration of the 'end of history',[6] and Boutros Boutros-Ghali's conviction that

> an opportunity has been regained to achieve the great objectives of the charter – a united nations capable of maintaining international peace and security, of securing justice and human rights and of promoting, in the words of the charter, 'social progress and better standards of life in larger freedom'.[7]

This vision has been broadly associated in an influential strand of Western thinking with ideals of 'cosmopolitanism' and 'liberal internationalism'.[8] These ideals combine the agency of engaged global citizens, via the proliferating media of transnational technologies, to envision a 'globalization from below'[9] in which international communities of volunteers work to promote the common interests of mankind. Frequently, such communities are envisaged as working in partnership with intergovernmental organizations such as the United Nations and the World Bank.

Ramsbotham and Woodhouse regard the 'international community' as 'the collectivity which faces the challenge of what to do or not to do in the face of humanitarian suffering in other countries'.[10] This descriptive definition is then given a normative status through their conceptualization of the international community as a 'realm of legitimacy' located on a continuum somewhere between an 'international society' or realm of order, and a 'world community' or realm of justice. The suggestion that the decision made by the 'international community' regarding 'what to do or not to do' is subject to concerns of legitimacy, rather than merely *realpolitik*, introduces a normative aspect to the international realm.

Ramsbotham and Woodhouse's 'international community' comprises, primarily, interventionist states and United Nations peacekeepers. They distinguish the 'international community' thus from the 'world community' in which the distinction between states has broken down, and the decision-makers who face the challenge of humanitarian response become an undifferentiated public of global citizens. For Chris Brown, the concept of 'world community' requires a 'growing awareness of common interest and identity'.[11] The extension of compassion across borders transforms here into a decreasing awareness of borders as salient at all. This transformation implies that the view of humanitarian action as the promotion of particular values universally by an 'international community' has been supplanted by the defence of universal values presupposed. David Held perceives an internationalization of political communities, in response to economic globalization, in the following manner:

> The determination of political community and the nature of political identity within it become less a territorial matter and more a matter of transaction, exchange, and bargaining across a complex set of

> transnational networks. At the very least, national political communities by no means simply determine the structure, education, and cultural flows in and through which their citizens are cultivated. Citizens' values and judgements are now formed in a complex web of national, international and global cultural exchange.[12]

As a result of this transformation of political community, different nations are 'enmeshed and entrenched in complex structures of overlapping forces, relations, and movements'.[13] These different accounts suggest a dual transformation taking place in the classical division between the national and the international realm, largely in response to forces of economic globalization. These transformations comprise, on the one hand, an increasing tendency on the part of states and inter-state organizations to seek to legitimize intervention on the grounds of defending common values; and secondly, on the other hand, an increasing complexity of enmeshed transnational networks operating across state borders, to promote common values.

It is significant that the conceptions of an international society, co-operating in pursuit of order, an international community of legitimate compassionate intervention, and a world community of solidarity are viewed as points upon a temporal continuum in which the driving force is economic globalization. The current phase of 'international community' is often seen by liberal internationalists as trapped between increasingly outdated but still powerful conceptions of *realpolitik* and a more expansive future freed from the bonds of exclusionary conceptions of citizenship and sovereignty. Consequently, the interventionary tendencies of states and inter-state organizations has been viewed, since the end of the Cold War, as ambiguous in ethical terms. The new humanitarianism has been criticized as insufficiently disinterested, tending, as it does, to promote ethical objectives that accord with great power interests and to de-emphasize ethical imperatives that are costly, inconvenient, or simply irrelevant to the pursuit of power. Richard Falk regards obstacles to the achievement of 'global justice' as arising from 'the persisting fragmentation of the world in terms of sovereign territorial states' while promising developments as emerging from the 'plausibility of conceiving the world as a unity and from the beginnings of a global civil society due to the efforts of transnational forces'.[14] He views as 'encouraging' the 'various collaborations between transnational social forces and those governments that are more value-oriented and sensitive to the claims of global justice, as opposed to those that define their role according to the maximization of power, wealth, and influence'.[15] Similarly, Ramsbotham and Woodhouse regard the current status of the 'international community' as

> struggling into existence within the nexus of the international society of states, summoned to act in accordance with humanitarian values derived from the possibility of a world community of humankind, but

> at the same time having to rely on means provided by the most powerful states within the international anarchy, confronts the most vicious atavistic forces unleashed by the eruption of international-social conflict.[16]

In the *Agenda for Peace*, Boutros-Ghali offers a more benevolent view of state sovereignty as 'the foundation stone' of a new order. He added, 'the time of absolute and exclusive sovereignty, however, has passed'.[17]

Equally, Boutros-Ghali emphasises in the *Agenda*, and elsewhere, a sense of the diversity of actors constituting this understanding of 'international community' and the complex relationships of influence and legitimacy in which they exist. For example:

> Today, we are well aware that the international community must address a human community that is transnational in every way ... The mobilization mission that the international community fully expects of non-governmental organizations will be possible only if the organizations are in their totality representative of international society.[18]

This view of 'international community' captures a sense of complex cross-cutting networks for political influence, representation and mobilization, which operate across state boundaries and within and between inter-governmental organizations. It further suggests the diversification of democratic representation, away from the bounds of the state–society relationship, and into a transnational plane of voluntary engagement in the pursuit of the common good.

In this study, the term 'international community' will be used to identify the full range of interveners in Cambodia, acknowledging that these interveners are motivated both by *realpolitik* and by an emerging sense of universal norms and standards of political action. In this sense, it will be used in a descriptive rather than a normative sense. The tension between ethical concerns and promotion of interest in international action will be viewed as a constituent component of the 'international community' as it currently exists, and as explaining the diversity of forms of international interventionary policy. However, the teleological characterization of an international community engaged in a temporal transition of its own – away from the *realpolitik* of the past, and towards a humanitarian future – is rejected. The international community is viewed here neither as a nascent benevolent force for good nor as an anachronistic neo-imperialist drive for power. Rather, it is viewed as a complex set of overlapping and often contradictory networks and forums in which diverse political struggles over Cambodia's past, present and future can take place, within different discursive frameworks. In totality, these comprise a set of interconnected publics, which offer discursive and material resources to both the local and international actors who have access to them. It will be argued that, to a great extent, the international publics created by the engagement of the international community in Cambodia offer a significant sphere for political struggle, in a polity where the unambiguously domestic turf is increasingly dominated by the repressive entrepreneurial networks of the dominant party and the state.

International intervention from Paris to UNTAC

In the case of Cambodia, the decline of bipolarity in the mid- to late 1980s led to a decreased Western interest in maintaining the civil war as a means for 'bleeding' the embroiled communist states. Instead, a new interest in the promotion of international stability as a more solid platform for the smoother functioning of international markets became a key concern. Surin Maisrikrod attributes the change in Thai policies towards Cambodia from 1988 as economically driven, reflecting new Prime Minister Chatichai Choonhaven's vision of 'turning Indochina from a battlefield into a marketplace'.[19] Similarly, Vietnam's changing perspective on its onerously supportive relations with Cambodia and Laos, in a context of isolation from the thriving economies of ASEAN, were important in prompting Vietnam's withdrawal of troops from Cambodia and subsequent incorporation into the ASEAN community. The reorientation of Soviet policy from 1986, and the subsequent cuts in aid to Vietnam and Cambodia in the late 1980s and early 1990s, offered opportunities, from both the side of the capital-rich ASEAN tigers and the capital-starved orphans of the CMEA, to articulate ambitions for greater regional integration in the form of an expansion of ASEAN to include all the countries of the region, and regional economic policies in the form of the ASEAN Free Trade Area.

While these regional ambitions were tempered by the financial crisis that hit South East Asia in 1997, Thai foreign policy under the Chuan Leekpai government showed clear continuities with the Chatichai philosophy. In the wake of the financial crisis, and in response to the cross-border problems of refugees, drug trafficking and illegal immigration that accompanied economic liberalization and ongoing political strife in both Cambodia and Laos to the East, and Burma to the West, Thailand adopted a foreign policy rationale that focused on proactive promotion of regional stability in the latter half of the 1990s. This rationale was framed in terms strongly influenced by idealistic views of post-Cold War community, and it regarded 'peace, happiness and the well-being of neighbouring countries' as promoting the prosperity of Thailand.[20]

Proactive measures included promotion of policies such as 'flexible engagement' or 'enhanced interaction' at the regional level, to facilitate ASEAN's ability to intervene in the problems of its members – particularly the more problematic new entrants of Vietnam, Laos, Burma and Cambodia. These formulations briefly included a commitment by the Chuan government to Thai promotion of human rights in the region, but, by the end of the 1990s, this commitment was tempered by the resistance of other ASEAN countries.[21]

The changing approach of Thailand over the course of the 1990s reflected changing understandings of the relationship between politics and economics in the aftermath of the Cold War. Early connections were drawn between democracy and political and economic stability, particularly by Western countries. Australian foreign minister Gareth Evans contended in 1994 that:

> In-country peace-building is a long-term preventive strategy that focuses on potential causes of insecurity ... It seeks to encourage equitable economic development, to enhance human rights broadly defined and to facilitate good governance. These goals should be pursued not only for their own sakes, but also because making progress toward them contributes powerfully to national and international security.[22]

As the drafter of a document which finally provided the framework for United Nations intervention in Cambodia, Evans was an influential figure in the 'international community' which addressed Cambodia in the early 1990s. In the context of the Paris Peace Conference of 1991 and the deployment of UNTAC in 1992 and 1993, these views were significant in framing Cambodia's relationship with a posited 'international community' in those years.

At the start of the 1990s, arguably, an 'international community' was formed from the countries represented at the Paris Peace Conference. These signatories comprised a number of international states' groupings. The Non-Aligned Movement was represented by the participation of Yugoslavia. All the states of the ASEAN[23] and communist Indochina[24] attended, along with all the powers comprising the Security Council Permanent Five.[25] By this means both the regional and Cold War dynamics of the conflict in Cambodia were reflected. The co-presidents of the Paris Conference of October 1991, the Indonesian and French foreign ministers, were drawn from ASEAN and the Permanent Five respectively. In addition, influential Asia–Pacific powers and prospective donors were included in the conference in the shape of Japan, India, Australia and Canada.

In what sense did these groupings of states constitute an international community? The primary sense of community sprang from a common interest in ridding themselves of an onerous burden that impeded the formation of new relations within the region and the world, following the end of the East–East Cold War in Asia. As an obstacle to the economically driven desires for closer relations between the Soviet Union and China, China and Vietnam, and Vietnam and the ASEAN nations, Cambodia's civil war became a common object of concern.

However, coincidental interests in Cambodia did not imply similar policy frameworks. In the West, the war resonated in two policy frameworks.

Firstly, the Cambodian civil war was seen as an obstacle to promotion of the idea of the 'Pacific Rim' as a new economic community. This view was articulated by Secretary of State James Baker in 1991, who tied the question of economic co-operation and prosperity instrumentally to the idea of a moral community 'for the next millennium to be one of the Pacific, a strong sense of community must emerge based on shared prosperity and common values'. He added that the end of the conflict in Cambodia was necessary to 'enhance the sense of the Asia–Pacific community'.[26]

Secondly, the war resonated in terms of a moral agenda that viewed peace, justice and rightful action in international affairs, rather than economic growth, as the primary goal. Within this framework, an important aspect of a peace process would be the extent to which it would allow Western powers to distance themselves from the National Army of Democratic Kampuchea, which had received their diplomatic support throughout the 1980s. The jettisoning of the PDK by means of a peace process was seen by some Western liberals as an act that could symbolize the end of the era when national interest would dominate over moral values in Western foreign policy making. For example, US Congressman Stephen Solarz commented:

> If the international community truly believes that humane treatment of the defenceless is a norm that should be applied wherever possible, it must act now and to the utter limits of its capacity to block a new round of genocide in Cambodia ... Cambodians have suffered too long because of the moral cynicism of others. We degrade our own values if we unnecessarily permit them to suffer any longer.[27]

Both these views underline the strong sense in the early 1990s that the Paris Agreements represented more than merely a means to end an inconvenient war. Rather, the Agreements represented the end of the Cold War divide, and the construction of a community of common values and interests in South East Asia that could not only rescue the West from the hypocrisy imposed upon it by the communist threat, but could also further unlock East Asia's rich economic potential. Regional actors, including China, Thailand, Vietnam and the Soviet Union, shared the latter goal, but paid less attention to the former. To the extent that the signatories to the Paris Agreements shared one or both of these goals, and were prepared to commit themselves to interventionary action in pursuit of them, an international community can be said to have formed around the peace process.

In committing themselves as signatories to the Paris Agreements, the states that attended the Paris Conference in 1991 formally took on certain responsibilities with regard to the future of Cambodia over and above the requirement to co-operate and assist in the implementation of UNTAC's mandate itself. In line with the UN's goals regarding peacekeeping between foreign-supported armies, and the concern of external parties to the

Cambodian war to withdraw from the protracted and expensive conflict, an important requirement placed upon the signatories regarded respect for, and non-interference in, Cambodia's 'sovereignty, independence, territorial integrity and inviolability, neutrality and national unity'. However, certain aspects of Cambodia's future political trajectory were excluded from this domain by the wording of the Agreements themselves, setting the scene for particular forms of international intervention that would continue long after the peacekeeping exercise itself was over.

Thus, for example, the Agreements awarded duties and responsibilities to the external signatories with reference to the question of human rights. While the *Agreement Concerning the Sovereignty, Independence, Territorial Integrity and Inviolability, Neutrality and National Unity of Cambodia* called upon states to 'refrain from any interference in any form whatsoever, whether direct or indirect, in the internal affairs of Cambodia', the same agreement also required the signatories to 'promote and encourage respect for and observance of human rights and fundamental freedoms in Cambodia as embodied in the relevant international instruments in order, in particular, to prevent the recurrence of human rights abuses'.[28] With regard to both the question of sovereignty, independence, territorial integrity and inviolability, neutrality and national unity and to the question of human rights, the signatories committed themselves to taking action in the event of violations. Such action could include referring the matter to various organs of the United Nations or to the Co-Chairmen of the Paris Conference.[29]

The *Principles for a New Constitution for Cambodia*, specified in the *Agreements*, clarified the types of human rights under discussion. The *Principles* stated:

> Cambodia's tragic recent history requires special measures to assure protection of human rights. Therefore the constitution will contain a declaration of fundamental rights, including the rights to life, personal liberty, security, freedom of movement, freedom of religion, assembly and association including political parties and trade unions, due process and equality before the law, protection from arbitrary deprivation of property or deprivation of private property without just compensation, and freedom from racial, ethnic, religious or sexual discrimination. It will prohibit the retroactive application of criminal law. The declaration will be consistent with the provisions of the Universal Declaration of Human rights and other relevant international instruments. Aggrieved individuals will be entitled to have the courts adjudicate and enforce these rights.[30]

Emphasis on civil, political and property rights reflected the powerful influence of liberal internationalism upon the thinking behind peacekeeping in the early 1990s. The *Principles* further stipulated that Cambodia should 'follow a system of liberal democracy' with 'periodic and genuine elections', and that an independent judiciary should be established. Economic, social and cultural issues that might be addressed by the new constitution were not stipulated, except insofar as they were covered by the blanket references to 'the Universal Declaration of Human Rights and other relevant international instruments'.[31]

Further, the signatory states 'urge[d] the international community provide generous economic and financial support'[32] for rehabilitation measures. While the *Declaration on the Rehabilitation and Reconstruction of Cambodia* insisted that 'no attempt should be made to impose a development strategy on Cambodia from any outside source',[33] nevertheless it was suggested that 'international, regional and bilateral assistance to Cambodia should be coordinated as much as possible', through the establishment of a 'consultative body' called the International Committee on the Reconstruction of Cambodia.[34] It was also suggested that, since 'no effective programme of national reconstruction can be initiated without detailed assessments of Cambodia's human, natural and other economic assets', that international 'fact-finding missions from the United Nations system, international financial institutions and other agencies' should be launched to 'identify' development priorities.[35] It was stipulated that 'the reconstruction phase should promote Cambodian entrepreneurship and make use of the private sector, among other sectors, to help advance self-sustaining economic growth'.[36] Participation by non-governmental organizations was also advocated.[37]

These provisions suggest that, while the military interventions of the 1980s were to be left behind, nevertheless a project was underway to bring Cambodia into line with liberal internationalist and free market principles aspired to under the New World Order. Despite the participation of states such as China and the ASEAN nations, that would later resist the notion of international human rights in UN forums and assert rights of sovereignty vis-à-vis forms of humanitarian intervention in pursuit of peacebuilding or human rights protection, the Paris Agreements arguably placed the resolution of the Cambodia conflict within the liberal internationalist framework that would be elaborated the following year in Boutros-Ghali's *Agenda for Peace*. Thus no contradiction was seen between the concern for non-intervention and protection of Cambodia's sovereignty and the erection in the Agreements themselves of an internationally-sponsored framework for ongoing human rights oversight, liberal democratic reform and free market development strategies.

When the United Nations' mandate in Cambodia came to be implemented, however, problems arose. In part, these reflected contradictions between diplomatic forms of international action between the UN, the Cambodian parties, and various governments which formed one aspect of international community, and more idealist attempts at structural reform pursued by another sub-community of international actors, which criticized the diplomatic approach. The latter prominently included UNTAC's Human

Rights Component but also incoming international NGOs including human rights watchdogs such as Human Rights Watch, which also criticized the UN mission.

Within UNTAC, two strands of opinion were evident with regard to the priorities of the Peace Process, reflecting the influence of both liberal internationalist and political economist philosophies, and of reformist and diplomatic forms of action. On the one hand, strong claims were made for taking the idea of structural reform in the interests of post-conflict peacebuilding seriously. In 1992, Yasushi Akashi, Special Representative of the Secretary-General, described UNTAC's role as 'to act as a facilitator for the peace process and as a catalyst for the political and structural reform of democracy',[38] suggesting the accords were intended to have a long-term democratizing effect on the country. In Akashi's words, the objective was no less than to 'build a new country' – a free market liberal democracy of rights bearing citizens and entrepreneurs, to replace the communism and barbarism of the past. This accorded with the provisions in the Agreements which empowered the external signatories to continue to monitor, promote, and if necessary take action regarding human rights.

The view that UNTAC had a part to play in 'political and structural reform' reflected the new concept of 'post-conflict peacebuilding' formulated by then UN Secretary General Boutros Boutros-Ghali in his 1992 *Agenda for Peace*. Boutros-Ghali defined this as 'the construction of a new environment' by means of 'rebuilding the institutions and infrastructures of nations torn by civil war and strife'.[39] He added:

> there is an obvious connection between democratic practices – such as the rule of law and transparency in decision-making – and the achievement of true peace and security in any new and stable political order.[40]

A similar view was promoted vigorously by UNTAC's Human Rights Component; yet UNTAC's record with regard to human rights practices in Cambodia during the transition period exemplifies the tension between the imperatives of diplomacy and the ideals of liberal internationalism in relations between Cambodia and the 'international community'. The Human Rights Component, along with many observers of the process, viewed the Agreements overall as indicating international policies for structural change of the Cambodian polity in pursuit of human rights. The Human Rights Component's final report criticized the failure to reflect this in the framing of UNTAC's mandate, which in their view did not adequately address 'a need for a radical overhaul of existing state institutions [and]... to urgently rebuild or build new structures of government'. The Component pointed out that the mandate did not provide for 'peacebuilding' activities, which the Component viewed as 'clearly ... necessary' for 'the success of human rights efforts in the future'.[41]

Other international actors saw the aims of the international community in Cambodia as more limited. For example, Stephen Heder and Judy Ledgerwood – former UNTAC staff reflecting on the operation in a 1996 volume – argued that while fulfilling the Agreements required some kind of democratic acclaim for the transition, structural reform to promote the 'consolidation of liberal democracy' was not a high priority. Despite the incorporation of requirements that the new Cambodian constitution contain provisions safeguarding liberal democracy, pluralism, and the free market, it was left to Cambodians to 'integrate this commitment with the political, military, social, economic, cultural and diplomatic realities facing Cambodia once UNTAC was gone'.[42]

The distinction between a view of UNTAC as a force for internal structural political reform, and the more pragmatic and limited view of Heder and Ledgerwood, foreshadowed an ongoing tension in conceptualizations of the guiding principles of international intervention in Cambodia. These tensions became more marked towards the mid-1990s as the relatively homogeneous unit of UNTAC was replaced by competitive and increasingly enmeshed networks of bilateral, multilateral and non-governmental interveners, with a variety of interests to defend and promote.

Broader initiatives in the region, such as the emergence from early 1993 of an 'Asian view' of human rights, strongly supported by regional powers such as China, has led to a retreat from the liberal internationalist position, such as it was in the immediate post-Cold War years. The difficulties experienced by US policy makers pursuing 'democratic enlargement' throughout the 1990s in transforming 'rogues' into good world citizens led to a new mood of pessimism noted in the calls for a return to the colonization of 'failed states' that have remained 'mired in history', to use Fukuyama's term. While Akashi's view that 'UNTAC's strength is derived from the unanimous support of the international community'[43] may have glossed significant differences in understandings of the relation between means and ends from the outset, the tensions in the idea of a principled 'international community' addressing Cambodia have become more evident as time has passed. Yet, significantly, the continued deployment of the term in Cambodian and international political discourse suggests that the turn retains some rhetorical power.

Arguably this is because the term 'international community' does not require a referent of ready and willing crusaders in order to have political significance. Like any other community, the members of the 'international community' have divergent interests and perspectives. What defines them is not their interest in common action towards common goals, but their engagement, in some fashion, with Cambodian politics. The diversity of the international community, of its perspectives, interventionary activities and proffered resources, has prompted a range of engagements between local and international actors, which both sides have creatively exploited.

Intervention from UNTAC to July 1997

Following UNTAC's departure, intervention took less direct forms, as Cambodia's international status became more normal with the creation of an elected and internationally recognised government in 1993. In terms of organized forums within which Cambodian political developments could be discussed, UNTAC left behind it a number of organizational legacies. The first of these was the Office of the United Nations Secretary General's Special Representative in Cambodia, responsible for observing Cambodia's continued adherence to the aims and objectives of the Paris Agreements.[44] The work of this office was complemented by that of the United Nations Centre for Human Rights, later renamed the Cambodia Office of the High Commission for Human Rights, which was mandated to continue the work of the Human Rights Component, in assisting, educating and funding human rights groups and assisting with the drafting of legislation, the building of institutions and judicial reform.[45] Following the closure of this office in 1999, co-ordination of the United Nations country team fell to the representative of the United Nations Development Programme in Cambodia. Alongside UNDP and the COHCHR, the country team comprised seven other UN agencies, UN volunteers and UNAIDS. These agencies have co-ordinated activities with respect to disaster management and the drafting of a development framework for Cambodia.

The advice of UN specialized agencies on Cambodia's development trajectory is fed into donor decision-making via UNDP representation at meetings of the Consultative Group of Donor Countries. Initially launched as the International Conference on the Reconstruction of Cambodia in 1993, this co-ordinating group now meets four times a year to review the Cambodian governments progress towards a set of goals in the economic and administrative spheres, and to co-ordinate pledges of funds by agencies and states to Cambodian development projects.

However, Grant Curtis points out that the co-ordinating efforts of donor states and agencies for much of the 1990s was lacking in substance, and from 1993 to 1997 in particular, failed to impose a 'donor discipline' upon the Cambodian government.[46] In fact, the Consultative Group of Donor Nations encompasses states with diverse attitudes towards Cambodia. Following UNTAC's departure, multilateral forums and agencies found their scope for articulating a 'community' voice increasingly inhibited by developing networks of bilateral relations. Consultative Group meetings from 1993 to 1997 increasingly focused upon 'technical issues' rather than 'real discussion on the direction of Cambodia's development path'.[47] Consequently, the sense of a unified international community, such as it was in 1993, receded in the period to 1997, as different engaged countries and agencies came to different accommodations with the newly legitimated Cambodian government, and the contending parties within it. Yet the perception of a community of interveners engaged in joint action, inherited from the UNTAC era, continued to be influential, so that the concept of an organized, rather than merely accidental 'international community' continued to be deployed, sometimes descriptively and sometimes prescriptively.

The form of this international community can perhaps be most appropriately conceived of as a matrix of cross-cutting networks of interest, accommodation and normative concern. Tapping into these networks is crucial for many organizations in Cambodia, both state and non-state, as international networks provide the financial resources for organized activity that is widely viewed as unavailable within the constraints of Cambodia's subsistence economy. Yet the plural nature of the international community offered opportunities for different actors within Cambodia to co-opt different international resources to their own ends, exploiting the different perspectives which prevented the emergence of a unified, disciplinary donor stance. Such opportunities were pointed out by then Second Prime Minister Hun Sen in 1996 when, in a speech denouncing US intervention in Cambodia's domestic affairs, he drew a contrast between Western and Japanese approaches to aid:

> Don't protest against Japan, it does not interfere, it is very good. Japanese assistance is the only one which does not have conditions.[48]

The divergence in approaches among donors entails that the politics of donor–state relations is complex. Between 1993 and 1997, the attachment of conditions regarding state reform to aid was generally avoided by international donors. This was not only because of the dire state of Cambodia's infrastructure, economy and services, and the counterproductive political and economic effects of halting reconstruction, but also because attaining unanimity among donors, in a context of promising economic growth, was problematic. The apparent early success of the peace process in providing a basis for economic growth inserted a wedge between those international actors who saw economic development as the appropriate goal, and those who sought to promote some sense of political, social and cultural development towards liberal democracy as an objective of equal status. Even within the United States, where Cambodian–American communities regularly lobbied for an interventionary policy in support of democracy in Cambodia, and where the Clinton administration had made international human rights promotion, particularly with respect to China, a campaign issue in the 1992 presidential elections, policy reversals took place. In 1994, President Clinton articulated a new policy of 'constructive engagement' towards China, largely in response to powerful business lobbies within America who emphasized the primacy of economic development as a prerequisite for political change.[49] Throughout the 1990s this stance has been contested by groups of senators who have repeatedly pressed for sanctions against a Hun Sen-led Cambodia, particularly in response to the anti-CPP lobbying of their Cambodian–American constituents. However, under the George W. Bush administration, the drift to constructive engagement with a Hun Sen-led government is likely to continue.

Divergences between donor states, within donor states and over time, as bilateral donors change governments and policies, is closely watched and exploited in Cambodia. The activities of American senators who denounced the integrity of the 1998 elections were watched closely and much discussed in Cambodia, particularly within newspapers sympathetic to FUNCINPEC and the SRP, leading to claims that a US invasion of Cambodia to oust Hun Sen was imminent. For example, one leaflet circulating in Phnom Penh during the demonstrations stated:

> Bill Clinton ... has decided to save the Khmer people on the basis of the request of the U.S. Congress. This action will help to liberate Cambodia, and Cambodian people from dictator Hun Sen, the puppet of Vietnamese ... Submarines are now ready to be deployed. So are battle ships that carry all types of aircraft and armed troops. They will act in cooperation to arrest Hun Sen and his group to be sentenced for crimes against humanity.[50]

Equally, differences in donor perspectives have been exploited, at least rhetorically, by Hun Sen. For example, in late 1995, a leading FUNCINPEC parliamentarian, Prince Norodom Sirivudh, was arrested, exiled and later tried and convicted in absentia on charges of plotting to assassinate Hun Sen. The case raised a number of issues regarding the status of Cambodia's newborn democracy; in particular, the principle of parliamentary immunity was seen by human rights workers to have been violated, rumours of death threats against the arrested politician circulated, and the exile deal, brokered by the king in response to these threats, directly breached the 1993 constitution, which stated, 'Khmer citizens shall not be ... exiled'.[51] Following these events, Hun Sen adopted an assertive line vis-à-vis the question of any possible connection between the Sirivudh case and international aid to Cambodia. He publicly defied the US to remove Cambodia's Most Favoured Nation (MFN) trading status, threatening popular demonstrations against the US embassy in Phnom Penh:

> For Americans, if they talk too much about Cambodian affairs, we'll stage another demonstration demanding them to pay us compensation [for the war] ... We're not going to die if they give MFN or not ... During the State of Cambodia era, we lived in a time when they attacked us, they surrounded us, they imposed sanctions against us. We survived [then] and why can't we survive now?[52]

Subsequently, Hun Sen tempered these remarks, but reiterated his intention 'to protect independence and sovereignty of the country, stopping you from interfering in the internal affairs and from considering my country as a small one of yours'.[53] Shortly afterwards, US Assistant Secretary of State for East Asia and Pacific Affairs Winston Lord said during a visit to Cambodia that the US Administration was in favour of unconditional renewal of MFN.[54] In another speech, in February 1996, Hun Sen offered a different account of US–Cambodia relations which suggested the threat had passed:

> officials from the United States had a meeting with me – we spent three hours talking and eating together – they told me they will grant aid to Cambodia despite their current [budget] problems.[55]

The affair illustrated the limits to US interventionary practices; yet, at the same time, among Cambodian human rights groups, the Sirivudh affair was regarded as appropriately an international matter. For example, two directors of leading Cambodian human rights NGOs, who refrained from commenting publicly on the Sirivudh affair despite their conviction that Sirivudh's rights had been violated and that this represented a serious setback to Cambodia's democratization process, reported that they felt the affair was most appropriately addressed in the realm of the 'international community':

> We cannot allow our organization to be destroyed by a confrontation like that. We need our organization to survive to protect other people. And also Sirivudh can be protected by the international community better than us.[56]
>
> For the problem of Sirivudh, we couldn't use a local fight in Cambodia – we don't want to make things worse, because we knew that the second Prime Minister was really angry at that time. But with the international community, we make our case.[57]

This use of the 'international community' as an arena for local political action that was viewed as too dangerous to be undertaken at home reflects the view of the 'international community', not necessarily as a unified actor capable of implementing particular policies, but as a realm of political contention, which offered different opportunities to those available at home. In this case, little action was taken internationally – one UN human rights worker said with regard to the case:

> What could be done? It wasn't Tiananmen Square.[58]

However, on other issues, displacement of local issues into the international realm did result in major interventionary action by international actors. The decision by the International Monetary Fund (IMF) to suspend loans to Cambodia in response to the issue of illegal forestry is an example of this. This decision was taken in reaction to reports produced by a British-based environmental NGO, Global Witness, which conducted investigations into logging in Cambodia in the 1990s. From January 1995, the Cambodian government had banned the export of logs and timber from Cambodia in order to gain control over the timber trade. This move was supported by the IMF and World Bank, which were attempting to restructure the forestry industry as a source of revenue for the Cambodian government. However, the practice of issuing export licences for 'old felled timber' provided a cover under which exports could continue and defiance of the law could be rendered profitable. According to Global Witness, 95 per cent of illegally logged timber was exported under the cover of such subterfuges between 1995 and 1999.[59]

In 1996, Global Witness obtained documents signed by Cambodia's co-Prime Ministers authorizing the export of 1.1 million cubic metres of 'old felled' logs to Thailand.[60] Global Witness campaigned against the deal, arguing that such quantities of 'old felled timber' did not exist and that consequently the documents simply provided the cover for unrestricted logging of Cambodia's remaining valuable forest resources. Global Witness's campaign over the issue adopted the economic concerns of the IMF and World Bank, pointing in particular to the failure of the Cambodian government to specify where revenue from the deal would go. Global Witness claimed that this 'represented a betrayal of the Cambodian government's partner in reconstruction – the donor community ... [who] were ... working with the Cambodian government, to increase revenues from forestry, and to reform the forestry sector'.[61]

The IMF suspended its Enhanced Structural Adjustment Facility to Cambodia in May 1996 in response to this lobbying campaign. It is significant that the key issue at stake in this lone example of the exercise of conditionality in the period from 1993 to July 1997 was fiscal transparency, rather than political reform. This reflects an overall trajectory in international interest in Cambodia; however, it also reaffirmed, for domestic political actors, the relevance of an interventionary international sphere to Cambodian politics.

Beyond the realms of conditionality, donors put money into a variety of non-state projects designed to support democratization, military reform and human rights in Cambodia. For example, USAID money was channelled through a variety of non-governmental organizations working in Cambodia in these issue areas. The Asia Foundation worked on projects to strengthen the legislative branch of government by, for example, the establishment of a Cambodian Hansard to provide a record of parliamentary debates, support for a parliamentary committee system and provision of advice for the drafting of contentious laws such as the 1994 Press Law. The International Human Rights Law Group, also funded by USAID, promoted judicial reform by means of the establishment of a public defenders' association, established to provide legal defence for prisoners at trial, and a Court Training Project which deployed American judges to provincial courts in

Cambodia to act as mentors for Cambodia's judiciary. These efforts were also important in promoting lower level forums for debate, formulation of plans for action and mobilization of resources. The more mundane level of day-to-day interactions between Cambodian state, non-governmental organizations and donors is a highly significant level for determining the scope available to different Cambodian actors to promote interests, whether in reform or in maintenance of the status quo.

Grant Curtis has been critical of the community relations constituted by these activities, regarding the various donors as comprising not a community, but a 'market' operating in dynamic conditions of deregulated competition and notable for the lack of moral principle applied. For Curtis, the contours of the Cambodian 'aid market' in the 1990s reflected, firstly, the incorporation of rehabilitation into the conception of 'peacebuilding' captured by the Paris Accords; secondly, a concern among Western governments to 'expiate guilt' with regard to Cambodia's suffering in the Cold War; and thirdly, a perception that Cambodia was 'wide open' to career-making developmental experiments.[62] While the second of these represents a moral impulse, the deregulated and competitive way in which aid projects were implemented undermined, in Curtis's view, the ability to apply principles in any sustained fashion.

However, the question of united or sustained principles of international action is less important for understanding the trajectories of Cambodian politics in the 1990s than the influence of a forum of international attention, debate and comment in which diverse ideational and material resources circulate and may be co-opted by Cambodian actors. This conception of the international community, not as a unified actor but as a range of commenting 'publics', with material resources to contribute, remained important even as the enthusiasm of the most powerful actors – namely, intergovernmental agencies and bilateral donors – for direct intervention to reform the Cambodian polity (as opposed to economy) in a liberal democratic direction appeared to ebb in the mid-1990s. Because Cambodian political actors remained convinced of the political, as opposed to merely economic, salience of an 'international community', and continued to use international networks as political, rather than merely economic resources, the international sphere remained an important realm of Cambodian political action.

The crisis of 1997–8

The military battle that broke out in July 1997 in Phnom Penh and the abrupt departure of sections of the coalition government, the pro-FUNCINPEC military, and the opposition Sam Rainsy Party from Cambodia, brought into clear relief the divergence in international perspectives on Cambodia's future. The earliest reactions of many embassies reflected two concerns. Firstly, there was international concern regarding the performance of FUNCINPEC in government. Prince Ranariddh's activities as First Prime Minister indicated a commitment to liberalism that was more equivocal than expected.[63] There was also concern that the party, as a political organization, had proved weak and inadequate to the task of leading Cambodia through the transition period. Increasing awareness that the breakdown in coalition relations in 1997 had occurred as FUNCINPEC and the CPP competed for the allegiances of defecting NADK units caused some nervousness amongst diplomats. Claims in the pro-CPP press that 'the Prince is really the Khmer Rouge's puppet'[64] perhaps resonated with this nervousness.

Secondly, in the mid-1990s, the first flush of post-Cold War idealism was over, sobered after international experiences in Somalia, Rwanda and Bosnia. Emphasis on the promotion of 'common values' as the sine qua non of post-Cold War prosperity and security had given way, in Cambodia and elsewhere, to pragmatic acceptance of governments which, while illiberal in terms of human rights, and inconsistent in promoting the rule of law, appeared to be delivering certain economic goods. The *Phnom Penh Post* noted the lack of any expression of disapproval from Japan and France regarding the military victory of the CPP over FUNCINPEC and reported:

> Privately many Phnom Penh diplomats from key donor nations have been dismissing the seriousness of recent events and seem eager to get on with a new political equation[65]

A notable early example of this pragmatism included the immediate response of the Australian embassy. Australian Ambassador Tony Kevin reportedly described the 1993–7 coalition government as 'sterile and unworkable', and wrote in a leaked communication to the Australian government that Hun Sen was working to restore stable government in Cambodia.[66]

The leak and publication of this communication caused considerable embarrassment for the Australian government, however, which desired to be seen to be promoting liberal democratic values – an example of the extent to which the pressure of a notional liberal 'international public opinion' could influence international stances vis-à-vis Cambodia. Also, in the context of the claims that had been made regarding the success of the 1993 UNTAC election as an expression of the will of the Cambodian people, this entailed that Ranariddh, winner of those elections, could not be allowed to fade from view.

On 15 July 1997 the Australian Minister for Foreign Affairs, Alexander Downer, announced a suspension of defence co-operation with Cambodia, while continuing humanitarian aid projects in the areas of education, health, rural development and de-mining. Downer described the 'overthrow by military action' of Ranariddh as 'completely unacceptable'. The Australian government's engagement with Cambodia was described as determined by four principles: commitment to the Paris Peace Accords, the Cambodian constitution, and the 'formulation of a broadly based government involving the participation and support of representatives of FUNCINPEC'; commitment to free and fair elections as scheduled, if not before; respect on for human rights and the rule of law; and interest in Cambodia's stability.[67]

Following initial hesitations, other bilateral donors and international agencies also responded to the events. The US took the most critical stance. The size of the US Embassy to Phnom Penh was reduced by two-thirds and a 30-day suspension of aid was imposed, which was later extended indefinitely. A US State Department official on 16 July specifically related this decision to the question of Cambodian democracy rather than merely to stability, commenting that 'we are not willing to concede that we should do nothing, when democracy has been so brazenly flouted'. Japan also suspended a $70 million aid programme.[68] The United Nations Secretary General's Special Representative for Human Rights, Thomas Hammarberg, was one of few international actors to refer to the military battle as a 'violent coup d'etat'.[69]

It is significant to note that the internal struggle in Cambodia was quickly displaced into three different international arenas by the activities of Cambodian political actors. Firstly, the flight of politicians from FUNCINPEC and the Sam Rainsy Party was followed by a media campaign launched by these parties in the West. This prompted a response from Khmer communities in the US, Australia and France, who held demonstrations which demanded recognition from Western governments that 'this is an international problem'.[70] Sam Rainsy released a statement in which he argued,

> The 1991 Paris Agreements constitute a unique legal instrument for the international community to actively help Cambodia achieve peace and stability, while promoting democracy and development at the same time. They do not only give the right but they also create the obligation for all the signatories to intervene in a country where human rights are seriously and continuously violated.

According to Rainsy, UN reports of 'serious and continuous human rights violations implying the derailment of the democratization process' thus imposed a 'moral and legal obligation' upon eighteen countries 'to use all their influence to put Cambodia back on the democratic path, and to ensure the holding of free and fair elections in 1998'.[71]

The international campaign of public and diplomatic protests launched by FUNCINPEC and the Sam Rainsy Party – now united with two other parties in a political coalition called the 'Union of Cambodian Democrats' – brought the struggle within Cambodia, literally, onto the doorsteps of Western governments, as lobbyists were employed and groups of Khmers abroad gathered to protest in front of government offices. The exploitation of these international forums by these parties was given added weight by two further circumstances. The first was the expectation of Cambodia's imminent entry into ASEAN. The flight of FUNCINPEC troops and refugees to an enclave on the Thai border, while senior politicians based in Bangkok denounced the legitimacy of the post-July government, rendered this entry problematic, for Thailand and consequently for ASEAN as a whole. On 10 July, ASEAN foreign ministers held a crisis meeting in Kuala Lumpur at which they decided to delay Cambodia's admission 'in the light of the unfortunate circumstances which have resulted from the use of force'. The Thai Prime Minister Chuan Leekpai offered to mediate between Hun Sen and Ranariddh, although Hun Sen rejected this offer, and Indonesian foreign minister Ali Alatas visited Phnom Penh in an unsuccessful attempt to bring about dialogue between the two. These activities reflected the extent to which Cambodia's internal strife continued to be seen as a regional problem, perhaps the more so given Cambodia's impending entry into ASEAN.

A further international response was forced when the post-July coalition in Phnom Penh and the Union of Cambodian Democrats in Bangkok sent rival delegations to represent Cambodia at the opening debate of the United Nations General Assembly in October. Faced with a choice, the United Nations General Assembly's Credentials Committee in October 1997 refused to take a decision on which of two delegations should be recognized. As a consequence, Cambodia's seat at the assembly remained empty. A UN human rights official in Phnom Penh saw this decision as a decisive intervention in Cambodian affairs:

> That was the international community – in the form of the General Assembly which is the most authoritative form of the international community that there is – the body that can claim to be the international community more than any other body – refused to recognise the July events. Failed to recognize Ung Huot as first prime minister.[72]

New diplomatic forums were formed in attempt to salvage the situation. One such forum was the ASEAN 'Troika' comprising the foreign ministers of Thailand, the Philippines, and Indonesia. Another was the self-styled 'Friends of Cambodia', a group of representatives of the governments of Australia, Britain, Canada, France, Germany, Japan, New Zealand, South Korea, Russia and the United States. The mobilization of international and regional forums in response to the crisis reflects the unusual degree of international intervention in Cambodian politics, compared to other small states, and also offered considerable political resources to the parties that had been decisively defeated in military terms in July 1997. The resources made available to these parties by the pursuit of political and diplomatic campaigns in international forums crucially influenced the gradual return of their senior politicians to Phnom Penh from November 1997 to participate in elections the following year.

At a meeting in February 1998, the ASEAN troika and the 'Friends of Cambodia' adopted a four-pillar plan put forward by Japan, as conditions for finance and support for Cambodian elections scheduled for 1998. These elections were vital to the post-July government as a means to regain, not only American and Australian aid, but its seat at the UN General Assembly. According to the Japanese plan, Ranariddh would break all ties with the PDK and declare a ceasefire, allowing his forces on the border to be reintegrated with the Royal Cambodian Armed Forces. In return, the trial of Ranariddh, on charges of illegal weapons imports, would proceed immediately, and would be followed by an immediate pardon granted by the king, allowing Ranariddh to participate in elections.[73]

Monitoring the implementation of this plan required the establishment of further interventionary forums, in the form of networks of international observers to monitor the 1998 elections and the lead-up to them. These networks comprised a number of different strands. Firstly, donors sent country delegations, most of whom were subsumed under the auspices of the European Union's Joint International Observer Group (JIOG). Exceptions to this were the United States observers, who made a separate statement on the elections. Two separate groups of United Nations observers were also in evidence: monitors deployed by the Cambodia Office of the High Commissioner for Human Rights to oversee the human rights situation across the country, and monitors deployed by the Office of the Secretary General's Personal Representative to Cambodia, to monitor the security of the returning 'self-exiles', including Ranariddh and Rainsy. Finally, a variety of non-governmental groups fielded observers, including the Asian Network for Free Elections, the Volunteer Observers for the Cambodian Elections and the Independent International Observers Group. Human rights monitoring during the election period was conducted by delegations of Amnesty International and Human Rights Watch. Monitoring by some of these groups, particularly by UN monitors and international human rights organizations, continued after the elections and encompassed the period of demonstrations that took place in August 1998, after FUNCINPEC, the Sam Rainsy Party and other political parties rejected the results of the election.

The intervention of these international monitors was, at times, significant in an increasingly tense situation. Early international acclaim for the conduct of the election, especially by the Joint International Observer Group, was widely criticized by local political actors, as it was seen as having closed down prematurely international arenas for contesting the election results. These critics included not only the parties that lost the election and rejected the results, but also members of Cambodian election observer groups. A member of the Board of Directors of one of the Cambodian election observer networks commented after the elections that the preemptive recognition of the elections by JIOG 'jeopardized the whole process' by restricting opportunities to harness international resources as a means of promoting the stance of election observers vis-à-vis election organizers in the post-election phase, when important procedural issues regarding handling complaints and reconciling ballots remained outstanding.[74]

Regarding the human rights situation, however, international monitoring had a different effect. For example, UN officials intervened twice in circumstances where Sam Rainsy appeared to be under threat of detention during this period. In mid-August, a grenade was thrown at a group of SRP members staging a vigil outside the Ministry of Interior in protest over alleged irregularities in ballot counting. A member of the attending press corps was killed and Sam Rainsy was briefly detained inside the Ministry of Interior, along with other members of his party, until monitors from the UN Secretary-General's Personal Representative's office negotiated his release. Later, as demonstrations against the election results gathered momentum, Sam Rainsy took refuge in the UN Secretary-General's Personal Representative's office after it was rumoured that a warrant for his arrest had been issued. He remained there for several days as the Secretary-General's Personal Representative and foreign ambassadors consulted with representatives of the government-elect, and with UN Headquarters in New York, in an effort to resolve the situation.[75] Once again, the engagement of international actors in Cambodian political struggles, and the use by Cambodian actors of international political spaces and resources, was clearly demonstrated.

In short, the crisis period from 1997 to 1998 prompted the emergence of a more public international engagement in Cambodia. International actors engaged in a dialogue with Cambodian political actors who were once again divided as a consequence of military action. Consequently, Cambodian actors competed for international support, and attempted to provoke international declarations on the political situation in the country. The struggle between the former coalition partners was conducted in front of an international public, not only because of the presence of CNN cameras in Phnom Penh during the military battle, but also because of the attempt by Cambodian actors to use international forums and resources as sites of political contestation. This constituted a more visible international–local engagement than had been evident in the period from 1993 to 1997, and there was more evidence of specifically principled action in support of articulated ideals of 'democracy' and 'freedom' on the part of international actors than there had been in the years immediately preceding the crisis. Arguably, this represented the response of the international community to an increased polarization of local actors, and the latter's more forceful attempts to press their disputes in international arenas during this period, rather than a dramatic change in the nature of international–local engagement itself.

The Hun Sen government from 1998

Following the formation of a new government, incorporating FUNCINPEC as junior partner to the CPP, in 1998, the nature of international intervention transformed once again. The agreement of the two most powerful political parties on a recipe for government entailed a lessening of the extent to which Cambodian political struggles were played out in the international arena. Once again, international engagement in Cambodian politics operated on the level of diplomacy, negotiations and debates over aid programmes, and interaction with non-governmental actors. The emphasis of donors now shifted to the question of 'good governance' on a day-to-day level, rather than addressing the larger questions of the legitimacy and sovereignty of the Cambodian government.

'Good governance' is defined by donors in accordance with international standards. While defined in such a way as to routinely include references to democracy and participation, it views the efficiency of government as a prerequisite. Thus a UNDP representative to the 2001 Consultative Group meeting in Tokyo commented:

> On the occasion of the UN Millennium Summit, UN Member States made the strongest, most unanimous and explicit statement to date in support of democratic and participatory governance ... The international community has not set specific development targets to measure progress towards good governance, democracy and peace. However, it is widely accepted that an effective system of government underpins the prospect of achieving International Development Targets.[76]

The sense of measured professionalism inherent in such an interpretation has largely replaced the political zeal of a decade earlier in international pronouncements on Cambodia.

The new agenda for intervention involves a closer focus on the Cambodian state, rather than on Cambodian political society, and the Consultative Group meeting in May 2000 generated a working group for public administration reform. The government's plans for reform, as submitted to the donors' meeting, included aspects of state practice that have long been heavily politicized and supportive to the CPP. 'Critical' areas for reform included the judicial and legal systems, public finance, civil administration, anti-corruption measures, natural resource management and military demobilization.[77]

International intervention on these issues has been reorganized under the rubric of 'credible partnerships'. These were discussed by Keat Chhon , Senior Minister for Economics and Finance, in a presentation to the 2001 CG meeting, as involving a 'major shift from the way things are currently done' in order to 'allow for and address ... capacity gaps, constraints and burden'.[78] This implied, Keat Chhon averred, 'major transformational change on the part of all the Partners – the Government in combination with civil society, the private corporate sector, and the International Donor Community', and particularly involved changes in 'the way in which internal and external relationships are to be managed'.[79] The new sense of partnership would comprise 'a focused and measured way of sharing experiences and capacities to meet challenges larger than one partner alone can manage'. It would be aimed at 'speed[ing] up our ... path up the learning curve'.[80]

The emphasis upon a co-operative, professional and, above all, technical engagement suggests a concern, by the Cambodian government at least, to depoliticize international engagement in Cambodia in order to facilitate a withdrawal of access to international arenas and forums from non-state actors and political opponents. However, the technical agenda put forward by international actors since the 1998 elections constitutes an assault on some of the key planks of CPP power, as this was consolidated between 1989 and 1998. Demands for greater transparency in decision-making, a rationalization of the military and bureaucracy, and new emphasis upon legality restrict the ability of the CPP government to exclude its competitors from access to key domestic arenas. The impact of this upon political and civil society is discussed further in succeeding chapters.

The international community and the domestic realm

This overview of intervention suggests that the sheer variety of agents, rhetoric and practice belies the notion of an 'international community' as a potentially unified ethical actor, so often invoked with respect to Cambodia. However, a comparison of the penetrative multilateral international intervention into the process of politics and government in the 1990s, with the practices of military engagement evident in the 1970s and 1980s, suggests that changes in the form of international intervention have had certain net effects on the functioning of Cambodian state and society. Specifically, international policies described above have had a powerful impact on the strategies and resources available to state and non-state actors in their ongoing negotiation of Cambodia's political trajectory.

The dramatic changes, described in previous chapters, in the nature and extent of terrain for political and civil action in Cambodia over the 1990s have emerged from the changing nature of state power and international intervention over the period. The most important trend in the transformation of the state has been the commodification of personal relationships of patronage and violence, in the context of a privatized economy of power. By contrast, the major impact of international intervention into the 1990s has been twofold. With regard to the state, international intervention has focused upon the public constitutional forms of the state, rather than the private networks of transformed patronage which underlie these. Consequently, international statements, donations and technical assistance programmes, while of limited success in determining the nature of state action, have helped to support a continuing notion of the state as it exists on paper in the 1993 constitution. Support to the National Assembly and judiciary and continuing rhetoric regarding civil service reform prevents the abandonment of notions of the separation of powers and neutralization of the state, so that these rhetorical goals continue to provide a basis for criticism for non-state and opposition political actors.

Secondly, the greater availability of international resources, beyond the purview of the state, has altered the political economy of power in favour of greater pluralism and the empowerment of new, non-state political actors. In creating and sustaining platforms for public debate and activism, international intervention has become integrally intertwined with the current Cambodian political landscape as the foundation of various types of political terrain that are increasingly used with familiarity and imagination by Cambodian non-state actors.

The increasing importance worldwide of international political spaces for non-state politics has been noted by recent theorists of transnational activism. Thomas Risse-Kappen suggests that the impact of transnational movements, such as those dedicated to the promotion of human rights and environmental concerns by non-governmental actors around the world, can be analysed not only in terms of the penetrability of domestic institutions in the target state, but also in terms of the degree to which a co-operative international regime of institutions regulate the issue in international relations. Risse-Kappen comments that such an international regime offers international norms which can legitimize local action and 'lowers state boundaries, thereby allowing for flourishing transnational relations'.[81]

Equally, a relatively thick web of international institutions offers space for activism by non-governmental actors. Risse-Kappen points to the multiple channels offered by international institutions for NGO input, while Keck and Sikkink write that if the claims of non-governmental actors 'resonate' beyond the borders of the state, then the problem of an inaccessible local state structure can be overcome by international contacts which 'amplify the demands of domestic groups, pry open space for new issues, and then echo back these demands into the domestic arena'.[82]

These analyses suggest that terrain for political action can be established beyond the state in certain issue areas because of the resonance of local struggles in a broader context, and because of the establishment of international structures which support non-governmental political action. However, the case of Cambodia illustrates that international intervention can also produce new spaces within the polity in which political and civil action can become more confident and self-assured. Consequently, the borders of Cambodian politics are not merely blurred by the projection of issues outwards to a broader international community, they are also blurred by the inward projection of international power to change the terrain of engagement for struggles in the local community.

International policies have profoundly affected the landscape of Cambodian political terrain in this respect. Firstly, international policies brought new resources for political activity to Cambodia, which have sustained a multi-party political sphere and an arena of organized non-governmental action, hopefully dubbed 'civil society' by many commentators. Secondly, international policies in themselves operated as exemplars of and arenas for critical scrutiny, debate and oppositional action vis-à-vis the state and led to new forms of political contestation. The interaction of these new international and local realms of political action is explored in detail in the remaining chapters.

Before addressing in detail the use made by local actors of international interventionary practices, two qualifications should be addressed. The penetration of international resources into Cambodian politics has been highly variable, not only over time, as described above, but also across Cambodian territory. The rural–urban divide is the most prominent example of this, and security, infrastructural and political barriers to international intervention in rural areas has significantly affected Cambodia's political trajectory. Secondly, to the extent that Cambodian politics is based upon international resources and displaced into international arenas in order to take advantage of these resources, international intervention runs the risk of disrupting relations of accountability between the Cambodian state and Cambodian society.

Representative liberal democracy is based upon the conception of a binary relation between state and society. Society elects official representatives, and engages in a critical dialogue with and scrutiny over them. The state guarantees order in society through the administration and enforcement of law, while safeguarding the rights of the individual. The binary nature of notions of legitimacy and accountability mediated in this encounter is central both to contractarian notions of liberal democracy, and to conceptions of civil society. Society both legitimizes the state and holds it accountable by means of elections and other forms of organized representation; the state guarantees the status of the individual person through recognition of rights of citizenship, and holds him or her accountable through the due process of law.

The internationalization of a polity disrupts this binary relationship and introduces an array of sources of legitimacy and avenues of accountability that exist beyond the state–society relationship. For example, as theorists of transnational activism point out, the intrusion of 'international norms and standards' regarding respect for human rights represents a set of legitimizing criteria capable, at certain critical moments at least, of beckoning considerable international resources or outrage. Yet neither these norms and standards themselves, nor the resources they can summon, are internal to the state–society relationship. They represent a third party in the state–society relationship to be appealed to by local actors, with significant implications for the practice of local politics.

Facility in the process of appeal to such powerful external resources consequently emerges as a significant factor in domestic politics. The ability to invoke international norms in the context of local disputes, to enter into relationships with international actors on the basis of such norms, and to deploy skilfully the resources made available becomes an important determinant of political success. This can occur at the expense of local concerns and norms, which are downplayed insofar as they diverge from donor priorities.

Furthermore, the displacement of political activism into international arenas precludes the participation of many local actors. An example of this is the flight from Cambodia of opposition politicians in the aftermath of the fighting of July 1997. These politicians subsequently pursued a diplomatic offensive at the UN and ASEAN. While activity at this level enhances the safety of the movement's leaders, it also reduced the extent to which ordinary Cambodians could engage in their campaign.

At the end of the 1990s, strong links between Cambodian political actors in Phnom Penh and influential international forums are rarely mirrored by equally strong links between urban and rural spheres, or by international–rural links. This runs the risk of excluding the rural poor from active participation in transnational democratization projects and campaigns. To the extent that international scrutiny and legitimation come to replace local and, especially, rural input into Cambodia's democratization process, this process may emerge as democratic in form only, and anti-democratic in substance.

The remaining chapters examine the ways in which the emergence of a multi-party political sphere and a sphere of 'civil society' has occurred in the light of this analysis. Emphasis is placed upon these spheres as intermediate, products of the activities of an urban elite which has access to international resources, and which attempts to a greater or lesser extent to use these international resources to form alliances with the rural poor. The political economy of international–local interaction, in the context of a local government network which is highly politicized and antipathetic to pluralism at the village level, goes some way to explain the elitist nature of Cambodian politics, and the poor quality of democracy that has emerged over the course of the 1990s.

6 Multi-party politics in the 1990s

The successful transformation of the Cambodian People's Party in response to international promotion of multi-party politics in the 1990s, described in Chapter 4, has led a number of observers of Cambodian politics to question whether Cambodia's political culture offers fertile ground for democratization. The extent to which the CPP's supposedly 'traditional' policies were actually embedded in the transition to the free market and in specifically modern administrative practices, and were facilitated by the marginal nature of subsistence in the rural economy, has been addressed. The failure of new and returning parties in the 1990s to combat the consolidation of CPP power over the 1990s is also best explained with reference to the political economy of Cambodia's transition. It is argued that, in view of the impoverishment of rural Cambodia, these parties were inevitably organized from the top down.They were based in the capital city of Phnom Penh, attempting to project power out into the provinces, and to reach rural voters through campaigning activities.

This strategy was dictated by the paucity of resources for organizing political movements in rural Cambodia. It was thwarted because of the fragmentation of the Cambodian political community into isolated arenas that were easily monopolized by local authorities, and difficult to reach from the centre. Consequently, the parties that opposed the CPP in the 1990s remained preoccupied by politics at the top and failed to gain any close appreciation of the concerns and grievances of villagers in the countryside. Indeed, fearing reprisals against their followers in the villages, they conceded the public sphere of village politics to the CPP, urging their supporters to keep their allegiances hidden. As a result, the quality of campaigning and political debate in Cambodia has remained poor, and the ability of villagers to influence elite political agendas remains low.

The result has been a consolidation of power in the hands of ever fewer parties. Twenty political parties contested the UNTAC-organized election of 1993. Of these, four – FUNCINPEC, the CPP, the Buddhist Liberal Democratic Party (BLDP) and the Moulinaka and Combattants for Liberty Party – were returned to the National Assembly in 1993. All four parties were attached to armies that had fought in the civil war in the 1980s. In

1998, thirty-nine parties ran, and three – the CPP, FUNCINPEC, and the Sam Rainsy Party, launched in 1995 as a breakaway group from FUNCINPEC – were returned. The BLDP, which by 1998 had split into a number of separate parties, and Moulinaka lost their seats. In 2002, only the CPP, FUNCINPEC and the SRP remained as contenders for seats in Cambodia's commune council elections.

Over the course of the three elections, FUNCINPEC's share of the vote declined, falling from 45 per cent in 1993 to 32 per cent in 1998 and 22 per cent in 2002. The SRP's vote increased from 14 per cent in 1998 to 17 per cent in 2002.[1] In particular, the SRP made gains at FUNCINPEC's expense in the cities. In 2002, FUNCINPEC's share of the vote dropped to 14 per cent in Phnom Penh, compared to 36.4 per cent for the SRP and 49.8 per cent for the CPP. The SRP, consequently, gained the commune chief's position in six Phnom Penh communes, while FUNCINPEC gained none. At the same time, voter turnout dropped from between 90 and 95 per cent in the elections of 1993 and 1998 to around 70 per cent in 2002.[2]

The decline of FUNCINPEC is indicative of the ways in which the political economy of Cambodia's transition enabled the exclusion of an initially vigorous and successful political party. In much of the literature on Cambodia in the 1990s, the decline of FUNCINPEC is attributed to either the overbearing nature of the CPP or the weakness of FUNCINPEC president Prince Norodom Ranariddh. While both these factors are important, arguably they were rendered significant by the poverty of rural Cambodia, which permitted the monopolization of rural politics by the CPP, as described, and severely limited the options available to FUNCINPEC. FUNCINPEC was forced to rely heavily on its royalist identity, and this saddled the party with a weak leader, whose sole qualification for the job was the fact that he was the son of the king. The formal emergence of multiparty democracy, and the incorporation of FUNCINPEC as senior partner in the governing coalition in Phnom Penh in 1993 was not accompanied by a pluralization of executive power, nor an increased richness of political debate, either within the National Assembly or during election campaigns. The means by which FUNCINPEC was excluded from executive power, despite its 1993 electoral victory, have been widely discussed by observers of Cambodian politics in the 1990s.

The weakness of the legislative power was also swiftly apparent. From 1993 to 1996, all the parliamentary parties joined in a governing coalition, rendering legislative scrutiny of the executive weak. At key moments, the National Assembly proved ready to surrender its privileges vis-à-vis the executive with very little show of resistance, as when deputies voted unanimously to strip the prominent FUNCINPEC parliamentarian, Norodom Sirivudh, of his parliamentary immunity amid a climate of threat and intimidation. The leaders of FUNCINPEC and the CPP were heavily implicated in private deals with foreign investors that enriched them personally, while removing lucrative industries – primarily the logging industry – from the legislative purview of the National Assembly. Accusations that the National Assembly was swiftly turning into a rubber stamp were frequently heard.

At the same time, parliamentary parties have failed to cultivate strong representative ties with their constituents, both because of CPP tactics to exclude them from the local arena, and because of their own lack of familiarity with, and concern for, village politics. Consequently, on occasions when tensions increased within the coalition, political competition continued to be transformed into military contests. This ultimately led to the breakdown of relations within the coalition in 1997, and military battles between forces loyal to FUNCINPEC and the CPP, most prominently in Phnom Penh in July 1997. FUNCINPEC's weakness in policy terms, its failure to build on its 1993 electoral victory through forging strong ties with a sympathetic electorate, the risk associated with its military policy and bribes offered by the CPP led to a splintering of FUNCINPEC into several different parties between 1995 and 1998, although the lack of success of these splinter groups in the 1998 elections led to a return to the fold following the 1998 elections. Despite this ample evidence of the bitterness of the ongoing divisions within the political elite, in policy terms the parties have offered little of substance to voters during electoral campaigns.

This chapter explores the weakness of Cambodian political society with reference to a number of factors based in the political economy of the past decade. The most important factor is the reconsolidation of the CPP, which has operated to exclude its opponents from effective participation in, or oversight of, executive power, and from the rural political arena. This exclusion has occurred in a context where international efforts to promote multi-partyism have not penetrated far beyond the capital city of Phnom Penh, rendering economic resources easily captured by partisan local authorities. Because subsistence farmers have few means for launching grassroots-based parties to represent their interests independent of the elite, political parties opposing the CPP in the 1990s have tended to be built from the top down, attempting to project resources attracted from overseas into rural Cambodia. The implications of this are a form of politics characterized by populism, elitism and a tendency to search for international, rather than local, support in intra-elite power struggles. Arguably, this is a form of politics that has militated against the active participation of the average voter.

The decline of FUNCINPEC

The strategy adopted by the CPP to rebuild, following the defeat of the party in the 1993 elections, has already been described. However, the difficulties faced by other parties in attempting to resist this reconsolidation of CPP power are an important aspect of the weakness of Cambodian democracy at the start of the twenty-first century. The case of FUNCINPEC – the party which, as the victor of the 1993 elections, had the most opportunity to resist the CPP's rebirth – is instructive in illustrating the problems of party organization in impoverished rural areas.

FUNCINPEC was launched by King (then Prince) Norodom Sihanouk in the early 1980s, while in exile, as a movement to resist the Vietnamese occupation. It operated under the umbrella Coalition Government of Democratic Kampuchea (CGDK), a formation also including the remnants of the DK regime and the Khmer People's National Liberation Front, led by Son Sann. The Coalition Government was, to a great extent, a marriage of convenience formed in response to international concerns. Militarily it was dominated by the DK, and David Chandler suggests that Sihanouk's return to political life at this time was prompted by pressure from China as a means to facilitate Western recognition of the resistance in spite of its connection with the Pol Pot regime. The CGDK operated out of refugee camps on the Thai border, and its major political activities comprised canvassing international support for the continued isolation of the PRK. Chandler remarks that, beyond this, the CGDK had no political programme and attracted little support within Cambodia, despite the unpopularity of the PRK regime.[3]

The problems associated with FUNCINPEC's entry into multi-party politics in the 1990s reflected both the nature of the party's development as essentially a diplomatic and military organization in the 1980s, and the economic situation in Cambodia's villages in the 1990s. Initially, the party enjoyed high popularity due to its association with returning King Sihanouk. The restoration of the monarchy marked a return to a constitutional regime similar to that of the pre-war era, which, consequently, was viewed with a great deal of nostalgia by the war-weary population of the early-1990s. FUNCINPEC, in election campaigning in 1993 and 1998, focused almost exclusively upon the association of the party with the king. In 1998, one FUNCINPEC National Assembly candidate commented:

> People aren't interested in economic policy. The prince is the symbol of the nation, of peace. That's what people are interested in ... Actually we don't need to do much campaigning. We just need to tell people that FUNCINPEC is here. Because the people know us already ... People will vote for Ranariddh because it is the tradition for Cambodia to have a monarchy. And Cambodian people are very traditional.[4]

Arguably, however, this belief made a virtue of necessity. While presenting a vote for FUNCINPEC as a vote for the king was effective electorally in 1993, the subsequent decline in FUNCINPEC's share of the vote in 1998, and in commune elections in 2002, suggests that the party's failure, in government, to convert its royalist appeal into real benefits for voters was noted by the electorate.

FUNCINPEC had found the business of effective party building and effective government, between 1993 and 1997, problematic. With the ministries and local government dominated by a consolidating CPP,

FUNCINPEC found great difficulties exercising influence over the executive. For FUNCINPEC's leaders, coming into Cambodia for the first time in a decade or more, unfamiliar with government and with local conditions, and without any coherent policy platform to guide their activities, the business of attempting to wrest executive power from the CPP's grasp proved too challenging. During the 1993 election campaign, conducted in a heady climate of insecurity under the auspices of foreign election organizers, FUNCINPEC had done little to establish a clear relationship of representation with its rural campaigners and supporters. The party portrayed itself as possessed of a right to rule by virtue of its status as the embodiment of the natural aspirations of 'traditional' Cambodians for a monarchical system. Kate Frieson quotes a FUNCINPEC party bulletin from 1993 which offered this rationale for a vote for the party:

> FUNCINPEC favors royalism more than any other party ... FUNCINPEC is a child which follows the Khmer tradition of listening to its father ... Our nation's father says the Khmer are having problems and ... the king also says wait until Khmer have independence, peace and territorial integrity then it will be up to him to decide.[5]

Consequently, FUNCINPEC was elected in 1993 with as little in the way of a clear policy programme as it had had as a diplomatic front in exile in the 1980s. Subsequently, this limitation was not addressed and after 1993 FUNCINPEC became preoccupied with politics at the centre, within the coalition, losing touch with its rural structures, as Ranariddh freely admitted in 1998:

> I am very sorry that FUNCINPEC made its biggest mistake in 1993, because it forgot its rural structures. This was the biggest mistake of the FUNCINPEC leaders.[6]

Equally, the UN-sponsored settlement left FUNCINPEC without its longstanding foreign policy rationale of gathering international support against the Vietnamese-installed regime in Phnom Penh. Indeed, in the early years of the coalition, Ranariddh tended to distance himself from his erstwhile Western supporters, as in 1995 when he made a speech suggesting an 'Asian' consensual approach to political competition was more appropriate for Cambodia than Western-style civil and political rights. He further alienated former international allies by his participation in the acceptance of large cash 'gifts' from foreign investors and through his expulsion from FUNCINPEC and the National Assembly of the internationally respected Minister of Economics and Finance, Sam Rainsy, after Rainsy criticized the acceptance of such 'gifts'.

The split between Ranariddh and Rainsy reflected a difference of opinion within FUNCINPEC over the party's tactics. Rainsy's close relationship with international donors and his espousal of free market policies reflected a concern to mobilize international resources in support of the party, in its relations with its coalition partners in the CPP. Rainsy saw the beckoning of international pressure and resources could offer a policy agenda that would consolidate FUNCINPEC's position in the coalition, and, perhaps, in the eyes of the electorate. One National Assembly deputy, who joined Sam Rainsy in splitting from FUNCINPEC, spelt out this perceived opportunity and the disillusionment within the parliamentary party that followed Ranariddh's failure to grasp it:

> many in FUNCINPEC, not just us ... were disappointed with the leadership ... the leadership was very weak. He forgets his supporters, his members only take care of a small group ... ... Ranariddh was very good and very democratic before the election, but after the election he changed, he joined Hun Sen. Because of interest. He betrayed the nation. After 1993, Hun Sen was very low. Very weak. He was afraid of the UN – UNTAC was still here. Ranariddh could have made some changes but he didn't.[7]

Instead, Ranariddh attempted to rebuild the party in a manner reflecting the ideas of monarchism, which protected his own position as party leader and was perceived as a sure-fire means of mobilizing electoral support when necessary, even given the difficulties of organizing effectively in the countryside. Instead of following international initiatives in exchange for international support in the coalition, Ranariddh attempted to compete with the CPP's model of party relations via transformed patronage. In doing so, FUNCINPEC adopted the CPP's agenda and attempted to beat the party at its own game. Pro-CPP newspaper *Reasmei Kampuchea* editorialized in 1996 that:

> The best way to beat the People's Party is to compete to develop the countryside. Even though the People's Party has set out very far ahead of other parties, only if they use this strategy to compete can they have some hope.[8]

Second Prime Minister Hun Sen equally threw down a challenge to Ranariddh to compete with the CPP's development programmes in the countryside in a 1996 speech:

> They tried to build schools, but ultimately they just changed the school signboard, changed the name ... What sort of nonsense is that! ... Yesterday the people said they received one toilet and the name was changed ... Just one toilet and they change the name of the school, whereas for that I build three buildings ... [P]ut your own, you build one, I'll build ten. We're a superpower too, when it comes to doing that![9]

Such policies were unsuccessful, however, in part because FUNCINPEC did not enjoy the same level of control over local political arenas and local sources of revenue to make outbidding of the CPP possible. Increasingly, FUNCINPEC officials publicly denounced their exclusion from government. Consequently, in 1996, FUNCINPEC adopted a new and highly risky strategy of attempting to engage the faltering PDK as a political ally that controlled territory, substantial resources in the form of timber and gem mines, and armed forces. Through alliance with the PDK, FUNCINPEC saw a possibility to challenge the power of the CPP military and its transformed patronage structure on a more equal footing.

The CPP was determined to prevent this. Through 1996 and 1997, relations between the coalition partners deteriorated drastically. In February 1997, fighting broke out in the north-western province of Battambang as FUNCINPEC Deputy Provincial Governor Serey Kosal sent forces to stop and disarm 200 CPP soldiers on their way to the area of Samlot. Samlot was controlled by the Democratic National United Movement (DNUM) – a sector of the PDK that had split from the Pol Pot leadership and defected to the government in 1996, retaining control of its bases in the North West. Local control of loyalties in Samlot was the prize in this fight: FUNCINPEC claimed that the troops were 'unauthorized' and were to be used to intimidate Samlot voters into joining the CPP.[10] The CPP claimed that the affair represented a rebellion by former PDK guerrillas armed by FUNCINPEC 'in a bid to offset CPP's strong grip on the area.'[11]

The incident was a symptom of the increasing intransigence of FUNCINPEC's military chiefs in 1997. These chiefs believed that confrontation, backed by enhanced military capability, to attack CPP control of rural security was the only strategy to advance FUNCINPEC's political presence in the countryside. FUNCINPEC needed to show strength vis-à-vis the CPP, to regain the initiative in government and to open up at least some local areas for FUNCINPEC prior to the next elections.

For FUNCINPEC's generals, the aim of reasserting FUNCINPEC's strength was central. After the Battambang skirmish, Serey Kosal justified his actions:

> I want them to fairly see that no longer can they use force to suppress any single Khmer citizen ... So what I did was to stop the CPP boasting about shooting, about killing, about how strong they are. Because to boast about how capable you are at chopping and killing – other people are also capable of that. They cannot sit with their arms folded while allowing you to attack them any longer.[12]

Shortly before the July fighting in Phnom Penh, a FUNCINPEC Secretary of State at the Ministry of the Interior, Ho Sok, echoed these sentiments and expressed the feelings of personal insecurity of FUNCINPEC members, commenting:

> If it were not for Ho Sok and General Bun Chhay, Hun Sen could do anything to FUNCINPEC – make the rain and the thunder.[13]

The CPP termed this 'a calculated policy of provocation', and 'an attempt to recover political ground lost during a series of political blunders by Prince Ranariddh'.[14] It is indeed likely that the attempt was aimed at securing a material foundation for FUNCINPEC, in terms of territory, resources and military power, as a basis for building support for future elections. Once again, however, this strategy led to splits in the party as senior members, doubting FUNCINPEC's ability to survive outright confrontation with the CPP, formed new parties of their own, often with CPP assistance.

Eventually, FUNCINPEC's efforts to beat the CPP at its own game ended in disaster. Following months of tension, a military battle between the two sides broke out in Phnom Penh in July 1997. Each side claimed the other began the fighting; the outcome, however, was clear, as FUNCINPEC's leaders fled to Bangkok, and Generals Serei Kosal and Nhek Bun Chhay escaped to the border, where they mounted an essentially token military resistance.

Although FUNCINPEC subsequently campaigned relatively successfully internationally for support in negotiating Ranariddh's return to Cambodia and participation in the 1998 elections, the July fighting weakened the party significantly. The period that FUNCINPEC leaders spent in exile in Bangkok from July 1997 to March 1998 were expensive for rural activists. A series of killings of key figures in the FUNCINPEC military occurred in a campaign of terror that UN officials believed was aimed at destroying finally FUNCINPEC's ability to organize itself in the Cambodian countryside:

> In the 1980s, FUNCINPEC and the KPNLF had secret networks inside the country, and after 1991 those people identified themselves … They came out of hiding and got government positions. Those people fit the political and professional profile of people in the August 21 report.[15] There are still executions going on of people fitting that profile, people who are presumed to be ardent loyalists, the internal network of Nhek Bun Chhay. They are still being sought out and eliminated.[16]

May Sam Oeun, chairman of FUNCINPEC's election campaign, commented that following the July fighting FUNCINPEC's ability to organize in the countryside had been reduced still further:

> the infrastructure was destroyed, party members were killed – extra-judicial killings – the human structure or political structure of the party

> was destroyed ... They even destroyed the homes of FUNCINPEC members.[17]

May Sam Oeun estimated that $25,000 worth of equipment had been lost since the July fighting. The funds to replace this were raised from FUNCINPEC supporters abroad, including by offering National Assembly candidacies in the 1998 elections to Khmers in Western countries who wished to return and enter politics. This, again, exacerbated the elitism of the party, distancing it further from the grassroots in Cambodia.

More problematic was the task of rebuilding a network of organized activists at local level. May Sam Oeun reported that FUNCINPEC's grassroots activists were in hiding, and that precious months for contacting and developing the party structure and circulating the political platform had been spent by the leadership in exile. The CPP, on the other hand, had 'half a million CPP propagandists to bring the message of our political platform to our people', organized into a party structure operating and strengthening itself continuously since 7 January 1979.[18]

A key concern of FUNCINPEC's 'advance parties', which returned in early 1998, was to establish whether a grassroots network could be rebuilt in time for the elections. May Sam Oeun indicated that CPP local control, tightened following July 1997, was problematic for this process:

> Many farmers – we can't reach them. They are organized into a cell structure, and they are so aggressive and violent ... We had 100,000 members. We don't know where they are now.[19]

Given these problems, reliance upon a broad appeal to monarchism represented the most effective strategy for FUNCINPEC in 1998 as in 1993. Again, however, following the 1998 elections the party rejoined a coalition with the CPP and oriented its focus towards the politics of transformed patronage in Phnom Penh. Again, this was necessary to reward the returnees who had financed the rebuilding of the party with government positions and National Assembly candidacies. Once again, the party found that the source of material resources distanced the party from the electorate. Forging meaningful links of representation between rural villagers and Cambodian expatriates returning from the United States and Australia, sometimes after a lifetime away from Cambodia, was difficult, particularly in the light of CPP propaganda presenting such prospective politicians as fearful foreigners, who would flee Cambodia, abandoning their followers, at the first sign of trouble.

Politics from the top

In this regard, the experience of FUNCINPEC mirrored the experience of many other Cambodian parties. All the parties competing in Cambodian elections in the 1990s were elite-led, built from the top down and many comprised returnees from Western countries. The CPP had the significant advantage of time and military power in its efforts in this regard. For other parties attempting to enter Cambodian politics, campaigning entailed an attempt to penetrate a rural electoral sphere that was often unfamiliar to them, and that was already organized, surveyed and controlled by an armed and combative CPP.

A survey of political party leaders in 1998, gleaned from biographies penned by the leaders themselves and submitted to a 'Voters Guide' published and distributed by an election observer NGO, shows the nature of the elite from which these individuals were drawn. In the main, party leaders were born in Cambodia's densely populated central and southern provinces, and were aged between 40 and 60 years old at the time of the 1998 election. They differed markedly from the majority of Cambodians of this generation, however, in that they were highly educated, well-travelled and professionally qualified.

Fifteen of the 39 party leaders standing in 1998 had postgraduate qualifications, including seven doctorates (plus one honorary doctorate); only four ended their studies at high school level. Twenty-three of the 39 had attended educational institutions abroad, mainly in France (14), the US (7), Vietnam (2) and Australia (2), some in more than one country. Fewer than half were present in Cambodia during the Pol Pot regime from 1975 to 1979. Only eight had lived in government-controlled areas during the 1980s, while twelve resided, for at least part of that decade, with the resistance on the border and three were in jail for political reasons. Eight spent most of the KPRP/SoC regime in France, four in the US, three in Australia and one in Switzerland. While the urban–rural divide is in itself extraordinarily marked; greater distance is imposed between campaigning party presidents and the electorate by the fact that 25 of the 39 party leaders competing in 1998 returned to government-controlled Cambodia after 1990, with six of these only returning after 1995. Many sustained homes, families and businesses abroad to which they returned when their election bids were unsuccessful.

The career paths of these politicians were also distinct from those of the wider electorate. Nine were senior officers in the police or military, while the rest were uniformly professional, encompassing business, medicine, education, the media, law and engineering.[20] Frequently these careers had been pursued mostly or exclusively abroad. None of the party presidents standing in 1998 were rice farmers, although a few claimed to be the children of farmers.

Similarly, among the parliamentary candidates for the three major parties, most were educated professionals. Less comprehensive data is available on this group, but some general characteristics were observed in 1998. While CPP candidates were generally long-standing party members, with long careers in the military or state of the 1980s, FUNCINPEC candidates contained a large proportion of returnees – including some who returned to Cambodia only days before the start of the election campaign – alongside members of the Royal Family and officers from the former military resistance. The Sam Rainsy Party's candidates were more youthful and contained more representatives of white-collar Phnom Penh society, many emerging from the ministries and professions such as journalism, NGOs and teaching, and many having spent time in refuges on the Thai border prior to 1993.[21]

That politicians should be drawn from an elite strata of society is nothing new; but the sheer scale of the elite–mass gap in the context of Cambodia is extraordinary, particularly to the extent that it spans not merely a contemporary rural–urban divide but, in many cases, decades and continents also. These origins combined with circumstances in which entry into Cambodia's rural political arena was heavily policed by the controlling SoC/CPP. In these conditions, the possibilities for forging meaningful links of representation were limited.

This was reflected in the organization, attitudes, ambitions and campaigning styles of the political elite described. It is worth noting that party leaders often justified their practices in terms of a Khmer tradition of deference, patronage and hierarchy. However, as in the references to tradition in CPP campaigning described in Chapter 4, the transposition of electoral campaigning into this framework reflects a virtue made of economic necessity. The distribution of access to the kinds of resources necessary to sustain a political party was such that top-down politics was almost inevitable. The access to funds, information and security required to start and register a political party was absent in rural areas, and was concentrated most heavily in the hands of wealthy and professionally experienced returnees. Ouk Phourrik, president of the Khmer Democratic Party which narrowly missed securing a single seat in the 1998 election, said he personally provided 80 per cent of the $500,000 spent on the party's campaign, due both to the poverty and the expectations of party members:

> After our congress I could hardly collect even 1,000 riel from each representative. They don't earn much. And it is hard to convince the members – some members say that the other big political parties support their members, the members don't support the party ... I don't like that – I don't want to be like the employer of the party. But that's the Cambodian way ... If I don't spend money, maybe the party won't exist.[22]

Similarly, Chhim Oum Yun of the Liberal Democratic Party commented:

> In the West, members give dollars to the party. In Cambodia, the party goes to help the members instead. Only the rich man can be the leader of a party.[23]

The outcome of this organizational imperative, in terms of elite attitudes to politics, was a view of democracy as comprising the co-optation of the broader population into elite-determined political trajectories, rather than the emergence at national level of organs that represented social forces on the ground. This was a view widespread among political party leaders, and coincided with further perceptions of government as the business of the elite and a matter appropriately determined by intellectual skill and professional training rather than brute democratic preference. This attitude was revealed in a number of ways. For example, both Ouk Phourrik and a provincial SRP activist, interviewed in 1998, articulated similar recruitment strategies:

> We want educated members. So far we have students and intellectuals – about 281 officials. We selected these members through a network from the provinces. So we select intellectuals to join the party. And among the 240 candidates for the election, almost 160 graduated from secondary school, have a degree, for example are doctors – have a good educational standard. *Why is that important to you?* Firstly, to have a stronger organizational structure, more effective for campaigning. One reason is that when intellectuals join the party it is easier to train them.[24]

> We don't want uneducated people to work in our network – it gives a bad reputation to the party.[25]

In emphasizing the importance of education and intellectual status, the political elite makes a virtue of necessity, justifying its own separateness as a function of the unattractiveness of the average 'uneducated' voter. This also happily promotes the idea that members of the elite enjoy a right to rule. Frequently, this right was presented as an obligation to the motherland. Two party presidents explained:

> I consider myself to be an intellectual, so I am obligated to serve my country.[26]

> Most of us feel obliged to help. In big countries like the US, if we have some qualification, like I have a PhD, it is a big plus for Cambodia if we can contribute in a positive way.[27]

Yet the jockeying for government positions that took place following the elections, when the leaders of small parties found their electoral bids unsuccessful, suggest that this obligation was pursued with a disregard for democratic preference that essentially transformed it into a belief among wealthy political aspirants in their own right to share power. After the 1998 elections, one president of an unsuccessful party, Nguon Soeur of the Khmer Citizens Party, called for all unsuccessful party leaders to be represented, as of right, in the newly formed upper house of parliament, the

Cambodian Senate. This call was rejected, but the Senate was used to house prominent politicians from outside the three main parties who had been ill-judged or unsuccessful in their choice of alignment in 1998, but who retained sufficient influence to make deals with more successful parties, as well as to reward unsuccessful but important campaigners and financiers from within the three parties returned to the lower house.

The poverty of campaigning

An analysis of party manifestos in the 1998 elections found little significant difference between the parties, many parties putting forward lists of 'principles' rather than policies as such. Such manifestos invariably included references to protection of territorial integrity, respect for 'human rights and democratic principles', support for the constitutional monarchy and 'national reconciliation', preservation of natural resources, and a solution to the border problem and illegal immigration.[28] Little difference was found between the principles espoused by parties allied to the CPP and parties which stood in opposition to it.

Low levels of education and literacy in rural Cambodia entailed that campaign messages should be simple and easy to remember. Yet in simplifying their programmes, many of the parties failed to distinguish themselves from other parties by offering a meaningful agenda for political debate. Buzzwords such as 'human rights', 'rule of law', 'territorial integrity' and 'national reconciliation' were used again and again during the election campaign, yet there was little discussion in campaign activities of the meaning of these slogans, the causes of problems in connection with them, or, of particular importance, strategies for tackling the vested interests which abused these ideals.

Almost all parties adopted a slogan for their letterhead which comprised a triad of liberal values, such as 'Democracy, Justice, Equality',[29] or 'Freedom, Civilisation, Compassion.'[30] While these may have been adopted in an attempt to provide illiterate voters with a simple ideological mantra to identify the party's political stance, the fact that the same concepts were used in different combinations by most of the parties meant that it became impossible to remember which slogan went with which party. For example, the word 'Justice' was used by 15 of the 39 parties, 'Freedom' by 14, 'Peace' by 13, and 'Development' by 11. Alongside liberal and modernist concepts, also popular were nationalist and religious ideals, with 'Nation', 'Motherland', 'Independence', 'Tolerance' and 'Compassion' all chosen by more than one party. Conversations with voters attending party rallies during the election campaign in 1998 suggested that such anodyne statements were unimpressive to voters. From these conversations, it appeared that voters' major concerns focused upon jobs, education for their children and the problem of shrinking access to public resources, and that they were by and large extremely sceptical of the ability or willingness of politicians to resolve these problems. 'Wait until tomorrow' was a phrase frequently used by villagers to satirize the promises of campaigning politicians.[31]

The poverty of ideas emerging from the parties for application to local conditions, and the difficulty in harnessing these to meaningful political action in the villages, reflects the emergence of democracy in Cambodia primarily as a set of national procedures. These were erected and enabled, with significant international funding and expertise, in the absence of a prior integration of local and national political arenas into a substantive political community in which democratic competition could be played out. Political society exists as a multi-party space for contention in the urban areas of Phnom Penh, where different party headquarters are relatively well-established, where street protests over political issues are increasingly common and where newspapers supporting different personalities and parties have published almost continuously since 1993, providing a broad sense of citizens' engagement with and orientation to a political sphere. However, in the various isolated rural political arenas, the ability to maintain offices, to campaign and to debate political issues is far more constrained, and the dominance of the Cambodian People's Party over public space is more evident and assertive. The loyalties of the rural electorate are decisive in determining electoral success, yet, under these circumstances, these loyalties are also the least accessible and the least understandable to parties led by urban intellectuals, members of the elite and returnees from abroad.

The nature of the gap between politicians and villagers, and mutual recognition of it, was revealed in two incidents observed on the campaign trail in 1998. For example, one exchange – between a campaigning FUNCINPEC parliamentary candidate, who had returned to Cambodia from life as a businessman in Seattle just the day before, and rural voters in a village in Kandal province – indicated reluctance on the part of the villagers to place their political faith in a stranger. When urged to vote for the FUNCINPEC candidate as their political representative, villagers replied, 'We don't know you.' The candidate answered,

> Don't vote for me. Vote for FUNCINPEC, whose president is Prince Ranariddh. The King is not in a particular party, he is the nation.[32]

It is significant that the response of the candidate did not seek to overcome the personal gap between himself and the villagers. Rather the candidate attempted to identify himself with an immediately recognizable figure, who, as a function of his royalty, combines an assumed and appropriate separateness with an innate (but not necessarily democratic) representative function. Similarly, during the 1998 election campaign, an SRP organizer commented on the difference in the reactions of crowds to Sam Rainsy's political speeches in the peri-urban constituency of Kien Svay, as opposed to rural constituencies in Svay Rieng and Prey Veng visited on the same day:

> In the towns, the people know our party well. In the countryside it is different. They just stand and watch. It's difficult to tell what they're thinking.[33]

The impression of mutual incomprehension reflects the fact that the structure of the party system emerging in the early 1990s did not primarily reflect organically formed communities of interest within Cambodia. Rather, the party system reflected a drive by members of the elite to carve out an economic niche for themselves in the country through entry into politics. Frequently, this drive is motivated by idealism and a belief in their own ability, as individuals, to promote Cambodia's well-being. However, this is an idealism derived from the self-confidence and benevolence of returning members of the elite, empowered by economic resources acquired abroad, rather than emerging from empathy or identification with the struggles of ordinary members of society.

A further response of the major parties to their lack of familiarity with the rural electorate has been the emergence, in electoral rhetoric, of broad nationalist themes designed to appeal to a lowest common denominator of 'Khmer-ness' in the face of an alleged ongoing attack from Vietnam. This has been most prominent in the rhetoric of the Sam Rainsy Party, which lacks FUNCINPEC's immediately recognizable royalist credentials with which to make an immediate impact upon the rural population.

In the 1998 election campaign and during post-election demonstrations, Sam Rainsy personally toured the country making speeches to mass rallies in which he repeatedly denounced the CPP as '*yuon* puppets' and communists. For example, he told crowds in Kraceh Province:

> we have seen foreigners invading Khmer territory, moving the border, illegal *yuon* immigrants coming to live all over Cambodia. Because our leaders are in debt to foreigners. So they have to repay their debt to the foreigners, they give the Khmer land to the foreigners, they cut down the trees and sell them to the *yuon* and the *yuon* people can move into Cambodia and catch the young fish and destroy all the fishing grounds. They destroy Cambodia. Our country will be gone as long as we have this kind of leader.[34]

This rhetoric presented real economic insecurities in the impoverished rural areas in a simplistic and xenophobic framework, which offered little of concrete significance to voters in terms of a programme of political change. While party activists and supporters interviewed from both FUNCINPEC and the SRP were clearly influenced by these kinds of rhetorical flights and spoke of their concern over alleged Vietnamese incursions and Vietnamese immigration, they had little concept of how an electoral victory might solve the asserted problem given the obvious military power of the CPP.

The positing of such problems, while failing to offer any proposals for solving them, was not only uninspiring but positively disempowering for voters supporting the SRP and FUNCINPEC, who continually questioned the value of their vote in the face of such an adversary. Activists from the SRP and FUNCINPEC propagated the view that the CPP were preparing a military offensive if they lost the election. For example, an SRP activist in Kompong Cham province claimed in a 1998 interview:

> Right now Hun Sen has sent a lot of killing forces to hide in Memot, to make a reserve force for when he loses the election. Right now the people related to Hun Sen, the Mafia guys like Mr Soeun, have set up their own forces. They have cut down a lot of forest and killed a lot of people. Maybe there will be fighting.[35]

These claims were alarming and undermined the election, particularly given the failure of FUNCINPEC to gain control following its electoral victory in 1993. A FUNCINPEC voter, an education trainer in Koh Thom Province, Kandal, reported the cynicism of villagers regarding the power of the vote in this context:

> last time after the election in 1993, they tore up the Paris Peace Agreements and they went for 'national reconciliation' – gave the loser a chance to share government. One man [in the training session] cried and said, they'll do that again. He said, my support [for FUNCINPEC] means nothing.[36]

This cynicism regarding the relation of the electoral process to the basis of political power in Cambodia can only have been heightened by the campaigning of the SRP and FUNCINPEC. The rhetoric of both parties portrayed the CPP as bloodthirsty warmongers intent upon the destruction of the Khmer race. At the same time, both parties urged their supporters not to antagonize CPP village organizers publicly, and to co-operate with the CPP's mobilization campaigns. While they reminded voters continually that doing so did not compromise villagers' right to vote for the party they liked best in the polling booth, they effectively ceded control of public political debate in the villages to the CPP. This had two effects. Firstly, it underlined an apparent powerlessness on the part of the opposition and prevented the emergence of any obvious popular momentum behind the two parties, leading voters to question the likelihood of a transfer of power following a CPP electoral defeat. Secondly, it prevented the parties from strengthening their links with the voters, isolating party activists in the villages and preventing party leaders gaining a clear idea of how villagers really thought and felt.

In this context, the CPP's articulated 'win–win' policy of promoting national reconciliation through coalitions between winners and losers on the battlefield against the 'Khmer Rouge', as well as in the electoral competition, aroused particular fears. It was interpreted by FUNCINPEC supporters to imply that the CPP would still be in a position to take revenge on them after the election:

> People have heard that even if they lose they will still win – so we are concerned ... they say, 'if they win, they win. If they lose, they still win'. It means the authorities still win – they never transfer power to anyone. They have everything – the police, the military force.[37]

> I have doubts – the CPP said even if they lose they will still win. They depend on their military forces.[38]

For the SRP and FUNCINPEC, the poverty of election campaigning led to attempts to mobilize voters through the presentation of the CPP as the marauding puppets of foreign powers. However, in adopting this rhetoric, the parties merely increased fears among voters regarding the likelihood of a return to warfare. In failing to articulate any policies to tackle the problems they asserted, the parties left voters uncertain of what they were voting for and thus unable to make an informed decision over their preferred political future. Rather, the parties continued to present international rescue as the only possible future for Cambodia, given the allegedly continuing depradations of the Vietnamese under the guise of the CPP.

The search for international solutions

The search for international solutions as a substitute for the engagement and representation of voters in substantive discussion of policy issues has been particularly prominent in the strategies of the SRP, which has tirelessly lobbied various forums of the international community in an attempt to attract greater international intervention in opposition to the CPP. In adopting this strategy, the SRP has enjoyed success in areas where international influence is greatest – namely, in Phnom Penh and its environs. However, the lack of international penetration of rural Cambodia entails that the party's portrayal of itself as the vector of international power in Cambodia merely underlines its weakness.

SRP strategies to beckon greater international intervention have varied since the party's launch in 1995 in response to the changing contours of the international community addressed. From 1995 to 1997, party members repeatedly referred to obligations of the international community which they believed were mandated under the terms of the Paris Agreements. Article 29 of the Agreements stated that the members of the Paris Conference could be consulted at the request of the UN Secretary-General 'in the event of a violation or the threat of a violation of these Agreements', with the aim of 'taking appropriate steps to ensure respect for these commitments'.[39]

A senior SRP official interpreted this in 1996 as follows:

> The international community has already made a lot of sacrifices, spent a lot of money, raised a lot of hopes and expectations. They can't let us down now ... We have the Paris Peace Agreements – eighteen countries committed themselves to ensure respect for democracy. Through this unique agreement the international community is committed.[40]

This view was supported by a pro-SRP newspaper editor who commented, 'The Paris Peace Accords said very precisely that the international community must make Cambodia democratic and have respect for human rights.'[41]

Trajectories of international intervention, discussed in the previous chapter, suggest that this faith in international action was misplaced. Although the fighting in July 1997 prompted greater direct intervention for a period of eighteen months, including the imposition of limited sanctions, greater international monitoring and international sponsorship of peace plans, this soon declined once again following the emergence of a new CPP–FUNCINPEC coalition in 1998. The SRP has continued to attempt to beckon international intervention throughout, however. Surrounding the 1998 elections, Sam Rainsy was an active lobbyist in the various international forums that appeared at that time, testifying before the US Senate Foreign Relations Committee, the 'Friends of Cambodia' group and the ASEAN Troika.[42] He repeatedly called for more stringent international control of election preparations, demanding that international donors withdraw support for the elections pending reform of the National Election Committee and aspects of the legislative framework for the elections, both of which were created during the months that the SRP and FUNCINPEC spent in exile in 1997.

Similarly, post-election demonstrations called by the SRP and FUNCINPEC were oriented towards an international audience. In August and September 1998, the SRP and FUNCINPEC organized a three-week long sit-in in a park opposite the National Assembly building to protest alleged election fraud and to demand proper investigation of complaints surrounding the conduct of the election. In speeches made to demonstrators, it became clear that Rainsy regarded the demonstrations as primarily useful as a means of communicating with international observers and donors in a bid to reverse international recognition of the election results and, consequently, to deny the legitimacy of a Hun Sen dominated government. This idea was evident in the remarks of protesters interviewed on the site. One protester commented that she had attended because 'I was afraid that the UN was going to support the result of the election.'[43] A student involved in an associated protest outside the EU headquarters in Phnom Penh at the same time commented: 'We came here to oppose the EU for supporting the result of the election, saying the election is free and fair, and we reject the result.'[44]

In interviews, protesters repeatedly declared that they were demonstrating in order to ask for international assistance in gaining freedom for Cambodia, for the international community of election observers to reconsider their assessment of the election, and for direct intervention

> I will stay until Hun Sen resigns. Even if it takes a long time I don't care. If we act appropriately, the international community will help.[45]

> I believe in the international community. If the Cambodian people try to demonstrate by themselves, and behave well, do not act angrily, then the international community will help them to find democracy.[46]

In speeches to supporters and demonstrators both Ranariddh and Rainsy spoke of precedents for international intervention in support of democracy, reminding crowds of the US ousting of Manuel Noriega from Panama in 1989, air campaigns against Iraq in the 1990s, and the bombing of Afghanistan in response to Al Qaeda attacks on American embassies in Africa in 1998.[47] These speeches, and in particular, Rainsy's calls for the US to bomb Hun Sen's residence in Kandal province, were criticized internationally and no such action was forthcoming. However, the speeches were taken very seriously by demonstrators, and during the post-election demonstrations in 1998, leaflets circulated in Phnom Penh claiming that a US invasion of Cambodia, to liberate the country from the Vietnamese, was imminent.

It is unclear whether Rainsy and Ranariddh really believed their own claims in this respect, or whether they permitted themselves rhetorical flights of fancy in order to galvanize demonstrators in pursuit of the more modest goal of obtaining international pressure upon the National Election Committee to investigate seriously the conduct of the elections. Rainsy later claimed in a press conference to foreign journalists that his call for the US to bomb Hun Sen's residence was a joke. However, the trend in SRP campaigning of looking to international actors to supply the power to scrutinize and limit the activities of the CPP in government continued following the formation of a new coalition between FUNCINPEC and the CPP in late 1998.

Since 1998, Rainsy has continued to lobby internationally for greater controls over the CPP dominated government. The SRP regularly distributes press releases in French and English denouncing the activities of the Cambodian government, and calling for international donors to take action. Since 1998, the focus of these press releases has tended to be on issues of corruption and 'poor governance' rather than human rights and democracy, in line with the shift in donor attention described in Chapter 5. For example, during the Consultative Group meeting in May 2000 in Paris, Rainsy held a parallel press conference to 'give his point of view on solutions to make international assistance a more effective tool to reduce poverty in one of the world's poorest countries, while at the same time promoting democracy and social justice'.[48] These consistent calls for the imposition of conditionality on international aid to Cambodia, positan international duty to protect the people of Cambodia from what the SRP views as a corrupt and illegitimate government.

Such appeals to international power are intended to promote continued international support to correct the poor functioning of the democratic process. However, they have the effect of further problematizing democratization, since they implicitly subordinate local political action to international power. The international sphere – a sphere that is distant from the lives of ordinary people – is portrayed as the decisive sphere in which political action can take place. This operates to the advantage of political leaders, such as Rainsy and Ranariddh, who have the appropriate expertise, experience and contacts to operate confidently internationally. It further promotes the view of politics as distant from the everyday level of village life, and as an activity that is reserved for professionals, with appropriate qualifications. Although Rainsy, in particular, has mobilized popular protests in support of this policy, this is regarded as promoting an appeal to international power, rather than being viewed as an exercise of popular power in itself.

In this way, extensive internationalization of politics can become anti-democratic in downplaying the importance of the role of the people themselves. The professionalizing and distancing impact of this approach is perhaps best exemplified in a quotation from a campaign speech of another politician, Tik Ngoy, president of the Free Democratic Republican Party, who campaigned almost exclusively on a portrayal of himself as an adept at international networking. Ngoy's rallies were notable for the waving of the Stars and Stripes, and the distribution of photographs of Ngoy in the company of US presidents such as Richard Nixon. Ngoy's campaign speeches emphasized the importance of international connections for Cambodia's future:

> Why does our party fly the American flag with the Cambodian flag? This is what we take pride in. Our party has two main things to do – firstly, promote economic development and, secondly, to promote free international relations, especially between Cambodia and Washington … I will do my best to improve the living condition and the health of the people – by means of my relationship with the superpowers, America and China.[49]

The view that a politician is empowered by his or her credentials vis-à-vis 'the superpowers' rather than in respect of the people reflects a view of Cambodian politics as beyond the capacities of ordinary Cambodians. Given the heavy toll taken by international politics upon Cambodia in the recent past, and Cambodia's contemporary dependence upon international aid and investment, this is perhaps a realistic portrayal of the country's current political situation. However, in capitulating to the imperatives of international aid and investment decisions, the concept of a Cambodia in which the 'Cambodian people are the masters of their own country', as the 1993 constitution puts it, is lost.[50]

In Cambodia in the 1990s, then, an emphasis upon international rather than local solutions has been common in electioneering, particularly by returnees who view themselves as uniquely qualified to facilitate such solutions. This has precluded the promotion of democracy as a means of harnessing local ideas and preferences to provide solutions to national problems. Although the voter is engaged as a chooser, selecting between different mediators of international interventionary policy, democracy is not viewed as a conduit for translating into national policy the ideas and contributions of voters themselves. This reflects the fact that, for party leaders, local ideas are unfamiliar and often inaccessible. Elite and transnational politicians find the solutions of international technocracy more comprehensible and more convincing, and tend to regard electioneering as a matter of achieving the acquiescence, rather than empowered participation, of rural Cambodians.

The voters' response

During the UNTAC era, and subsequently, democratization has been presented to voters very much as a procedural matter, strongly linked to periodic elections with election campaigns of limited duration, rather than focused upon the blossoming of political debate at the village level. Democratization has been promoted in rural villages through the activities of voter trainers and educators, rather than of political activists. These voter educators, along with opposition political party representatives and election observers, have concurred in exhorting villagers not to express political preferences publicly, thus contributing to the exclusion of urban-based political parties from forging solid links or achieving any detailed understanding of preferences and concerns in the villages.

In addition, in a climate of material dearth the appearance of wealthy politicians offering campaigning funds to local party members, gifts to those willing to join the party and promises of aid if elected, awarded a more immediate and certain return to voters than that offered by vague assertions of a better life in the future when conditions of democratic governance might have been achieved. This did not always amount directly to vote-buying. The centrality of money to campaigning was also described by a FUNCINPEC candidate in Kandal Province:

> You cannot run a campaign without money. Every time [I visit the districts] I spend $300 – they say, oh this has not been repaired, we need dollars for this, $30, $10, $20 ... You have to spend money because the CPP is there all the time making donations. [51]

FUNCINPEC parliamentary candidates, to a great extent, financed the district activists associated with their own campaign, and were also required to contribute to central party funds as a condition of their candidacy. Funding of local activists by candidates was central to the ability to organize a campaign in Cambodia's subsistence economy, yet it also inserted a steep hierarchical association into relations between local activists and party candidates recruited by the party centre.

Other practices, such as the offering of incentives to people joining the party, were more directly related to vote-buying. The problems of vote-buying in the context of a secret ballot have been described in Chapter 4 – the politician is unable to ascertain whether the voter has kept his or her end of the deal. For the CPP, as described, this problem was dealt with by the exertion of a stifling surveillance, accompanied by the circulation of rumoured threats against entire villages, designed to exert maximum pressure on the individual. For smaller and more distant parties such supplementary tactics were impossible. Vote-buying represented less a reward for loyalty than a hopeful shot in the dark.

Following the elections, politicians were divided on how successful the distribution of money had been in terms of determining voter preferences. The day after the election, as the first results (favourable to FUNCINPEC) were released, the FUNCINPEC candidate for Phnom Penh, Ahmed Yahya, commented that the single most important lesson learned during the election campaign had been

> the importance of funds. If we had more money we would get more votes. We have to start now putting money aside for next time.[52]

However, campaigners from less successful parties, who had also distributed considerable sums of money to their supposed members, held a different view:

> The reports [from local activists] are always very sweet – they never tell us about the problems ... When one supporter joins they get 100 riel, or 500 riel – they just put their name down as a voter. So we thought we had 80,000–100,000 members, but really we only had 10,000. Like the CPP – three million became one million. There is a real lack of control – one person is a member of five or six political parties so he can get the 500 riel five times. To get support.[53]

> The brokers are very good at cheating political parties. For example ... a guy comes to see you and says he can get 10,000 votes for you, can guarantee a seat for you in that province. And on the back of his motorbike he has pictures, thumbprints, names, addresses. Many political parties say, OK I'll give you $1,000 or $2,000 for that. But then he goes to another party office and says the same thing.[54]

While the willingness of Cambodian voters to join any number of parties, without necessarily voting for them, has been seen as an important indication that Cambodian voters maintain their freedom of conscience in the polling booth, the price has been the reduction of the public sphere of voter–party relations to a set of politically irrelevant financial transactions. Arguably, this reflects, also, a certain cynicism regarding the campaign promises of politicians, acknowledged in occasional complaints by voters and demonstrators interviewed that politicians had not worked to construct representative channels for popular engagement in government in the past, and were not offering them concrete, deliverable and debatable policies for the future. The question of whether and how this public sphere can be recovered for democratic political activity and debate in the face of continuing rural poverty remains unresolved. Throughout the 1990s, the implications of these features of the local political environment for the emergence of substantive relations of democratic representation between voters and parties were profound.

A concern of international democracy promotion in the 1990s has been to promote democracy in countries that have not achieved the levels of economic development that correlated positively with democracy in the past. The experience of Cambodia suggests that doing so is problematic for both the technical aspects of procedural democracy and the quality of the democratic debate produced. This is not primarily because economic development creates better citizens, but because in a context characterized by poor infrastructure, limited communications, and, consequently, poor access to fragmented political arenas, the ability of incumbents to dominate is high. The spectacular campaigning that this promotes does not generate a high level of debate. It rather promotes, on the part of parties, a rousing populist rhetoric that is ill-fitted to the transformation of politics in an oppressive and highly secretive atmosphere. For voters, it encourages a cynical approach to politics in which they become acutely aware that their role is little more than that of spectator and rubber-stamp legitimator of activities into which their input is not required. The tendency, on the part of politicians, to attempt to compensate for the dearth of organizational connections between the sphere of multi-party activity and the remote and unfamiliar sphere of the village by a resort to flows of funding, further distorts the political aspects of the elite–local relationship. The aspirations of leaders and voters alike are thwarted by the lacuna between them – a gap which the elitist political party in an atmosphere of tension and threat is ill-equipped to bridge.

7 Promoting democracy

NGOs and 'civil society'[1]

Alongside the constitutional reforms indicated in the Paris Agreements and the creation of a multi-party sphere for political competition envisaged in UNTAC's mandate, the UN-supervised transition of the early 1990s also featured references to promotion of 'civil society' as a plank of peace-building. This began with the formation of local partners to assist with UNTAC's mandated tasks. Thus, in his report to the Security Council on the implementation of the Paris Agreements, Boutros-Ghali stipulated with respect to the human rights mandate that UNTAC 'would ... expect to ... encourage the establishment of indigenous human rights associations' and 'may also wish to associate indigenous human rights monitoring groups with its [investigations and provision of redress for abuse], with the agreement of the parties concerned'.[2]

As in the case of UNTAC initiatives surrounding the promotion of democratic procedures, it was the Human Rights Component that emphasized the importance and long-term possibilities of such associations in terms of larger visions of Cambodia's political development towards a 'civil society'. The Human Rights Component stated that 'the strengthening of civil society is the most essential guarantee against the recurrence of the state repression of the past'.[3] By the time of the UN's departure, the Human Rights Component was cautiously optimistic in this regard, reporting that 'Cambodian political and civil society began a process of re-establishment, many aspects of which are even now perhaps irreversible'.[4]

Evaluation of the contribution of this 'process of re-establishment' to Cambodia's political trajectory in the 1990s is problematic due to the widely varying manner in which the term 'civil society' is deployed, both as a concept in political science, and as a category in Cambodian politics. Like the phrase 'international community', the term 'civil society' (*sangkum civil*) has been popularized and instrumentalized in the Cambodian context. Like the 'international community', Cambodian 'civil society' is frequently and loosely viewed as a distinct set of actors – namely, Cambodia's most prominent local NGOs. Consequently, 'civil society representatives', 'civil society leaders', or sometimes 'civil society' itself are often represented unproblematically in the media and in the reports of

NGOs themselves as acting, thinking, making statements and pursuing the cause of democracy.

This use of the term 'civil society' contrasts with its use in political science to denote, broadly, 'the organizational and co-ordinating capabilities of non-state society'.[5] While the status of civil society as a theoretical concept is not uncontested, this definition broadly captures the sense of civil society, not as an actor or set of actors, but as a realm in which certain actions are possible. Gordon White defines civil society as

> An intermediate associational realm between state and family populated by organizations which are separate from the state, enjoy autonomy in relation to the state and are formed voluntarily by members of society to protect or extend their interests or values.[6]

This definition contains two distinct parts: firstly, the existence of a realm in which the resources for autonomous association are available, and, secondly, the furnishing of that realm with actual associations which use it to protect or extend their interests. This distinction is significant in view of an increasingly powerful presumptive connection in the 1990s between the development of 'civil society' in the South and an impulse towards democracy.[7] Michael Bratton views this connection as emerging from the ability of NGOs to facilitate 'full political and economic participation by the poor'. He comments:

> By their very existence, NGOs help to pluralize the institutional environment and, to the extent that they encourage participation in decision making, to promote a democratic political culture.[8]

Larry Diamond sees a wider range of democratizing functions associated with civil society, including: the monitoring of state behaviour; the building of channels for communication between state and society, and between different sectors of society; the promotion of political participation; the acculturation of citizens to liberal conceptions of their rights and duties; the encouragement of free pursuit of one's own interests and acknowledgement of the validity of the interests of others; the dissemination of information; and the recruitment and training of political leaders. By these means, the legitimacy and accountability of the state is enhanced, and the socialization of citizens into liberal democratic attitudes and norms of behaviour is achieved.[9]

In both these conceptions of the role of civil society, however, the existence of NGOs and the established nature of their links with the state are assumed. Analysis of the role of NGOs and civil associations in Cambodia in the 1990s must come to terms with the fact that such links had not been established; indeed, given the success with which state and party monopolized economic and political life in rural Cambodia, particularly the existence of a non-state realm with the resources to make autonomous association was possible was highly uncertain.

Consequently, the 'civil society' that the Human Rights Component regarded as promisingly and perhaps irreversibly established differed from the theoretical models put forward by White, Bratton and Diamond. While NGOs may have been irreversibly established, the terrain on which they operated and the nature of their links with the broader population and the state were both highly unstable. Consequently, their ability to promote either political participation amongst the public at large, or the interests of their members in particular, was uncertain also. To this extent, their ability to promote democracy was also contingent.

Many commentaries on Cambodian 'civil society', including that of UNTAC's Human Rights Component, in focusing on the organizations themselves have overlooked analysis of the terrain they inhabit. This is significant in that the requirement for a non-state terrain on which non-governmental organizations can confidently exist is, in fact, a taller order for early post-authoritarian and highly intervened societies than the requirement of non-governmental organizations themselves. The experience of Cambodian NGOs in the 1990s suggests that while international backing can lead to the creation of large, professional and fully functioning NGOs, a realm of freedom of association that is independent of international scrutiny and support is much more difficult to engineer in the absence of economic conditions that tend towards the diffusion of power more widely amongst society.[10]

NGOs emerging in Cambodia in the 1990s thus faced similar problems to political parties with respect to promoting the empowered political participation of citizens in Cambodia's rural villages. NGOs were significantly more successful in securing international aid and assistance for their projects; however, this was a double-edged victory in that dependence upon international resources also entailed subordination of local imperatives and objectives to international ones.

This chapter examines that aspect of 'civil society' which is commonly identified as such in Cambodia – namely, the sector of non-governmental organizations formed since 1992. The nature of these organizations and the difficulties they face in their relations with, primarily, rural society are investigated in the light of two major constraints: namely, the pressures imposed by close relations of dependence upon international donors; and, secondly, the problems of operating in an impoverished rural Cambodia. It is argued that the problems of a lack of autonomous local terrain upon which activities can be conducted and representative links constructed has, to some extent, created an NGO sector in limbo, which increasingly regards the pursuit of international links and resources as their priority. This disempowers local NGOs in their relationship with international NGOs, and increases the difficulties faced in forging representative links with rural society that can facilitate local participation in politics. It encourages a lack of self-confidence which induces further dependency, and, consequently, sterility in terms of potential contributions to democratization.

However, the final chapter of this study argues that the major contribution of both the multi-party sphere and the NGO sector in the area where these have been most consistently sustained – namely, the city of Phnom Penh – has been to engender a precedent for, and exemplify strategies of, non-state action in pursuit of personal interests and grievances. This has encouraged the emergence, particularly since the late 1990s, of a panoply of small-scale, interest-based movements lobbying government over issues of policy. While these have largely been confined to the capital city, they have nevertheless offered opportunities for a new form of politics based upon the mobilization by citizens of their own resources. It is argued that this represents the best opportunity for revitalizing Cambodia's democratic aspirations.

Building civil society in Cambodia

Interest in promoting civil society in Cambodia coincided with a number of analyses of a wave of democratization noted in East and South East Asia in the late 1980s and early 1990s in which democratic opening was widely attributed to the emergence of a civil society as a consequence of the fruits of economic success. John Girling, for example, commenting upon the emerging civil societies that prompted a range of transitions or attempted transitions in Asia in the late 1980s, draws attention to economic factors as vital in constituting the terrain upon which civil associations emerge as empowered interlocuters with the state. He argues:

> Economic development gives rise to civil society – i.e. new intermediate groups ranging from middle-class professionals to labour organizers and party officials – which in turn creates pressures for the development of representative institutions enabling the 'new social forces' to take part in decisions affecting them.[11]

In the case of Cambodia, economic development since the late 1980s has, as described, been highly skewed towards promoting the cohesion of the state through a strategy of using state power to privilege access to material resources and profit-making activities. The benefits of economic activity have thus been distributed primarily according to criteria determined by loyalty and power rather than by reference to either efficiency or need. The private sector remains small and underdeveloped, and growth in the rural economy has been minimal. The gains have been concentrated in a very few hands.

Under these circumstances, economic development is unlikely to create a resource-rich terrain that can sustain a democratizing civil society in the short term. This does not necessarily mean that aspirations for political participation were absent in Cambodia in the early 1990s; merely that the economic power, necessary to transform aspirations into a stable platform from which organized pressure for political change could be exerted, was not available to ordinary people. However, international assistance in the establishment of NGOs was available from the early 1990s, raising the question of whether international aid, training and protection to individuals could substitute for the emergence of an 'intermediate level operating between economic structure on the one hand, and the state apparatus on the other', as Girling defines the terrain of civil society.[12]

Benefiting from such international assistance, the Phnom Penh NGO movement grew rapidly over the 1990s. By 1995, 90 Cambodian organizations were members of the umbrella Cambodian Co-operation Committee, although Yukiko suggests that at least 164 NGOs were operating in Cambodia in 1996.[13] Of the 90 CCC members, 41 were development organizations, 30 were organizations catering to the needs of minorities, special interest groups or professionals, 10 were human rights organizations, 5 were cultural organizations and 4 were smaller umbrella groupings of NGOs. By 1999, the organization PONLOK estimated that between 400 and 900 NGOs were operating in Cambodia.[14]

Heder and Ledgerwood comment on the unusual nature of the NGOs that emerged in Cambodia under UNTAC's auspices. They suggest that 'the implementation of the Paris Agreements created conditions in which fledgling facsimiles of archetypical bodies of civil society might play a disproportionate role alongside other political forces organized along communist or insurgent military lines'. Yet they regard these civil bodies as liable to be overpowered by 'the general refusal of elite culture to recognize the legitimacy of difference and opposition'.[15]

Yukiko Yonekura, in a later study of civil associations in Cambodia in 1995, found that NGOs in Cambodia performed poorly in promoting democracy, measured in terms of success in advocacy, representation of target beneficiaries and the ability to defend their autonomy from both donors and the state. However, Yukiko rejects the notion that Khmer cultural traits are necessarily antithetical to civil action. Rather, she attributes the limitations of Cambodian civil society to a failure of international political will, which, she argues, failed to live up to its task of securing terrain for civil action in the early years when civil associations were first forming and attempting to strengthen themselves.[16]

In 2001, a democratic audit of human rights and democracy NGOs commissioned by the Swedish International Development Agency – one of the major donors supporting these organizations – found that many of the major pro-democracy NGOs in Cambodia were not themselves internally democratic, and consequently had limited power as exemplars and training grounds for democratic action and attitudes. In fact, the auditors concluded, the development of these organizations appeared to have been driven by many of the presumed cultural propensities often considered to undermine

Cambodia's democratization. The audit suggested that these organizations were often grouped around charismatic leaders, had poor internal procedures for consultation with their own staff and operated in a didactic rather than a representative manner with respect to their target beneficiaries in the population at large. The auditors concluded, in line with Heder and Ledgerwood's earlier assessment, that these features were attributable to 'the cultural context of Khmer society' which led to excessive deference on the part of Cambodian NGO staff members, and distrust of them on the part of their charismatic leaders.[17]

These analyses suggest, once again, a view of Cambodian politics either as a function of international agency and Cambodian weakness and passivity, or as a function of international efforts at democracy promotion blocked by anti-democratic Khmer cultural attitudes. Curiously, little attention has been paid to the question of whether international promotion of civil society in the impoverished environment of Cambodia raises problems of its own.

Evidence from studies of Cambodian NGOs from 1995 onwards suggests that, in fact, the poverty of rural Cambodia and the politicization of local government posed considerable problems for the emergence of a 'civil society' comprised of NGOs. Furthermore, it is suggested that international assistance, far from helping to overcome these problems, actually exacerbates them by further complicating the nature of NGO relations with the population, particularly in rural areas. Norman Uphoff draws a distinction between the 'grassroots organizations' and 'non-governmental organizations' which together comprise a third, civil, sector between the market and the state.[18] Uphoff views grassroots organizations as 'any and all organizations at the group, community or locality level'.[19] He defines the 'group level' as 'a self-identified set of persons with some common interest, such as occupational, age, gender, ethnic or other grouping'; the 'community' level is defined as 'an established socio-economic residential unit, often referred to as the village level'; while the 'locality' is viewed as 'a set of communities having social and economic relations, usually with interactions centred around a market town'.[20]

While grassroots organizations are defined in terms of the spatial level at which they operate, non-governmental organizations, which include grassroots organizations, are better defined in terms of the 'incentives used to get co-operation or compliance'.[21] While the state uses bureaucratic mechanisms and enforcement, and the market uses calculations of private interest, the 'third sector depends more on voluntaristic mechanisms, involving processes of bargaining, discussion, accommodation and persuasion'.[22] In Cambodia, the NGOs that emerged in the early 1990s formed a 'third sector' in Cambodian society; however, their status as 'grassroots organizations' – and consequently, their impact upon substantive opportunities for political participation in rural areas – is less clear.

International–local relationships in Cambodian NGOs

A wide variety of international interveners developed close relations with Cambodian NGOs in the 1990s. International NGOs, such as Oxfam, Save the Children, the International Human Rights Law Group, Co-operation Internationale pour le Développement et la Solidarité (CIDSE) and American Friends Service Committee, were important in offering funding, training and support to local NGOs. Many of these were grouped under the Cambodian Co-operation Committee, formed 'to share the lessons of the NGO experience, to monitor development assistance and to promote partnership between international and national NGOs'.[23]

Also important were the various United Nations offices that remained in Phnom Penh after the departure of UNTAC. The UN Centre for Human Rights Field Office in Cambodia, later renamed the Cambodia Office of the High Commissioner for Human Rights, worked closely with human rights groups, while the United Nations Development Programme, UNAIDS, the United Nations Centre for Housing, the United Nations Children's Fund (UNICEF), and the United Nations Economic, Social and Cultural Organization (UNESCO) also aided Cambodian NGOs pursuing activities in their areas of interest. Alongside these agencies, bilateral donors channelled aid to Cambodian NGOs also. The various embassies and the European Union mission to Cambodia made small grants to NGO programmes and organized small-scale workshops directly.

Many bilateral donor countries also sustained offices for their government aid agencies in Phnom Penh; prominent among them in sponsoring NGO activities were the Swedish International Development Agency (SIDA), the Canadian International Development Agency (CIDA), AusAid, and the Japan International Cooperation Agency (JICA). International sponsorship of Cambodian NGOs also took place via quasi-governmental organizations, funded by bilateral donor governments. These included organizations of the US Democracy Project, funded by USAID – the Asia Foundation, a Court Training Project, working with the Cambodian judiciary, and a Human Rights Task Force, working with Cambodian human rights NGOs. The German government also funded quasi-governmental foundations, which were active in supporting human rights and democracy NGOs, while SIDA funded two Swedish NGO umbrella organizations, Forum Syd and Diakonia, to collaborate with local NGOs on its behalf. Finally, international assistance occurred via various organizations, including the British organization Voluntary Service Overseas and the Australian Volunteers Service Overseas Service Bureau, which facilitated the deployment of volunteers from Western countries to work as trainers within Cambodian NGOs.

In the 1990s, a momentum emerged behind the drive to international civil society promotion in Cambodia, which reflected both contemporary thinking in international developmental circles, and the interests of individual donors and donor agencies. Grant Curtis suggests that Cambodia became, at this time, an 'aid market'. He argues that a combination of international guilt over the international connivance in Cambodia's civil war, and the exciting challenge presented by a Cambodia which was viewed as a blank slate in developmental terms, all led to an influx of aid that far exceeded Cambodia's 'absorptive capacity'.[24] In the NGO sector, Curtis, like many other commentators, ascribes limits to the ability to transform donors' funds into the appropriate democratizing activities to mental health problems and a cultural attachment to patron–client relations amongst Cambodian NGO staff.[25]

However, the nature of the relationship between these various international donors and supporters and their Cambodian 'partner' NGOs arises, perhaps more obviously, from a hierarchy emerging from material inequalities in power between international and local NGOs, and a condescending attitude internationally that has been empowered by the greater economic power of international donors. This follows a pattern set in the earliest days of UNTAC's support for human rights associations. The importance of UNTAC in providing the arena in which these NGOs could operate is reflected in the fact that the first local human rights NGOs established in Cambodia opened their headquarters within UNTAC compounds, the better to enable effective United Nations protection of them.[26] It was clear, from the emergence of these organizations, that it was international policies and practices that sustained the political space in which they operated, building an inequality into the relationship between international and local organizations from the very beginning. The ongoing relationship between these organizations and the UN Centre for Human Rights was summed up by another UN official in 1996 as follows:

> The UN just has a support role – political, financial, technical ... Especially how to lobby, how to set up systems of communications. And when the political authorities give trouble – intervene and bail them out.[27]

Over the course of the 1990s, arguably, the inequality between international donors and local NGOs has hardened, rather than reducing. From the earliest days, some international observers criticized the relationship cultivated by UNTAC with local NGOs as saturated with 'paternalism'[28] and 'colonialism'[29]:

> During UNTAC ... there was a patronising attitude, they are like children, they can't stand on their own feet, they don't know what they are doing ... [UNTAC] failed to think of the NGOs as independent, self-sustaining, domestic entities. It thought of them as outgrowths of the UN.[30]

Heder and Ledgerwood suggest that Cambodian NGO leaders and workers were complicit in fostering this attitude because of cultural predispositions towards deference and patronage:

> UNTAC at times seemed pervaded with the condescending belief that 'the Cambodians' were incapable of anything unless UNTAC held their hands and walked them through it ... the hierarchical nature of Cambodian political/social patron–client networks fit all too nicely with such attitudes.[31]

Equally, however, the emergence of Cambodian NGOs in an environment constructed and dominated by the language and material resources of international intervention and assistance has entailed a relative lack of space in which Cambodian NGOs can articulate their own vision. International dominance and leadership became the norm, and the availability of international funds has entailed that those Cambodian NGOs who conformed to international agendas have flourished, permitting the consolidation of the power of international perspectives.

International perspectives have emphasized professionalism in NGO formation, particularly with regard to providing financial transparency and value for money. In a country where the possibilities for local organization at the village level were constrained, this aspect of NGO operations has been disproportionately emphasized by local NGOs seeking to demonstrate some kind of progress or achievements to their international 'partners'. In line with this professional agenda, Cambodian NGOs have come to view their own environment as lacking in two key areas. Firstly, many in the Cambodian NGO movement view themselves, or at least their compatriots, as lacking in 'capacity'. Secondly, the central objectives of NGOs, such as 'human rights', 'development' and 'democracy', are viewed either as foreign imports or as practices which once flourished in Cambodia but were lost. Consequently, external input is needed to revitalize them.

Lack of capacity

It is widely recognized that the authoritarian style of government in the areas held by both the Phnom Penh-based administration and the resistance armies in the 1980s was not conducive to the promotion of 'civil society' in Cambodia. Equally, international discussions of the Cambodian social context have focused upon the long-term and irreparable nature of damage inflicted in these years, and have presumed that the psychological and social traumas suffered by Cambodians have led them to internalize the violence of the 1980s and reproduce it in their post-war social relations.[32] The trauma of war is viewed as exacerbated by the destruction of such limited manifestation of 'civil society' as existed in the pre-war era, and as unleavened by the enlightening power of education, following the policies of extermination pursued towards the educated and professional classes by Pol Pot's Democratic Kampuchea regime.

For these reasons, Cambodians themselves, and the organizations they form, are frequently viewed by international interveners as inherently problematic and in need of international tutelage and guardianship. This view is clearly articulated in the language of international assistance. For example, the Cambodian human rights associations set up during the UNTAC era as the vanguard of 'civil society' were characterized by the then Special Representative of the UN Secretary General for Human Rights in Cambodia in 1995 as the 'children of the UN'.[33] This view is echoed in CIDSE's analysis of its 'partner' Cambodian NGOs. Like many international organizations working with Cambodian NGOs, CIDSE frames its goals in terms of 'capacity building'. In embarking on a programme of capacity building, with respect to a local partner NGO, CIDSE conducts an initial analysis of 22 capacity areas it considers necessary for the efficient functioning of the organization. Yukiko reports, 'Based on ... capacity indicators, the progressive growth of capacity [among Cambodian partners] is divided into four stages: infancy, growing-up, adulthood and maturity'.[34]

The language of 'capacity building' and the attribution of 'childishness' to Cambodian NGOs not only suggests an inequality of power in the relationship between international organizations and their local 'partners', but also attributes that inequality to the nature of the Cambodian organizations themselves, rather than primarily to the circumstances in which they operated or the resources available to them. This kind of language suggests that the Cambodians themselves bring little to the relationship by comparison with their international contacts Such a view is in line with a number of analyses that saw Cambodians as either ruthlessly individualistic as a consequence of the traumatic experiences of the 1970s and 80s or bound by cultural norms that precluded co-operation on a basis of equality. In this way, many international analyses of Cambodian civil society took, as a starting point, the inadequacy of Cambodian efforts to engage in partnership, rather than questioning the possibility of genuine partnership in conditions characterized by a marked inequality in power.

This attitude coincides with a common focus, by theorists of democracy promotion, on international strategies for building the capacity of local NGOs that are presumed to be inherently inadequate. In a general survey of international civil society promotion strategies implemented in the 1990s, Larry Diamond describes a plethora of such activities. These include:

> Education and training (including the training of trainers and associational leaders (in forming, building and running an organization democratically: drafting a constitution or by-laws, facilitating meetings, recruiting volunteers, eliciting active participation, expanding membership, holding elections, tolerating differences, resolving conflict, raising funds, managing projects, advocating policies, building associational networks, and relating to the press, public and government.

To this he further adds:

> Training in more specialized skills – grant proposal writing, financial accounting, curriculum development, civic education, program evaluation, computer networking, public opinion polling, and statistical analysis – are often also needed, along with equipment, infrastructure, project funding, and general operational subsistence.

In addition he comments that 'it is often unrealistic to expect that groups seeking to reform the political process, empower marginalized groups, and challenge established interests can maintain ambitious agendas while being (or becoming) self-supporting', suggesting a funding role for international democracy promoters also.[35]

Three features of Diamond's characterization are striking. Firstly, it is a view that instrumentalizes the emergence of civil society, regarding it as a function of the capacity to have meetings, plan projects and calculate budgets rather than as a more organic process of empowerment. There is no suggestion here of local input into determining the shape of the organizations that should emerge – one size fits all. Secondly, it is a view of civil society that emphasizes the professional over the political. Any sense of radicalism is explicitly marginalized through an emphasis upon resolution of conflict and tolerance of difference, begging the question of how pro-democracy NGOs operating in an environment of intolerable authoritarianism can promote political change without in some way provoking conflict. Thirdly, it is significant that Diamond does not regard the international–local relationship of tutelage that he advocates as hierarchical or involving a far-reaching international imposition of understandings of the appropriate methods and scope of NGO activity. On the contrary, he describes this as a 'bottom up' strategy for democratization.[36]

There is evidence that Cambodian NGO workers have themselves adopted this view of their own organizations as weak, lacking in capacity, and dependent upon the initiatives, funding and methods of international 'partners'. Interviews conducted in 1996 suggested a widespread view that, in terms of the emergence of a free and democratic 'civil society', Cambodia was indeed immature, requiring instruction and discipline in order to conform to internationally imposed standards. For example, a FUNCINPEC National Assembly deputy commented:

> Human rights have to be respected because … we are like UNTAC's baby and we have to behave well. The West wanted to stop the fighting and invested $2 billion. Of course they expect a good job. So this is one of the fundamental things we must do – protect human rights compared with Western standards.[37]

Such immaturity was also commonly rendered in terms of dependence on international support. Staff of human rights NGOs in 1996 still viewed their continued existence as dependent upon the presence of the UN Centre for Human Rights Field Office in Phnom Penh:[38]

> Previously the Royal Government wanted to close the UN Centre in Phnom Penh – if that happened other human rights organizations would lose their will and their independence because of the security situation and because working in the provinces is not secure.[39]

> International organizations are very important for us. Without the UN office in Cambodia, the government would violate everywhere.[40]

> We are lucky to have the UN Centre. Otherwise, NGOs might not be able to work.[41]

Significantly, similar views were elicited from representatives of government, NGOs and academic institutions surveyed by the Cambodian Institute for Cooperation and Peace in 1999. Based upon the responses of these interviewees, the Institute concluded that 'Cambodian democracy during the period between 1993 and 1999 has been like a baby growing up on a daily basis'.[42]

In examining the strategies by which Cambodian NGOs could contribute to this process of maturation, the CICP survey found that NGO workers considered 'capacity building' to be the first priority. This was placed above the mobilization of local expertise and knowledge.[43] Similarly, in the same survey, priorities identified with regard to 'needs' of Cambodian NGOs were remarkably similar to those advocated by Diamond. The first priority listed was external funding, followed by 'capacity building or human resource development', strategy building, 'professionalism, transparency, accountability and credibility'. It was noted, with regard to the latter, that NGOs 'will need to ensure that they have strong administrative capacity, including accounting and public relations, not only with the government and the donors, but also with the people'. The perceived necessity of attaching this last, cautionary, reminder is perhaps significant.

Beyond this, NGO priorities included 'expertise' to contribute to 'the people and society' – this was particularly necessary because of the need to 'compete for assistance in a time of increasingly scarce funds and the increasing demands of assistance worldwide'. The remaining priorities listed were international networking and communication, information dissemination through publications and development of leadership and management skills.[44] International NGOs were seen by their local Cambodian counterparts as the answer to these problems. Eight roles were envisaged for international NGOS: provision of funding, capacity building, provision of office equipment, sharing of experience, help with networking, expressions of moral support, facilitation of local NGOs' relations with the Cambodian government and evaluation of local NGO work. In this set of functions, the dominant role awarded to international NGOs by their Cambodian counterparts is clear.

To suggest that this is inevitable, given Cambodian culture, is to deny the transformative power of civil society. The award of such a dominant position to international NGOs has not occurred because Cambodians are somehow trapped by their culture in a way that other democratizing peoples are not; rather, it has occurred because of the extraordinary dependence of Cambodian NGOs on international donors in a situation where the fast-track promotion of civil society was attempted in an environment which lacked local resources to empower local NGOs vis-à-vis their international partners.

Consequently, 'professionalism' has been defined by Cambodian NGOs in terms of Western knowledge and, consequently, has come to represent a lack in the abilities of Cambodians who have not been schooled in Western management practices, and whose pre-war intellectuals were largely wiped out by the Pol Pot regime. The leaders of two of the largest and most prominent Cambodian human rights organizations interviewed in 1996 commented that human resources were a significant problem for their organization:

> When we set up our NGO, the UN was here so the UN took all the best elements … Cambodians who know English, French, anything … they pay well, so how can we compete with the UN? …. Only after the UN departure could we get some … But then some went to the embassies, private companies, as they have some knowledge, how to deal with people, how to work, how to co-ordinate, how to use English, so off they went to have a good salary and we had to take elements that weren't really good. But we train, train, train.[45]

> the people who came [to join us] are teachers … or students or ordinary people – they helped our organization and worked with us from the beginning, at first as volunteers, receiving only a small fee. That's why we could not select the good people for our activity.[46]

The suggestion that recruiting the 'best elements' or the 'good people' is difficult unless a high salary is on offer is interesting in that it suggests a prioritization of professional skills and capacities, such as a knowledge of 'French, English, anything' over political commitment within human rights organizations. It is also significant that the skills given as examples here – skills in European languages – are quintessentially foreign, and Western, rather than arising from local knowledge. Similar valorization of foreign over local knowledge was exhibited in meetings to discuss capacity-building held between the Swedish donor Forum Syd and the Cambodian organizations it funds in 1999. Forum Syd reported that:

> training in accounting, English, computer skills and report writing were mostly demanded. Some, but very few organizations, requested assis-

> tance in professional staff development in the operational areas of the organizations, i.e. how to conduct audience surveys, deeper knowledge of election systems and local governance, and deeper knowledge of anti-crime investigations.[47]

These priorities suggest that the NGOs felt their most urgent need was for training in methods of communicating with international donors – whether through bookkeeping or report writing – rather than methods of communicating with a broad public.

Some NGOs emerged, particularly in the early 1990s, without international funding or support. The president of a smaller human rights NGO, which lacks the funding to offer salaries to its staff, commented in 1996:

> I think it seems very strange to people that they volunteer. But actually they volunteer because most of them have just finished school or university and they have no job to do. So I just try to persuade them to work here because even if now we have no salary, we hope that in the future if we are doing a good job, somebody might help us.[48]

Again, even in a volunteer organization, it is significant that volunteering for NGO work was represented as attractive, in the context of an interview about the nature of human rights work in Cambodia, because of the hope of eliciting external funding in the future. It is important to note that this kind of statement does not necessarily imply that voluntarism or public-spiritedness is absent in the Cambodian NGO movement. For example, many human rights and electoral observer NGOs rely upon the voluntary efforts of a network of 'activists' to pass on to them information regarding human rights abuse and electoral violations in rural areas. Such efforts are viewed as involving both risk and expense in making journeys to provincial NGO offices to make a report. In a survey of 107 volunteer activists associated with the human rights NGO Adhoc conducted in 2000, only two respondents indicated that they had become activists to get money.[49]

However, what these comments do suggest is a belief that voluntary activity, particularly if motivated by political beliefs, is second-best, and that human rights work is appropriately the work of trained and salaried professional staff in collaboration with international human rights networks. Arguably, this belief pervades that part of the NGO movement that is to be found in regular attendance at the internationally funded workshops and seminars held almost daily in Phnom Penh's hotels.

Lack of capacity and lack of funds

It is significant that both the CICP study and the comments of human rights NGO directors linked 'capacity building' to funding. The CICP study saw capacity building as necessary to 'compete for assistance in a time of increasingly scarce funds and the increasing demands of assistance worldwide', while the human rights directors viewed the ability to offer salaries as essential to attract staff whose capacity was already 'built'. In this relationship, voluntarism is subordinated to professionalism, which is necessary to attract the funds to pay professional salaries. The operation of this virtuous circle increasingly distances the professional NGO staff member from the ordinary activist or citizen who lacks professional knowledge but possesses political commitment, running the risk of constituting paid NGO workers as an elite. The extreme competition surrounding access to NGO jobs in Phnom Penh, where unemployment among university and high school graduates alike is extremely high, and where the only major alternative employment is as a public servant on a minimal salary, contributes to the potential for elitism in the movement. It also fuels a significant subsidiary industry in private English language and computer-training schools, catering to the professional aspirations of would-be NGO workers.

However, this trend is, to a significant extent, driven not by Khmer culture but by the demands of international donors themselves. In his study of local NGOs in Cambodia, Grant Curtis cites a report produced by the Council for the Development of Cambodia, which commented:

> If local NGOs want funding from international donors, they must meet certain [donor-determined] criteria. They must be able to write detailed, structured applications [in either English or the language of the donor, rarely in Khmer]. They must have qualified, competent staff. They must have a record of success and they must meet the development goals of the donor. In other words, if a local NGO wants project funding it must accept the donor's rules and play the donor's game.[50]

Some national NGOs established in the 1990s, whose leaders had not mastered these skills, found it difficult to compete or quickly fell by the wayside, and a number lost their funding due to problems in maintaining international standards in financial accounting or adhering to international spending priorities.[51] In the climate of uncertainty regarding both political trends and donor commitment that followed the fighting in Phnom Penh in 1997 in particular, a number of NGOs withered away. Yukiko reports that between 1999, while the total amount of international aid to Cambodian NGOs had increased in comparison to 1996, each donor funded on average 25–30 per cent fewer organizations. Donors were looking to the larger, better established NGOs with whom they were familiar, and who, Yukiko suggests, were more easily supervised.[52]

Some international NGO activists have recognized a contradiction between the competitive pursuit of professional commitment that both facilitates, and is facilitated by, the availability of international funding, and the cultivation of political commitment. One international human rights promoter interviewed in 1996 contrasted the emphasis on professionalism among human rights NGOs unfavourably with more spontaneous and radical human rights movements that had emerged elsewhere in Asia. He commented:

> The strength of a human rights organization is primarily based on the commitment of the people. Having so much money may give rise to a situation where you don't really get the right people to do human rights work – that's a reality in Cambodia.[53]

A suspicion that NGO work had become a 'good job for young, bright people', rather than a question of political commitment, was widespread among international human rights workers collaborating with the Cambodian human rights associations in the mid-1990s. Two American human rights activists commented:

> Foreign aid is coming in – it has prospects and a good salary ... A lot of hopeful mildly idealistic youngsters join because they get foreign aid. They do care, but enthusiasm for human rights is complex. It's perceived as a growth area.[54]

> [Cambodian human rights workers] didn't go in as human rights activists. They mainly went in for the salary.[55]

These characterizations are perhaps unfair to individuals who, particularly in rural areas, take considerable risks to engage in human rights work. However, they do underline the professionalizing pressures exerted on individuals by international aid policies. Yet, despite international unease at these tendencies, international donors have continued to enforce rigid control on local counterparts, who are expected to submit plans, reports, accounts and evaluations of their activities regularly in order to release new tranches of money. This has had a significant impact upon the nature of Cambodian non-governmental organizations. Dependent upon international organizations for material resources and protection, they are compelled to subscribe to international standards for managing such resources. Yet their efforts to comply with these standards have also led to international criticism for a failure to operate sufficiently democratic internal procedures for agenda setting and prioritization. For example, a major strand of the SIDA-commissioned Capacity Building through Participatory Evaluation of Human Rights NGOs in Cambodia project was an attempt to assess whether NGOs funded by SIDA were internally democratic along the lines of what was called 'the Swedish model'. It was concluded that 'in most of the partner organizations there is still a long way to go'.[56]

From the perspective of Cambodian NGO leaders, 'capacity building' offers a solution to this catch-22, in that sufficiently intensive staff training can socialize staff members into the norms and values of international organization, thus expanding the pool of staff that can be reliably involved in democratic internal decision-making. In the meantime, charismatic leaders who had proved successful in forging networks of close relationships of mutual respect with international donors dominated the movement throughout the 1990s, at the expense of the input of lower-profile or rural-based individuals.

There is a further dimension to the mutually sustaining relationship between 'capacity building' and reliance upon external funding. Not only does reliance upon external funding impel concerns to build the particular types of 'capacity' required to secure funds: conversely, the types of 'capacities' envisaged also affect the nature, and costliness, of the type of organization to be built. The highly managed and supervised nature of the kinds of projects funded in the Cambodian NGO movement suggests the need for a fairly large and well-equipped organization with computers, telephones, cars and educated personnel.

This has a centralizing imperative, as indicated by the experience of Cambodia's three election monitoring organizations, the Committee for Free and Fair Elections (COMFREL), the Coalition for Free and Fair Elections (COFFEL), and the Neutral and Independent Committee for Free Elections in Cambodia (NICFEC). Of these organizations, COMFREL and COFFEL are the largest, sustaining networks of election observers in 24 and 15 provinces respectively. Both organizations have professionally staffed central headquarters in Phnom Penh, plus provincial teams in the provincial towns, and, in between elections, sustain a network of district and commune activists who report on any election-related issues arising in their areas. NICFEC has a small headquarters in Phnom Penh and organizes commune-level activities through the voluntary participation of students from arts colleges across Cambodia into a variety of programmes, prominently including voter education by means of student-directed and performed travelling theatre and puppet shows.

While all three observer networks are internationally funded, COMFREL and COFFEL are significantly more 'professional' and internationalized in their functioning and outlook, sending staff members to study abroad, and employing expatriate advisors – COMFREL on a part-time basis, and COFFEL under the auspices of Voluntary Service Overseas. Their objectives are couched in terms of promoting human rights, free and fair elections and the democratic freedoms of citizens. NICFEC is a more modest organization with a smaller permanent staff, approximately half as many commune activists, about half the funding of the other two organizations, and a mission statement that elevates the protection of Khmer culture over the promotion of respect for human rights and democracy. It is significant that donor representatives based in Phnom Penh regarded NICFEC as the most cost-effective of the three coalitions.[57] It is also significant that the budgets of the organizations, for overlapping and roughly equivalent periods between the end of the elections in 1998 and 2000, indicate that NICFEC spent three-quarters of its budget on activities taking place in the provinces in this period, while COFFEL spent more than three-quarters of its budget, and COMFREL 97 per cent of its budget, on activities in Phnom Penh.[58]

This example suggests that while a high national and international profile and intensive efforts at promoting professionalism through capacity building are useful in attracting international funding, these attributes do not necessarily promote political change in rural Cambodia. The CICP survey of governmental and non-governmental representatives significantly found that NGOs generally were believed to be more effective in Phnom Penh than in rural Cambodia. Among the strengths of NGOs, respondents to this survey listed the following:

> clear planning and strategy; budget assistance; recognition by the government, people and donors; close cooperation with the government; evaluation/feedback; 'many' forums and seminars; auditing by donors; self-education and improvement; capacity-building/staff training; dissemination of information; research capacity and exchange of experience and information; collaboration among the NGOs; pro-reforms; and commitment/will.[59]

It is significant that these 'strengths' fit closely with the priorities of 'capacity-building' programmes offered by donors. Indeed, the survey's respondents appeared to feel confident that they had grasped the fundamentals of capacity building, and were able to communicate well with donors as a result. Foremost among NGO weaknesses, by contrast, were

> lack of understandings of the real needs and interests of people; too proud; ... too few NGO programmes in the rural areas, donor dependency ... some wasteful budget spending ... publication and dissemination of information are not widespread in the countryside.[60]

This self-evaluation suggests that the relationship with the international sphere has been pursued at the expense of relations in the rural arena in particular. Yet, in reporting on respondents' views of their strategic priorities, the CICP report placed the need to co-operate with 'other institutions and organizations, either within the country, the region or the world' ahead of 'working directly with the people'.[61] At a feedback workshop to discuss the findings of the SIDA evaluation of ten human rights and democracy promotion NGOs, the participants 'agreed that building grassroot support is vital to their future work in Cambodia'. However, they 'had trouble describing how their organizations could support local community activists or grassroots initiatives to help influence both community or national policy'.[62]

The disempowerment of local NGOs and the impoverished local sphere

Close but hierarchical relations between NGOs and the 'international community' that funds them reflects a relative lack of confidence in operating in rural political arenas, but also contributes to growing sense of distance between the increasingly professional NGOs and the people they purport to represent. These features emerge from the political economy of resources for civil action in Cambodia. In particular, they reflect the interrelationship between the exclusionary policies of the state, particularly with regard to rural political space, and the intensive and hierarchical displays of power by the international community of donors that sustains a civil associational realm.

The case of human rights NGOs is particularly acute in this regard. In their relationship with the state, human rights NGOs, in particular, have found negotiating with the state to secure terrain for action to be a difficult task, particularly in the countryside. From the early 1990s, the NGOs found that most complaints of abuse were emerging from rural areas, and particularly from remote communes and villages in heavily militarized areas. This occurred for three major reasons. Firstly, the emergence of private markets led to the expropriation of land and resources by the military and local officials, often violently and usually at the expense of the ordinary civilian. Secondly, the contest between the CPP and other parties over political access to rural areas prompted the reassertion of a political surveillance over the population by local officials, particularly at election time. Thirdly, the ongoing war and the lingering effects of war placed villagers at risk from random acts of violence and banditry. Human rights workers interviewed in 1996 saw the major victims of abuse in Cambodia as the 'poor', the 'grassroots' and the 'weak'. They viewed the major abusers as armed agents of the state, in particular local (commune) authorities, village militias, police and members of the military.

For human rights NGOs attempting to address these issues, the problem of fragmentation of rural political arenas was acute. Politics at the commune level in Cambodia is a highly fragmented affair, with many communes extremely remote, cut off seasonally by floods, or simply isolated by the dearth of transport and communications infrastructure in rural Cambodia. In the early to mid-1990s, when transport was not only difficult but insecure, in view of continuing insurgency, mine-laying and banditry along the roads, visits to outlying communes were expensive, uncomfortable and dangerous. For human rights investigators, there was a fear that their appearance might be seen as potentially embarrassing to local officials who controlled violence in the locality by means of the system of village militias. Consequently, penetrating isolated areas was highly dangerous for these organizations. Even at the end of the decade, with security much improved and political contestation dampened by the coalition between FUNCINPEC and CPP, the poor state of Cambodia's roads and the limited reach of telecommunications made the integration of such remote communes into a 'civil society' problematic.

Human rights NGO workers described these problems in interviews:

> There are some remote areas that we have never been to, to provide training. We just don't go there because we don't have good communication equipment. We just cannot trust the local authorities – they might kidnap or extort money from you.[63]

> In the places we've been to, there isn't much human rights abuse. But there are places that have a lot of human rights abuse on the other side of the Mekong River – Tboung Khmum District and Prek Kraek District. They are beyond the reach of non-governmental organizations. When we go there, they just point guns at us and ask for money. They are armed men … We don't know who they are. They just come from the jungle.[64]

Consequently, although human rights NGOs maintained offices in most of Cambodia's provincial towns and attempted to maintain contact with volunteer 'informants' at the subdistrict level, these NGOs pursued a top-down approach to human rights promotion. Activities were firmly anchored in the secure arena of the Phnom Penh headquarters from which collaboration with other NGOs or international actors offered protection and support that was not available in the countryside. At the village level, the NGOs' presence was intermittent and their activities were didactic. Activists arrived for week-long training sessions, and then departed. Those seeking to report human rights abuses in the countryside by and large had to travel to district or provincial towns to find human rights organizations.

These serious problems made human rights work in the provinces a risky business for much of the 1990s, and the courage of those who engaged in it is undoubted. Yet for much of the 1990s, human rights workers were unable to stake out a terrain of 'civil society' – an intermediate realm between the state and the individual – at the local level that was the immediate site of the abuse because of the insecurity and impenetrability of these areas. Consequently, human rights organizations functioned via the organization of channels for removing 'serious' problems from the politicized and state-dominated terrain of the isolated village, and placing these problems instead in the sphere of the international–NGO–state dialogue in Phnom Penh.

Human rights activists described this process:

> If we have a serious case – for example land grabbing – we send a complaint to the National Assembly or the Ministry of Interior, to get compensation for the victim, because it is a very serious case. When a group of soldiers decides to take land from the people, it is impossible to solve the problem for the victim in the provinces, because of the

> provincial and local authorities. So we always take the case to the regional [military] commander or to the Ministry of the Interior.[65]

> We had our most serious case around the [1993] election ... It was a complaint about land ownership – his land was taken by the district authorities, supported by the provincial authorities. They took about seven hectares of rubber – he was a representative for 30 families whose land was taken. The victim sent a complaint to this office, but he was intimidated by the abuser – even here, in the provincial town. So [another human rights organization] sent him to Phnom Penh.[66]

These and other accounts of rural cases handled by human rights organizations suggest that the tackling of abusers directly is avoided because of the difficulties of investigating under the observation of the abuser, and because of the prospect of intimidation against those who made the complaint. Consequently, information and sometimes even complainants are sent to Phnom Penh where the greater stability of both the (limited) public face of the government and the terrain of civil society allows the case to be dealt with more effectively.

These problems suggest, firstly, that the poor state of the Cambodian economy, particularly in terms of the lack of infrastructure and the availability of funds for travel which prevents the unifying of local political arenas, is a significant barrier to the emergence of a civil society, if that is conceived as both the existence of NGOs and the existence of terrain upon which they can operate. Human rights NGOs, at least, have discovered that the autonomous terrain for civil action is not readily available in the villages. It is significant that attempts to construct such terrain through the mobilization of villagers to resist abusive local authorities is rejected by NGO workers; this is because of concern that to do so would be to enter into the political contestation for the control of village loyalties which was at the heart of state strategies in the 1990s. For example, NGOs participating in the SIDA workshop in 2000 'expressed the need to be cautious about using the term "popular movement" as it will arouse government suspicion and possible charges of "anarchy"'.[67] To avoid this, NGO workers transferred serious cases to Phnom Penh, where advocacy could take place in safety.

Even at the national level, however, a public call for redress is not usually the strategy adopted by human rights organizations. Human rights leaders frequently avoided action in Phnom Penh's nascent civil terrain for fear that this sphere was still too fragile to support such activities without prompting threatening government action to exclude them from public activities altogether. Such a move would jeopardize the existence of human rights NGOs and the second strand of their work – human rights training for potential victims and abusers – and consequently was frequently avoided.

Human rights leaders, discussing their strategies for pursuing redress for human rights abuse at the national level in 1996, described a particular style of negotiation that they had developed in their relationship with the government. Meetings with the government were by and large private rather than public, and terms used to describe the contact made included: 'discuss'; 'exchange views with'; 'collaborate'; 'give *constructive* criticism'; 'persuade'; 'just say peacefully'; 'work out a solution with'; 'conciliate'; 'appeal to'. Words specifically rejected included 'confront', 'denounce', 'condemn', 'force', 'criticize'. For example, three senior members of the two urgent-action human rights committees, set up by NGOs to conduct joint advocacy on human rights cases, commented:

> We don't like to confront the government. This is our policy ... If we don't collaborate with the government now, I think we cannot solve the problem of human rights violation properly ... If we act like that, the government will be angry with us ... and they will make obstacles for our activity and they may cut off training with government officials.[68]

> Sometimes they are high-ranking but their knowledge is low. So we have to understand ... what kind of strategies we can use to discuss with them. How can we get feedback from them? We have to understand how to get a profit from them ... if we force them to have respect for human rights it's useless.[69]

> The Action Committee and the UN Centre for Human Rights are working very closely with the government to promote human rights in Cambodia.[70]

Such attitudes have been frequently attributed to the predispositions of Khmer culture, and some human rights NGO workers interviewed also regarded these strategies as emerging from efforts to promote culturally appropriate forms of human rights action. However, one of the roles ascribed to civil society by theorists such as Larry Diamond is that of transforming political culture in a pro-democratic direction. This begs the question of why human rights NGO workers felt the need to adhere so scrupulously to a perception of traditional etiquette in this particular field of activity, rather than attempting to transform cultural norms so as to incorporate into them the ability to demand redress for clear cases of serious human rights abuse.

Arguably, human rights activists were forced into the familiar role of supplicant, rather than sustaining the less familiar role of critic, as a result of the lack of independent resources available to empower them vis-à-vis the government. The emergence of relations of equality between power-holders within the state, on the one hand, and the ordinary civilian, on the other, has historically occurred in conditions where economic power became diffused beyond the control of the state. Under these conditions, economic power could be wielded through, for example, the non-payment of taxes, by (proto-)citizens, to force acceptance by the state of rights to political equality, including a right to demand redress for human rights abuse. In the context of Cambodia, such economic power as is wielded by the human rights NGOs is international in origin – a fact that is problematic in their attempts to present themselves as advocates of the 'grassroots'. If they are not to be denounced by the government as comprador agents of foreign intervention, the human rights organizations must take pains to present themselves as approaching the government on overtly Khmer, rather than international, terrain.

Cases considered too hot to be handled even at the level of the urgent action committees were passed even higher, to UN human rights workers and foreign diplomats. An example of this occurred in 1995 when the Secretary-General of FUNCINPEC was arrested, in violation of his parliamentary immunity, after allegations surfaced in the press that he had talked of an assassination plot against then Second Prime Minister Hun Sen. The leader of one of the largest human rights NGOs in Cambodia commented:

> We kept quiet. We discussed it and decided we shouldn't do anything. If we do something, we will become a government target. We think it would be stupid if our organization were destroyed by this event. And also, Sirivudh can be protected by the international community better than by us. Also – Sirivudh has a big house in Paris, he has French nationality. Whereas for us.[71]

Such comments indicated the extent to which even internationally guaranteed terrain was problematic for NGOs when they faced the task of approaching the government over a case considered to have political implications. This view persisted throughout the 1990s. In 1997–8, when a series of suspicious killings of FUNCINPEC supporters occurred in the aftermath of the July fighting, the Cambodia Office of the High Commissioner for Human Rights and local human rights NGOs worked closely together to gather evidence pertaining to human rights abuses. A senior United Nations human rights official reported that international and local human rights workers had worked out an informal division of labour – whereby local human rights NGOs gathered information from villagers regarding the location of bodies, and passed this information to the United Nations office which confronted the government with it. By this means, the local contacts of Cambodian NGOs could be used, but the risk of government oppression of them could be avoided.[72]

These relationships illustrate the extent to which the activities of human rights NGOs have formed in such a way as to mirror the distribution of power in the state which they address. The preference for private over public contacts, the emphasis on preserving hierarchical relationships of deference and respect and the concern to use private networks of influence and control to their own advantage clearly reflects the functioning of the transformed patronage networks which underpin state cohesion. In responding to this, the human rights NGOs exemplify the ways in which NGOs in Cambodia have felt the need to compromise between the real world, constituted from the configuration of international and state power, and the idealized notion of the autonomous associational realm of voluntary action put forward in concepts of civil society as a democratizing agent. This compromise was described graphically by two human rights directors, explaining the dangers inherent in over-reliance on the stability of the civic sphere in the mid-1990s:

> We are in the same boat. Our boat is [our organization]. We are here inside the boat ... I'm here to say, 'OK, look, here is a typhoon, so come to the port and we can moor our boat and then ... stay here until the typhoon has gone. Don't go, otherwise we are all going to sink and its useless'. So we don't fix objectives for one, two, five years' time – we say that we are going to one day arrive somewhere in a nice place.[73]

> For now we have to compromise ... a lot, so that we can do what we can do, slowly. There is a Cambodian proverb which says when the water flows strongly, if you put a piece of rock to stop the water, it will be washed away. You have to go slowly to reach your goal. Democracy is a very long way away.[74]

The instability of the terrain upon which NGOs operate is a function of the lack of internal resources to support such terrain. While international support and a busy round of workshopping, networking and discussion in Phnom Penh have developed a set of supportive relations between NGOs, this does not extend much further into a broader sphere of economically autonomous citizens. This lack of internal resources for support leaves NGOs exposed on public terrain that is largely internationally constructed and only intermittently stabilized by the weak constitutional guarantees of the state. Over-dependence on international resources of support leaves NGOs open to accusations that they are merely the lackeys of international interveners. Consequently, caution is dictated. Engagement with alternative faces of the state, on the private terrain of personal contact and in accordance with a perception of the legitimizing dictates of status and respect, offers a more effective and less risky, although also far less predictable, mode of response to abuse.

The importing of foreign norms

In discussing their relationship with the state, human rights NGOs frequently referred to the need to move cautiously on the question of human rights advocacy in order to preserve their extensive programmes of human rights education. This is significant in that it speaks to a further core presumption which emerges from international dominance of Cambodian civil society, and which has affected the continuing orientations and operations of civil society in Cambodia. That is, that the goals of civil society, whether democracy, development or human rights, are essentially foreign imports, or, at best, attributes of Khmer tradition that have long been lost in Cambodia itself.

In a survey of human rights activists in 1996, when asked whether human rights were a foreign idea brought to Cambodia from outside, half the respondents agreed with this statement, while the other half said that human rights were prefigured in Cambodian history, religion and moral codes. Most agreed, however, that the term 'human rights' had not been heard in Cambodia during the years of warfare and upheaval, and that most Cambodians did not know what it meant prior to the arrival of UNTAC. The 1999 CICP report similarly stated that 'before the arrival of the international peacekeeping forces, it was not possible to learn anything about human rights and democracy because the state, under the influence of the socialist/communist party, did not permit it'.[75] However, since 1991, the report commented 'everyone – including politicians and the people of Cambodia – have received more information and developed an understanding with regard to human rights and democracy through seminars, meetings, television, radio or newspapers in recent years'. Education and training programmes on human rights and democracy were considered to have had a 'far-reaching effect'.[76]

This characterization of the emergence of an awareness of human rights and democracy through attendance at NGO training sessions, rather than through actual grassroots action in organized pursuit of individual or community interests, represents a significant departure from the Diamond view of the democratizing impact of 'civil society'. The emergence of professional NGOs, strongly oriented in their internal functioning towards Western norms of management practice and drawing recruits from the urban educated class, has resulted in a gap between the NGO movement and the rural villagers they regard as their 'members' or beneficiaries.

This gap was illustrated in a cartoon produced by an artist at the Cambodian NGO, Center for Social Development, for the cover of the SIDA evaluation reports. It showed a group of smartly dressed NGO activists advancing across a narrow bridge over a vast chasm, carrying placards bearing the words 'human rights', 'good governance' and 'rule of law'. Far behind them, on the other side of the ravine, could be seen the major public buildings of Phnom Penh, including the Council of Ministers, the Parliament Building and the Royal Palace, along with NGO offices and donors – represented by stetson hats floating above the horizon. In front of them, on the near side of the gorge, were impoverished Cambodian villagers and corrupt local authority officials busy cutting down trees.[77] This unequivocal representation of the perceived gap between the urban and rural areas underlay the perceptions held by local NGOs of their own ability to promote political change.

More broadly, NGO workers believed that there was a difference between the level of comprehension of urban and rural dwellers. One human rights NGO director commented in 1996:

> The first step was to educate in the city, educate all police, soldier, social worker, teacher, *et cetera* ... I think that [at this] level, almost all of them studied in high school ... they understand about social activity. But the grassroots level do not understand about social activity and do not understand about human rights ... They ask the trainer, what are human rights? What is democracy? They don't know because they stay in the grassroots, far away from economic growth.[78]

Here the gap between the rural and urban areas was viewed as a function of the availability of schooling – minimally available in Phnom Penh in the 1980s, but much more restricted in the provinces. It was also viewed as a function of exposure to international ideas. The CICP reported that 'opening up Cambodian society will help to contribute to the internationalization of the country and bring the young generation of Cambodia a step closer to the doorstep of knowledge, skills and information technology'.[79]

A second common view was that human rights and democratic values had some roots in pre-war Khmer tradition but were lost during the war. For example, a senior monk who spent much time in the West and in refugee camps on the border, and is now active in an NGO working to promote peace, commented:

> Part of the problem is a problem with education in the past. During the long years of conflict, there was a lack of education, so the people imitated the evil ones – they believe in violence. Violence becomes something normal or ordinary. They have bad habits. We have to change the bad habits in the mind.[80]

Similarly, a provincial human rights NGO worker and a senior monk commented:

> Human rights so far have not existed in Cambodia – that's why I wanted to work in this organization ... but its difficult to do it well because Cambodia lost everything during the war.[81]

> During the three years, eight months [of the Pol Pot regime] it seemed that Cambodians lost their minds, lost all their values. Up to now, we have not been able to correct all. We just try to improve a little bit.[82]

The perception of the rural villager as unaware of the meaning of ideas such as democracy and human rights led to a strong emphasis upon training –

echoing Boutros-Ghali's prescription for UNTAC's promotion of human rights in Cambodia:

> the development and dissemination of a human rights education programme is foreseen as the cornerstone of UNTAC's activities in fostering respect for human rights and fundamental freedoms ... Cambodians must fully understand both the content and the significance of those rights and freedoms in order to be in a position to know when and how to protect them properly.[83]

UNTAC led the way in launching human rights and voter education programmes and education and training activities were prioritized by human rights and democracy promotion NGOs after UNTAC's departure. Arguably, this emphasis again emerges from the predispositions of NGOs towards a view of human rights and democracy as appropriately promoted by 'professionals' and 'experts'. Comments made by two staff members of Cambodian human rights organizations in 1996 underlined this point:

> I don't demand the same level of respect for human rights as in Western countries ... If we try to have all ... in Cambodia this is not good at all because Cambodian people mostly are illiterate so if we say we have all freedoms it is not good. It is dangerous for Cambodia [because] Cambodian people are not ready to get those rights, they don't well understand the Universal Declaration yet.[84]

> Democracy also can create big problems. For example, I vote for you ... because I think that you will do something for me; but after I've elected you, you don't do anything for me. I'm angry! I will vote for one of those other people without thinking that the other person might be even worse. That's why I think democracy may not be so good ... So if we want democracy, we should raise education.[85]

In both these comments, an explicit connection is drawn between education and readiness to exercise freedoms and democratic rights, indicating a certain degree of mistrust of the poor and a distancing of human rights professionals from them. SIDA's evaluation of human rights and democracy promotion NGOs in 2000 found that almost a decade after the initial launch of such education schemes in Cambodia these NGOs continued to be preoccupied with education at the expense of other activities such as advocacy. In response, the NGOs evaluated commented that 'they wanted to continue focusing most of their organization's activities on education and they cited the current stage of development in Cambodia as their reason for doing so'.[86] NGO representatives also commented that 'education was the more "safe" path to develop their agenda'.[87] These comments suggest that NGO staff draw explicit connections between the lack of development and education in Cambodia generally, and rural Cambodia particularly, and both a lack of stable ground upon which to mount a defence of human rights and democracy vis-à-vis the state and a lack of ability upon the part of ordinary rural Cambodians to understand and defend these principles by themselves. Drawing these connections has the significant advantage for NGO staff of rendering themselves and their connection with the resources and power of their international backers crucial to any effort to promote political reform in Cambodia.

The privileged place of the educated professional in this vision of reform was made explicit in the view of a university professor active in human rights causes in the 1990s:

> In Cambodia there are a lot of different classes. The class of farmers is very ignorant. They can't criticize – they are angry, but they don't know the way to criticize. Some, not a lot, but some of the intelligentsia, know about this.[88]

Arguably, this conception is informed by the belief that the entrenched division between elite and grassroots cannot be easily removed, except by long-term processes of economic change. Interviewees drawn from human rights NGOs characterized the class of people they represent as 'poor', 'illiterate', 'lacking in knowledge', 'simple' and 'weak'. Efforts to empower the grassroots in human rights NGO activities were viewed as secondary to the need to act in a professional manner, in concert with powerful international interveners, to protect the poor from the immediate abuses of the powerful.

As a result, educational curricula offered to villagers focused on two major themes. The first theme comprised the transmission of the content of international human rights instruments, which were translated into Khmer and circulated widely. The second theme comprised an interpretation of such instruments, with a heavy emphasis on how rights should be seen in relation to morality. One human rights NGO director described the curriculum as follows:

> We tell the people that when we have rights we have also duties, obligations. For example, we have the right to life. We must also have the obligation to respect the life of another ... It's the curriculum that we give them. Duty to the family, duty to yourself, duty to the community and duty to the nation, to society.[89]

This morally didactic emphasis arguably reflects a degree of distrust, on the part of educated and professional NGO workers, of ignorant 'grassroots' responses to a rhetoric of liberation. Such an attitude was obliquely noted by respondents to the CICP survey, who listed 'too proud' and 'inappropriate attitudes towards the people' as weaknesses and problems for NGOs in Cambodia in 1999.[90]

The close relationship between international organizations and local NGOs, and the tremendous influence exerted by international organizations in funding, training, supporting and, to a degree, protecting local NGOs has had a significant influence upon the trajectory of 'civil society' in Cambodia. Above all, the organized NGO sector is, and regards itself as, primarily urban, professional, intellectual and existing in a didactic relationship to the weak, uneducated and rather dangerous 'grassroots'. This has frequently been regarded as an outcome of the operations of Khmer culture in which patrimonial relationships between the wealthy and educated and the poor and illiterate have been common. However, any pre-existing impetus towards this kind of hierarchical relationship between the NGO community and its intended beneficiaries has been accelerated by the nature of international assistance. Particularly important in this respect has been the emphasis upon foreign knowledge in rendering NGOs acceptable as 'partners', assertions of 'lack of capacity' on the part of Cambodians in the eyes of their international benefactors, and international emphasis upon human rights and democracy as a reorientation, rather than an empowering, of attitudes within Cambodian society at large. All these attitudes have been transferred to the Cambodian NGO movement, strengthening perceptions of an urban–rural divide and the appropriacy of tutelage rather than solidarity in their relations vis-à-vis the poor. This significantly inhibits the extent to which civil society has emerged as a realm of equality in Cambodia; yet the inhibitions emerge, not from Khmer cultural propensities towards hierarchy per se, but from the political economy of international funding, which is inclined to strengthen rather than weaken these.

The role of the state, as an intervener in the three-way relationship between NGO, international donor and 'the grassroots' is also important. The cohesion and functioning of the state, as it has evolved over the course of the 1990s, has been heavily dependent upon personal networks of transformed patronage aimed at exploiting resources and populations alike in order to generate profit for state insiders. As such, it is incompatible with a tolerance of civilian challenges to its operations and with the language of professionalism, accountability and transparency promoted by NGOs.

In the rural political arenas, NGOs have hesitated to challenge the state directly, perceiving little secure public terrain upon which to mount such a challenge. In Phnom Penh, the political landscape is perceived as more open, particularly because of the protective presence of international observers, who, in the early days, often briefed, prepared and accompanied NGO workers to meetings with government officials. At this level, NGOs have initiated dialogue with the government on a range of issues, combining attempts to promote state adherence to and acknowledgement of principles of governance, and efforts to lobby privately through personal networks to achieve particular case-by-case interventions by the powerful to right wrongs perpetrated by their subordinates.

State responses to NGO lobbying have been varied, reflecting the discretionary use of power that sustains the transformed patronage relations upon which state cohesion has been largely based since the late 1980s. There have been few examples of major reversals of public policy as a result of NGO intervention, except where NGO interventions have been supported by international lobbying. This point has been well noted by NGOs, who regard advocacy to the 'international community' in an attempt to beckon international pressure onto the government, as a crucial strategy with more chance of success than direct lobbying of the government.[91] A lawyer, who headed one of the urgent action committees in Cambodia in 1996, commented:

> The international NGO has more power than the local NGO; for example, it is easy for them to have access to the prime minister, King or ministries ... because ... Cambodia is alive now because of the international community. Peace came here from the international community and development also ... If the government does something that is not in accordance with the ideas of the international community ... the international community will be unhappy ... The government has to be respectable in the eyes of the international community.[92]

Arguably, the NGOs' own conception of the 'grassroots' as poor, ignorant, weak and powerless prevented them from regarding community opinion at home as decisive in the same way. NGOs were unable to tap into local frustrations and grievances, and transform these into a public movement for change, due to the instability of terrain for doing so, and due to concern to preserve international linkages which promoted moderation and professionalism over mobilization and confrontation. Consequently, questions of human rights and democracy, as well as broader issues of governance, became questions for negotiation between professional NGOs, government and international donors, rather than questions demanding the political participation of the people.

Alternative approaches to NGO work

The characterization emerging so far of a professional NGO movement based in Phnom Penh and distanced from the 'grassroots' and closely associated with international resources and interventionary power, is not exhaustive. Alternative approaches to NGO work have emerged in response to the problems noted above. There have been attempts by some NGOs to promote a more rural 'grassroots' approach to issues such as development, peace and conflict resolution.

Analysing the impact of these programmes at the level of rural villages requires a more detailed account of the nature of political relations within the village. William Collins's analysis of the nature of civil space in rural

Cambodia provides a framework within which the impact of these three movements on Cambodian villages can be understood. Collins suggests that, at the village level, a sphere akin to 'civil society' exists in the tension between the spiritual or moral influence of individuals and organizations aligned with the village temple and the secular power of local officials associated with the state. Collins reports that the temple committee is an important actor in building community spirit in the village, through mobilizing village contributions to common enterprises, such as the maintenance of a racing boat to compete in the annual water festival, and the organization of other celebrations on the ritual calendar. The temple committee frequently also undertakes development initiatives, such as constructing and maintaining schools. However, Collins suggests that the temple and state are seen as distinct entities with separate jurisdictions. Where co-operation occurs between temple and state officials, it is on a personal basis rather than an institutional basis. The temple committee does not take on an advocacy or scrutinizing role vis-à-vis the state, and thus, while it may promote the strength of the community, the temple does not directly promote the accountability or democratization of the local state authorities – rather it attempts to promote the independence of the community from state-led development.[93] In this respect, the wat committee represents a form of civil society that corresponds to the political economy of rural Cambodia. The resources to challenge the state are difficult to mobilize in a context of state militarization and domination of political space. Consequently, civil action is confined to action that is pursued self-consciously in a sphere that is defined as separate from the state, rather than empowered engagement with the state on its own ground. It therefore differs from the democratizing civil society described by Diamond.

Non-governmental organizations attempting to work at the level of the rural village intrude in a sphere characterized by a temple-based hierarchy of officials and elders, whose power is based upon their moral authority and community building activities, and a local-authority comprising CPP-aligned village, commune, and district officials, with associated militias and partisan 'clienteles'. It is significant that many alternative approaches to NGO work opt to frame their work within the moral sphere, traditionally occupied by the wat, rather than in the politically partisan, entrepreneurial and militarized sphere of the secular authorities. Examples of this include the respected NGO *Krom Akphiwoat Phum*, set up in Battambang in the early 1990s, which focuses on the promotion of trust among villagers through the sponsoring of community development activities. Similarly, the *Dhammayietra* peace march, an annual pilgrimage led by monks and nuns which traversed rural Cambodia in the 1990s to promote a policy of an immediate end to the ongoing civil war, framed its message within Buddhist conceptions of peace, forgiveness and reconciliation. This permitted a moral approach to a highly charged political question that preserved the march from hostility from local officials or the military. The spiritual leader of the movement, the Ven. Maha Ghosananda, described this as follows:

> Everything has its cause and condition ... The cause of fighting and war is greed, anger, hatred and ignorance. The cause of peace is morality, concentration and wisdom. Also truthfulness and gratitude. When we have truth there is no more greed. When there is compassion there is no more anger. When there is wisdom there is no more ignorance. So there is no more fighting. We must keep morality.[94]

The Cambodia Centre for Peace and Development, a programme sponsored by the Phnom Penh-based economic research organization, the Cambodia Development Resource Institute, has also focused on locating peace and development in a moral sphere. This is achieved through the sponsoring of publications and training programmes which promote principles of conflict resolution based upon Buddhist teachings. A graduate of the programme described how she had established a local organization which taught the five principles of Buddhism as a basis for conflict resolution among villagers in her home province of Banteay Meanchey. She commented that in doing so she had extended the abstract principles of religion so as to imbue them with an everyday utility that had previously been missing:

> Previously people only heard the five precepts in Pali, but they couldn't understand them, they didn't know how to apply them in their everyday lives. We translate the five precepts into Khmer so they understand.[95]

The view that Buddhist teachings, widely revered in rural Cambodia, offer an opportunity to restore peaceful relations within society is widespread also among Phnom Penh-based NGOs. Human rights, in particular, are closely associated with Buddhist precepts, an association encouraged by international donors and trainers, who have sponsored projects designed to teach human rights within a Buddhist framework. Among human rights activists, there is widespread acceptance of the view that the distinctions between human rights, as formulated in the Universal Declaration of Human Rights, and Buddhist precepts are minimal and unimportant. This belief is highly significant for the development of relations between grass-roots civil society and local authorities in the villages. It locates human rights in the sphere of moral development, to be achieved by private personal reflection rather than in the sphere of public political contestation, and reflects a concern to disengage from the state rather than to engage more closely with it.

This view has been developed into a philosophy of political change by the spiritual leader of the *Dhammayietra* movement, the Ven. Maha Ghosananda. A leaflet distributed by marchers in 1996 captured the message:

First we meditate to have peace in our hearts,
Promote peace in our family,
Promote peace in our community,
Promote peace in our nation,
Promote peace in the world.[96]

That this view is prompted not by the imperatives of Khmer culture, but as a response to the political economy of rural Cambodia, is suggested by the dilemmas facing rural activists of human rights NGOs. The human rights movement encompasses both the professionalism of internationally sponsored NGOs, evident in the organization of headquarters in Phnom Penh, and the insecurity of existence in the militarized and authoritarian arenas of rural Cambodia. Consequently, the philosophies of human rights promoted by these organizations exhibit a certain ambiguity. Emphasis upon international norms and standards, as set out in the Universal Declaration and other international instruments, is accompanied by a belief, particularly among rural human rights activists, in human rights as the potential source of moral rebirth. For example, one human rights activist described the task of human rights organizations as follows: 'Before our young men used to go and live in the monastery and were taught by the monks how to live a good life. Now human rights organizations have to do this'.[97]

This conflation of human rights with moral action proceeding from religious practice locates human rights firmly in the sphere of the wat rather than in a public sphere where society holds the state accountable for its actions. It reflects the difficulty of promoting non-state action on issues of government – issues where the state has monopolized resources. This has practical implications for the trajectory of Cambodia's political transition. It implies that the mechanics of democratization require not an increase in the demands made of the state by civil society, but a personal conversion of individual officials and the spread of personal commitments to human rights across Cambodia. This is a radically different view from that of Larry Diamond, and it is a view that, in the decade between the signing of the Paris Accords and the first post-war commune elections, appeared to have had a limited impact on the arbitrary power of local officials. Complaints of violence, intimidation and vote-buying in rural villages in the run-up to the commune elections of 2002 suggested a continued dependence by local officials on transformed patronage, rather than a reformed conscience to uphold their authority. However, given the status of grassroots civil society, described by Collins, the militarization and partisanship of local authorities, the degree of surveillance they could exert over village life and, crucially, the hold of local authorities over economic resources, this conception offers perhaps the most feasible long-term strategy for the promotion of non-state action in rural Cambodia, in the absence of significant changes in the political economy of rural life.

Conclusion

This account of the emergence of 'civil society' suggests that a number of changes have taken place in Cambodian society since 1991 which are highly significant for Cambodia's political trajectory, even if they do not represent the smooth evolution towards democracy that many early commentators hoped for. A survey of non-governmental activities suggests that the arena of activity usually described in Cambodia as '*sangkum civil*' represents a group of organizations, by and large based in Phnom Penh, developing in a manner significantly determined by their heavy reliance upon and close orientation to international power and resources. These organizations tend to be centralized and hierarchical with a heavy emphasis upon the didactic transmission of foreign knowledge and a cautious and professional approach to mediating between 'grassroots' and government.

While this approach is often characterized as emerging from Khmer cultural predispositions, it has been argued here that the political economy of international support has exacerbated these predispositions rather than ameliorating them, and international priorities have in fact made it very difficult for these organizations to become vectors of cultural change, as predicted by theorists of civil society-led democratization. The dependence upon international organizations noted is in part a consequence of the emerging nature of the Cambodian state, which has resisted the emergence of stable and unthreatening political space for civil contention with state actors. The emergence of such space, and the admission of a principle of transparency and accountability, would conflict with state strategies of transformed patronage, which have been used by the CPP in particular, and FUNCINPEC to an extent, to manage the transition from war to peace in the 1990s. Consequently, NGOs have been forced onto a heavy reliance upon international securing of political space in Phnom Penh and, like opposition political parties, have also tended to displace issues outwards into the 'international community' rather than attempting to enforce a direct scrutiny of the state by local actors.

As with political parties, an important corollary of these strategies has been a distant and hierarchical relationship between the leaders and professional staff of Cambodian NGOs and their 'members' in Cambodia's villages. Education through training schemes and representation of those who report abuses of their rights are the major modes of contact, and they reflect primarily a relationship of tutelage rather than of solidarity. Even this form of contact is extremely limited in the most remote areas. However, some alternative forms of outreach have been attempted by movements which have tried to locate themselves directly in rural communities, and, by doing so, have tried to alter power relations at the local level in a direction favourable to the emergence of political space.

The outcomes of these latter efforts have been variable. While there has been some diversification of channels of power and protection at the local level, this has often represented shifting relations between existing men of influence, rather than the empowerment of the poorest groups. Research by Ledgerwood, Vijghen and others suggests that open rebellion in the local sphere is rare, and that consequently there is little sense of civil space in the village in which the operations of power can be openly critiqued. At the local level, resistance remains covert. As the case of Kraingyov commune and a variety of land protesters since 1998 suggests, flight to Phnom Penh offers the best hope of claiming space for the expression of grievances.

8 Urban protest movements

The future of Cambodian democracy?

The ending of the war between 1996 and 1998, and the 1998 elections, marked a turning point in Cambodia's political trajectory in three ways. Firstly, the results permitted the CPP finally to achieve international legitimacy for the power it had continued to wield throughout the 1990s, through its colonization of the constitutional state with networks of transformed patronage. Secondly, and consequently, the results ushered in a new period in international–state relations in Cambodia. A new conciliatory spirit on both sides permitted some cosmetic movement, at least, on long-mooted plans for military demobilization, civil service reform and local democratization by means of commune elections. These plans had long been blocked by the tense situation between the coalition partners and the uses made by the CPP of its networks in the military, ministries and local authorities to consolidate power. FUNCINPEC's apparent acquiescence to the role of junior partner after 1998 permitted the CPP to begin to organize these reforms from a position of dominance, from which it could expect to manufacture a favourable outcome.

Greater stability in elite politics, however, does not amount to a deepening of democracy where democracy is viewed as the emergence of a lively, plural and powerful public sphere of debate that permits the participation of the ordinary citizen in the business of government. However, at the same time, beyond the narrow sphere of the elite, the period since the 1998 elections has seen new social forces flexing political muscles for the first time. These comprise protest movements of, primarily, the poor, who from 1998 have increasingly used public spaces in the capital city of Phnom Penh to publicly confront the government with lists of grievances. The present chapter investigates some of these movements, locating them in an urban economy which differs radically from the more easily monopolized arena of the rural village, examining their connections with national and international elites, and investigating their ability to provide new channels for substantive political participation by the poor.

The urban economy and the state

It has been suggested so far that a key aim of the state throughout the 1990s has been to strengthen itself through the violent monopoly of economic resources as a means to retain political power. This has occurred through the protection and expansion of transformed patronage networks which rewarded those state employees that were included in them at the expense of the poor farmer. It has been suggested also that in preserving this private domain of entrepreneurial and militarized activity, the ability of the state to evolve into a transparent and accountable body, that could be taken to task by either a political opposition or an activist civil society, was limited. While certain reforms were made in response to the Paris Peace Agreements, particularly the passage of a constitution which enshrined certain rights of citizenship, and the holding of elections which established at least formal links of representation between the individual and the government via the National Assembly, the continued operation of private relations of transformed patronage and mass surveillance prevented them from functioning to permit the participation of the poor in framing government agendas.

In this context, the emergence of channels by means of which the citizen could call the government to account was extremely limited. In the rural world of the village, continued domination by pro-CPP local authorities entailed that the space for free political action was by and large absent. In the cities, particularly in the early 1990s, CPP dominance of state workplaces was intended to reproduce the same effect. While multiple political parties existed, their efforts to wield public power, through parliament, the media, or the use of street protests, were resisted in a series of key assaults which had the combined effect of protecting the power of the executive vis-à-vis other political formations. For example, the 1995 arrest by the military of the prominent and progressive FUNCINPEC Secretary-General Prince Norodom Sirivudh, in violation of the constitutional award of parliamentary immunity, was a blow to the power of the National Assembly at the expense of the executive, at that time in the joint hands of Ranariddh and Hun Sen who, it appears, collaborated in the subordination of parliament in this way.

The assassination of a series of newspaper editors similarly represented an attack on the sphere of the press, while the March 1997 grenade attack on a demonstration led by Sam Rainsy outside the National Assembly building also reflected the imposition of limits to public use of the city's streets for political association. The 1997 military battle, which led to the departure of the leading opponents to the CPP from the FUNCINPEC, BLDP and KNP/SRP, may be regarded as a bid by the CPP to reclaim the city, following five years of uncertain multi-partyism and international sponsorship of civil space. Yet, in 2002, it appears that attempts to preserve the public spaces of the capital as spaces for free political association and peaceful mobilizations critical of the government have so far been relatively successful, sharply contrasting to the ousting of political activists from rural areas and the limiting of space in the villages for civil action.

For the Phnom Penh administration, from the late 1980s, the imminent peace process, which would bring the king, the parties of the former resistance and international interveners into the capital city, represented the end of the SoC's ability to maintain tight political control over the city. The move to the free market, so successful in shoring up state power in rural areas, had a contradictory effect on state control over urban loyalties and urban political action.

Not least, this control had been exercised in the 1980s through control of housing allocations and the rations made available to state workers in the city. The privatization process from 1989, however, permitted a rapid concentration of land, housing and amenities in private hands in Phnom Penh, as in the countryside. In part, the loyalty of these hands could be assured to the extent that their ownership rights were dependent upon the maintenance of private networks of connections within the state. This heightened the power of borough and municipal officials within the city, as well as opening up new sources of revenue in the form of pay-offs and commissions for issuing deeds and titles.

The move to private ownership in the 1990s favoured those with connections to the state over both returnees from the resistance or from refugee camps, and over the poor in Phnom Penh itself. For the urban poor, the complexity of the process and the discretionary nature of the control of officials over it entailed that widespread fraud was perpetrated against them. For example, the family book system, instituted in the 1980s as a tool of surveillance when families were supposed to register the identity and place of residence of members with local authorities, was abused as families in the 1990s paid local officials in Phnom Penh for this form of registration, presuming that this official endorsement of their residency was sufficient to establish ownership rights to their residences. Other families were given receipts on making applications for ownership and believed that these constituted ownership papers in themselves. Officials made money from the issue of papers that were later adjudged useless when families attempted to use them to defend their land on the basis of right.[1]

The system of land allocation at the start of the 1990s, although promulgated as a public decree to be implemented by public officials, again exhibited the discretionary mix of public principle and private power that ensured the subordination and exclusion of certain groups. For those able to enforce their claims through connections, money or force, ownership became a reality. Others found themselves dispossessed and excluded by processes of land allocation into which they could not tap. Although the privatization of the 1990s constituted a change of direction in comparison with the state control of the 1980s, in terms of the relationship between the allocation of space and the exercise of political power, the similarities are clear. The concentration of land in the hands of the loyal and the exclusion of the redundant occurred in both eras, while public principles remained subordinate to discretionary power exercised via private connections.

However, the privatization of resources in the city differed in its political impact, in comparison with the countryside, because of the proliferation of networks of power and favour in the city. In the villages, the concentration of resources in the hands of a small number of local officials permitted a more effective regimentation of village life, as villagers were sharply aware of the need to sustain personal or political connections with officials in order to share in newly available development resources. The 'local authorities' remained fairly indistinguishable, to those marginalized within the village. Furthermore, in the small and (locally) transparent world of the village, officials could distinguish easily between residents who were part of their networks of connections, and those who were not, and could discriminate accordingly in the distribution of resources – particularly development aid and protection – which they more or less monopolized.

Denser, more fluid and, consequently, more opaque populations in the city could not be treated in the same way, and inflowing resources, particularly after the arrival of UNTAC, were too numerous and diverse to be monopolized by local authorities. Consequently, in the city, different officials were able to corner different sets of resources in an ad hoc manner, and the benefits of discretionary official behaviour in different spheres of life became a commodity to be sold to the highest bidder accordingly. While citizens could and did seek connections with local authorities, courts and police, these connections could be pursued and drawn upon privately and discretely, and did not result in their definition as 'insiders' or 'outsiders' in every aspect of their lives. In terms of the patron–client relationship, transposition to the city allowed clients greater discretion to pursue a number of such relationships and to draw upon them only when needed, rather than organizing all aspects of daily life in the context of them.

The city offered clients multiple sources of patronage, as well as places to hide when patrons were crossed or abandoned. The depersonalization of such patronage links increasingly led to the commodification of these relationships, as the support of a judge or borough council chief, for example, need not be cultivated all year round, but simply bought for cash as circumstance dictated in the context of a particular dispute or problem. These developments both reflected and furthered the loss of political control that took place in the city from 1989, as support from the state was increasingly bought and sold on the open market rather than awarded on a discretionary basis to political loyalists. Indeed, over the course of the 1990s, the urban population has proved to be significantly more unruly than the rural population in its voting patterns and in its predilection for mobilization against government policies.

The emergence of a market for land in Phnom Penh did not merely make fortunes for those with wealth, but also created legal and illegal opportunities to lease land or to build for letting and renting. Alongside the sale of land and houses, the early 1990s saw the proliferation of squatter settlements on previously public land as state officials offered such land for sale illegally, at cut rates, to migrants from the countryside. The Tonle Bassac squatter area, which constituted an infamous city landmark from 1990 to 2001, is an example. The illegal housing appeared on the site of a former park in 1990, after soldiers who had formerly been camped there began to sell plots of land to incoming civilians, including those ousted from houses in Phnom Penh and migrants from the countryside seeking work in Phnom Penh.

The opening of such opportunities, combined with the associated boom in construction, as well as the so-called 'UNTAC boom' from 1992–3, led to new opportunities for rural families to migrate to the city. Income levels in the city were 3.6 times higher than in rural areas, and employment opportunities were more plentiful. In consequence, urbanization in Cambodia, although low, rose throughout the 1990s and was estimated at 15.7 per cent in 2001.[2] Push factors contributing to this rural–urban drift included insecurity and war in rural areas, the difficulty in gaining access to land for those returning to or coming of age in Cambodia after the 1989 decree, and the expropriation of rural land from the poor.[3] The repatriation of hundreds of thousands of refugees from camps in Thailand, under the auspices of the United Nations, created a further pool of migrants to the city. Construction, prostitution, the service industry, petty trading and, increasingly, manufacturing all offered opportunities for unskilled labour in the 1990s.

However, the ability to engage in these economic activities was contingent upon the ability to gain a foothold on the space of the city, for living and working. For the poor, gaining such a foothold in the early 1990s was possible through processes of private accommodation and negotiation. While land had ceased to be the property of the state, the ability to occupy land still depended upon the tolerance of state officials and powerful private citizens who wielded the power either to recognize or assault occupancy of space. A flourishing retail and rental market in squatter housing developed under the protection of borough officials within the city.[4] The determination of occupancy according to these factors extended to the micro-level of patches of pavement, which were occupied or 'owned' by stall-holders, hawkers and street sleepers, according to fluid and evolving negotiations with police and neighbouring landowners.[5]

The reorganization of the ownership and use of space in the city in this way was significant in reconstituting relationships between the state and the citizenry also. The new population of private entrepreneurs operated in a new set of relations to the state. Their activities were facilitated and tolerated by state agents, and particularly the police, to the extent that they were able to pay bribes, protection money and other kinds of informal fees. For these individuals, protective relationships were frequently cultivated with individual members of the security forces, but these differed from patronage relationships in that they usually implied the payment of fees. The burden of such fees on the poorest traders emerged in a 2001 survey of micro-vendors – people who have no fixed stalls, but sell produce out of baskets in or around Phnom Penh's markets. The survey found that sellers who fell foul of market regulations were subject to 'grabbing' – having their produce confiscated and either dumped on the ground or carted off to the market office, from where the vendors would have to buy it back.[6] Similarly, cyclo-drivers waiting for fares outside Phnom Penh's major markets reported that if they did not pay fees to the police, the police would seize the seats of their cyclos, and they too would have to pay to have these returned.[7] Micro-vendors further reported that the system of taxes and fees imposed upon market traders was opaque, and that lack of clarity about the legality of their position in the market left them open to the arbitrary imposition of fines, confiscation of goods, or banishment by market police.[8] Some micro-vendors who slept in the market also reported that they were sometimes rounded up and imprisoned for this practice and had to buy their freedom through paying fines.[9]

The fluidity of such arrangements left individual sellers at the mercy of market employees or state agents, yet they also permitted a certain degree of latitude. While cyclo-drivers, micro-vendors and other kinds of casual workers lived in conditions of very great hardship, and were constantly entangled in relationships of exploitation and dependence with more powerful individuals, such relationships were organized on a fluid, personal and ad hoc basis, rather than an official one. While harassment by officials was severe and frequent, it was not accompanied by the same degree of surveillance that existed within the rural village. Nor did these relationships imply long-term diadic ties, as in traditional forms of patron–client relationships. While frequently injurious or exploitative, they were also often fleeting and spontaneous. Consequently, these relationships offered greater room for manoeuvre, even if the only options were flight or concealment.

While there remained a core of state workers in the city, these were supplementarily engaged in the proliferating employment and business opportunities attendant upon the arrival of UNTAC. The decline in value of state salaries and the broadening opportunities for economic activity independent of the state transformed the relationship between the state and its workers. Some used their positions in the state apparatus to advantage them in private business. Others were increasingly able to distance themselves from the state altogether as they devoted the greater part of their energies to private work outside the state apparatus. The reconstitution of intra-state relationships also produced groups of losers previously associated with the state. For example, the sale of public facilities and enterprises to developers sometimes operated at the expense of workers employed in them. Some state-operated enterprises began to shed staff in preparation for privatization, and employees of state-operated enterprises were reportedly prominent in demonstrations against privatization that took place in 1991 in Phnom Penh.

Amnesty International observers reported that the protests began when workers and staff of state enterprises demonstrated, accusing their superiors of profiting from the illegal sale of factories and official residences to private businessmen. Civil servants, whose salaries were in arrears, and students also joined the demonstrations.[10] Such dissent from individuals within the state system indicates a difference between the operation of privatization in the city and in the countryside. In rural areas, privatization was effective in consolidating the state system because it empowered the military and local government officials at the expense, primarily, of poor farmers. In urban areas, by contrast, privatization tended to empower powerful state officials and their associates, often at the expense of those lower down the civil service hierarchy.

Such alienation of urban groups associated with the state continued throughout the 1990s. Facilities such as the Olympic and O'Russei markets were offered for redevelopment to private companies, who then charged traders for buying back their stalls in the refurbished markets. This attracted the ire of traders who had held stalls in the markets since the early 1980s. Interviews with traders in the O'Russei Market in 2000 revealed that the long-standing stall holders in the market were almost exclusively the wives of state employees.

Consequently, among state employees in the capital city, also, pockets of disillusionment emerged at an early stage, and the private allegiances of state employees proved to be much less manipulable than those of rural farmers in both the 1993 and 1998 elections. In both elections, the constituency of Phnom Penh voted by a majority for FUNCINPEC and the Sam Rainsy Party, rather than the CPP. This occurred despite the fact that the CPP was able to maintain a firm grip on overt loyalties within the ministries throughout the 1990s, preventing FUNCINPEC from transforming its electoral mandate into political action via the executive. This paradoxical situation can be explained with reference to the nature of the city, where private preferences could be kept private more easily than in the (locally) transparent world of the village, even though surveillance was prevalent within public sector workplaces.

Efforts made by the CPP to secure the votes of state employees through surveillance mounted primarily in workplaces continued to 1998 when, for example, all university staff members were issued with a CPP membership card and required to attend campaign events held on campus.[11] However, such surveillance was difficult to sustain in the city where population density and fluidity made the group system, practised to great effect in the countryside, unworkable.

The struggle for control of the city, 1993–8

Between 1993 and 1998, CPP attempts to resist the tide of pluralization were primarily exemplary, comprising high-level tolerance and frequently endorsement, if not organization, of acts of violence against opposition political activists. Between 1993 and 1998, contestation of the space for political action in the city took the form of a series of violent attacks against opposition political activities. These included a grenade attack on a congress of the divided Buddhist Liberal Democratic Party in 1995. The party had split, after 1993, into two factions contending for power. One faction, led by Minister for Information Ieng Mouly was seen as more sympathetic to the CPP, while the other, led by former resistance leader Son Sann, was viewed as more closely aligned with FUNCINPEC. Plans by the Son Sann grouping to hold its own party congress independently of the Ieng Mouly faction, attracted the ire of the government, which suggested that such activities were not only illegal but provocative and might cause trouble. When the group went ahead with its plans, grenades were thrown into a pagoda where delegates from rural areas were staying. There were also reports that some rural delegates had been prevented from travelling to Phnom Penh to participate in the congress.

This kind of violent act, often following public warnings from senior government figures that certain political activities were provocative, were common between 1993 and 1997. Pro-opposition newspapers were also the target for a series of assassinations and arrests. In the summer of 1994, two journalists were killed. One of these was the editor of *Antarakum News* (Intervention News), who was 'secretly and severely beaten on his head and neck' just a few days after his newspaper resumed publication following a bomb attack on its office in March 1994.[12] The second was Nguon Chan, editor of *Samleng Yuvachon Khmer* (Voice of Khmer Youth) who was shot dead in Phnom Penh on 7 September, following articles in this newspaper which criticized the government and the CPP-aligned Cambodian businessman Teng Bunma.

A third journalist, Chan Dara, of *Koh Santepheap* (Island of Peace) was murdered in Kompong Cham province, after writing articles criticizing unregulated timber exports from the province to Vietnam. CPP General Sat Soeun was indicted for the murder but acquitted by Kompong Cham provincial court. Soeun was later demoted for his alleged participation in the illegal timber industry by the newly elected CPP government in 1998. In February 1996, a FUNCINPEC radio disc jockey, Ek Mongkul, was seriously injured in an assassination attempt in February 1996, a few days after reading articles about alleged Vietnamese encroachment into Khmer territory.[13] In March 1996, Thun Bunly, publisher of the pro-SRP newspaper *Udam Kate Khmer* (Khmer Ideal) was shot dead in Phnom Penh, allegedly after publishing articles insulting a CPP general. In 1995 and 1996 three editors of pro-opposition newspapers, Thun Bunly, Chan Ratana, and Hen Vipheak, were sentenced to jail terms on charges of disinformation, after publishing articles critical of the government. Bunly was murdered before his case exhausted the appeals process, while Chan Ratana and Hen Vipheak were eventually pardoned by the king.

In 1995, the office of the opposition newspaper *Sereipheap Thmei* (New Liberty News) was attacked by a group of angry villagers from Kraingyov commune following a critical report published by the newspaper of the Hun Sen Development Zone. In the attack, newspaper equipment was destroyed and staff members were beaten. Afterwards, Second Prime Minister Hun Sen publicly defended the right of the villagers to launch such an attack, commenting:

> I just would like to exercise my right ... to express the opinion that Kraingyov people were not wrong in their action.[14]

The attack on *Sereipheap Thmei* symbolized the way in which rural allegiances, consolidated through the sponsoring of development projects more or less explicitly tied to political loyalty, could be mobilized to isolate and intimidate urban dissenters.

Violence against groups that took up publicly oppositional stances vis-à-vis the government reached their height in 1997. By this time, relations within the FUNCINPEC–CPP coalition had plummeted, as the parties engaged in competition to attract the loyalties of defecting NADK commanders in the North-West. FUNCINPEC had announced its entry into a political alliance, the National United Front for Cambodia, with the KNP and the Son Sann grouping of the BLDP. A series of incidents of violence followed against the National United Front. In March 1997, a demonstration led by Sam Rainsy in front of the National Assembly Building, protesting corruption in the courts and comprising mainly trade unionists from Phnom Penh's garment industry, was attacked by a grenade, killing twenty and wounding 100 people.

This was followed by a shoot-out between bodyguards loyal to Ranariddh and Hun Sen, in front of Ranariddh's house in June, followed by a full-fledged military battle between units loyal to the two leaders in July. Following the CPP's victory in this battle, soldiers looted areas of the city regarded as being loyal to FUNCINPEC, and members of FUNCINPEC's military network in the provinces were allegedly hunted and killed.

There remains a significant degree of disagreement among Cambodian political actors and foreign observers of Cambodian politics regarding the specifics of these events. The culpability of particular individuals or parties has not been proved in law in any of these cases, and analysts remain sharply divided in their attributions of responsibility. However, arguably, these details are unimportant in determining the significance of this period for Cambodia's overall political trajectory. The significance of the period emerges from the fact that the events can clearly be seen as a struggle for political control over the public spaces of the city. This interpretation of events is corroborated by the statements of political leaders regarding these events. From the vantage point of 2001, in particular, the rhetorical responses of Hun Sen to a number of these violent incidents are striking.

Hun Sen almost invariably responded to such incidents by increasing political tension through confrontational rhetoric, and by attributing the blame to provocateurs who engaged in political action in the city. For example, with reference to an alleged plot to assassinate him, which resulted in the arrest of Prince Sirivudh, Hun Sen told Kraingyov villagers:

> You have to destroy those forces from afar in all forms. No one would regret if they have to die because if they exist they are nothing but worms that destroy the society.[15]

In a later key speech to party members at the Ministry of Transport and Public Works, Hun Sen similarly remarked with reference to the deteriorating relationship between the CPP and FUNCINPEC: 'If it comes to fighting over this, so be it'.[16] In contrast with the measured, patriarchal and statesmanlike image Hun Sen has cultivated since the military victory of the CPP over FUNCINPEC in 1997, the inflammatory nature of his earlier speeches is marked.[17]

It is noticeable, too, that following the military victory over FUNCINPEC, security in the city much improved, particularly in response to a security drive launched by Hun Sen in August 1997. The drive was successful in reducing the prevalence of weapons carried openly on the streets, and was accompanied by a weapons amnesty which saw the collection of millions of weapons, which were destroyed at a ceremony presided over by Hun Sen at the Olympic Stadium. While this campaign transformed the security environment in Phnom Penh, at least during the day, it also represented a consolidation of power in the hands of those who had been victorious in July. The extent to which the security drive represented the disarming of opponents was reflected in the placing of a monument to the successful amnesty. The monument – in the shape of a gun pointing skyward with a knot tied in its barrel – was placed on a roundabout directly in front of the national headquarters of FUNCINPEC, neatly illustrating the way that FUNCINPEC's barrel had been securely knotted by the events of 1997.

The overall pattern of events in the period of political tension from early 1996 to late 1997 suggests that whether or not individual incidents of violence were instigated or perpetrated by the CPP, the CPP benefited significantly from them, particularly vis-à-vis FUNCINPEC. These benefits came at a price, however. The urban arena is the arena of Phnom Penh most closely supervised by the international community, and violence in this sphere had a significant impact upon international perceptions of Cambodia and its government. Between 1993 and 1997, the Royal Government was frequently criticized internationally with regard to acts of violence that occurred. Hun Sen's denunciation of provocative elements also led him into public condemnations of 'international intervention' – for example, in 1995 he threatened to launch demonstrations against the US and French Embassies in response to their criticism of the attack on the *Sereipheap Thmei* office.[18]

The military battle in Phnom Penh in 1997 led to a renewed bout of international scrutiny and intervention, and the imposition of conditionality on certain aid arrangements. This reflected the visibility of violence in Phnom Penh, internationally, and made continued violence a high-cost strategy. However, to an extent, the military and electoral defeats of FUNCINPEC in 1997 and 1998 also made further violence in the service of intra-elite struggle unnecessary. With FUNCINPEC in decline and the SRP excluded fairly effectively from rural areas, there was no further need on the part of the CPP to pursue intra-elite violence on this scale.

New social forces in the city

However, since the 1998 elections, demonstrations and protests appear to have become more, rather than less, common in Phnom Penh. Their emergence has also been difficult to attribute to opposition political parties. Rather, an upsurge in protest over the past few years appears to be linked to the perception, on the part of a range of discontented groups in the city, that a space for public expression of grievance has emerged. Some of these discontented groups represent new social forces emerging from the process of economic change that has taken place in the city over the past ten years. In the 1990s, new job opportunities opened up in the city, in private garment factories, construction and the sex industry. These complemented longstanding forms of seasonal employment offered to rural-dwellers in the city, such as cyclo- and moto-driving. At the same time, the unsupervised de facto privatization of public land in 1989 made areas of illegal housing available cheaply to the poor at a time when marginal families in the countryside were finding it difficult to support themselves on meagre distributions of land. The problems faced by female-headed households following the demise of the *krom samaki* system, continuing problems of displacement through warfare and the return of thousands of refugees from border camps created a steady stream of migrants to urban areas. In the heady days of privatization, these migrants and workers found themselves immediately in problematic relationships with the state officials that were supervising the reallocation of space and power in the city. The conflicts inherent in these relations lie at the heart of the new social movements that have emerged in Phnom Penh since 1991.

Equally, urban protest movements have emerged in Phnom Penh in response to more diffuse structures of power in the city. One aspect of this is the broader distribution of economic power in the urban service and manufacturing economy as compared to the subsistence agricultural economy of the countryside. While the private sector of the economy remains tiny, the appearance of garment factories in the environs of the capital prompted the emergence of the first significant protest movement – the trade union movement. This movement has been highly politicized, in particular through the alliance between one of the major unions and the SRP, but it is significant that it emerged initially in opposition to foreign (often Chinese) factory owners and managers, rather than in opposition to Khmer political powerholders. Equally, protests against the 'corruption' of individual government officials by their subordinates in various ministries are common. The proliferation of power through different networks of transformed patronage within the state apparatus in the city permits disputes between different coalitions within the state apparatus.

Furthermore, the urban arena differs from the rural arena in that there exists in the city at least nominal channels for the redress of grievance. The limits to the ability of political parties and non-governmental organizations in rural areas to represent local interests or demand redress for local grievances effectively at the local level has been discussed in previous chapters. Common strategies for such organizations is to forward concerns to headquarters in Phnom Penh, where greater possibilities exist for lobbying and advocacy. These opportunities have emerged from three aspects of city life.

Firstly, the city offers opportunities for public protest and discussion in a variety of forums, including specially created NGO forums and workshops, the media, the streets and parks used for demonstrations, and the floor of the National Assembly. Such forums not only offer ready-made space for association and expression of grievances that is not available in the tightly surveyed arena of the rural village, but also a pool of professional organizers of such activities in the form of NGO staff, journalists, and trade union and political party activists.

Secondly, the diffusion of power in the city, particularly pursuant to constitutional reforms, offers a range of targets for lobbying and advocacy, including parliamentary representatives, the various ministries which can sometimes be pitted against one another, the prime minister, the National Assembly Human Rights Commission, and the king. Thirdly, the greater connectedness of Phnom Penh to the outside world permits the use of the city as a point of access to a much wider political stage. This connectedness is manifest in the plethora of international NGO offices to be found there, the presence of two English-language newspapers and various foreign press agencies and correspondents, and the various embassies and international organizations in the city, as well as the availability of telecommunications and internet access which render Washington, Paris and Tokyo more accessible from Phnom Penh than many of Cambodia's rural communes. The resonance of protest activities amongst this wider audience both empowers and, to an extent, protects protesters.

The combination of space for protest, dedicated activists for organizing protest, a range of targets for lobbying and advocacy, and the sense of a broader, benevolent and powerful international audience combine to improve significantly the attractiveness of demonstrations as a form of political activity in the city as compared to the countryside. This was particularly the case following the emergence of the CPP as unquestionably the dominant party following the military battle in Phnom Penh in 1997.

Three protest movements that have developed in the late 1990s illustrate this point. The first of these is the trade union movement, which emerged in 1996, and was initially closely aligned with the SRP, but which has since become involved in a network of connections with governmental and non-governmental actors and international organizations. The second movement is the Democracy Square movement, which emerged following the elections in 1998. Again, this movement was instigated by political parties, but, arguably, took on a life of its own, has been emulated frequently since, and has been particularly significant in launching a new perception of the public uses of space in the city. A third movement examined is the movement of market traders which emerged in response to the redevelopment of the O'Russei Market in 2000.

In examining these movements, a number of trends become clear. First, they all represented attempts by marginalized constituencies to put grievances – primarily economic – onto the elite political agenda. They attempted to do this by engaging with a variety of organizations, including political parties, representative institutions of government such as the National Assembly and international organizations. Frequently, these organizations have found their attempts to engage these organizations in substantive debate over policy issues blocked or co-opted to a different elite agenda. Equally, however, elite efforts to co-opt these movements have prompted the injection of organizational skills, leading to the increasing dissemination of new strategies for protest to be used by later urban movements.

The trade union movement

Cambodia's trade union movement emerged in the late 1990s from the factories of the garment industry, which blossomed at the same time, following the promulgation by the Cambodian government of generous foreign investment laws. In 1995, twenty garment factories existed; this grew to eighty-nine by December 1997, bolstered by pull factors, which included cheap labour and a perception that Cambodia was more secure following the CPP victory in July 1997, and by push factors, such as the exhaustion of export quotas for the EU and US by garment industries elsewhere in the region.[19] By 2002, 220 factories were operating in Cambodia, producing exports worth nearly US$1 billion, 70 per cent of which were exported to the United States, under a quota system which permitted US imports of Cambodia-made goods to grow at 6 per cent per year.[20] Most of the factories were owned by firms from elsewhere in the region, particularly Hong Kong, Singapore, Taiwan and mainland China.[21] The industry provided jobs for approximately 160,000 workers, 85 per cent of whom were women, and 90 per cent of whom came from rural areas near Phnom Penh to the capital to work in the factories.[22]

The relationship between the garment factories, the workforce and the government is primarily economic, mediated by formal and informal payments. A survey of garment manufacturers in 2001 found that they estimated 'bureaucracy costs' – costs of permits to set up and operate factories, import raw materials and export garments, plus the costs of delays in obtaining these – at 7 per cent of total sales.[23] These bureaucracy costs also include the costs of gifts and bribes to bureaucrats and Ministry of Labour factory inspectors, and dividends to sleeping partners, who are often high-ranking officials in the Cambodian government. According to one survey of the industry, the acquisition of such a sleeping partner ensures the protection of the police for the factory – for example, in the event of a labour dispute.[24]

Workers in the garment industry also found their relations with their employers mediated by informal payments in the form of bribes and gifts paid for access to jobs, and formal payments in the form of nationally regulated wage and overtime rates. In this respect, work in the industry differed sharply both from the subsistence economy of the family farm, from which most workers came, and employment in the state apparatus, where the minimal salary was even lower than that earned by factory workers, and where the rewards for employment emerged rather from transformed patronage relations of exploitation and corruption. The nature of employer–employee relations as a matter of wage labour, largely unmediated by ties of patronage or kinship, placed the worker in an unfamiliar position, which could not be disguised by lip service to aspects of 'Khmer culture'. This feature was rendered more pronounced by the common practice in Cambodian garment factories of placing Chinese managers or interpreters in charge of the Khmer workforce. This fact, along with the many reports of racism displayed by such managers, had the effect of further alienating Khmer workers from their position as employees.

In this regard, the position of garment workers differed sharply from the position of state employees or farmers, and the activities of garment workers in engaging in collective action reflected this. The characteristics of the garment industry permitted the growth of militancy, and walk-outs and factory gate demonstrations in response to incidents of violence, racism, or poor working conditions emerged before unions were formed. This is significant, in that it suggests that relations of solidarity between workers are not the product of externally promoted unionization, but are the driving force behind the trade union movement. Since 1996, unions have been organized face-to-face at the factory level, maximizing the opportunities for horizontal solidarity and permitting immediate collective responses to workplace issues, resulting in the view among unionized workers interviewed that the establishment of a union had resulted in immediate improvements in working conditions in their factories.

A typical example of a spontaneous walk-out by workers, prior to their unionization, was related by a worker interviewed outside the Tak Fat Factory in Phnom Penh in August 2000:

> Previously I worked at GRC for four months, and I had a higher salary there, but then I had a dispute with the Chinese chief. The Chinese chief insulted Cambodia – he said Khmers would be servants all their lives because they didn't know anything ... I left immediately – in fact 17 people left. We went to the Ministry of Public Affairs to complain. We went in a group – not with the trade union, the union wasn't created yet at that time. I was the representative of that group. The Ministry was sympathetic, but we had to protest for a long time because the factory bribed the Ministry ... the Ministry told me that we had to wait to resolve this problem, and warned us not to hold any demonstrations outside the factory, because if we did so, the factory would close down. But we kept going to the Ministry and in the end the factory owners paid us $40 in compensation and we found new jobs.[25]

Other workers told of situations in which unionization occurred in response to concerns for workers' safety when confronted with violent employer reactions to early negotiating efforts. In the following account, the worker draws a contrast between the safety of demonstrations, even though these are frequently met with armed police and security guards, as opposed to the vulnerability of workers as individuals:

> I'm a member of the union. I paid 1000 riel to join. Because we had a demonstration – it was to complain about the salary payment. The factory paid us on the tenth or eleventh of each month, but we needed to get our wages on the seventh. We asked the factory owner, but he wouldn't agree, so we tried again, but the factory officials beat two or three workers on the head, in order to frighten the workers so they wouldn't hold demonstrations ... So then the workers decided all together to hold a demonstration. Then the trade union came. We just went to ask them to help us to conduct a demonstration, because we were all suffering together very much. But now we are afraid sometimes when we walk home somewhere. They can't beat us in the factory, but they could beat us somewhere quiet.[26]

The ease with which the protective relations of solidarity described in these accounts can be forged within the factories contrasts with the situations of other Cambodian workers. Efforts to organize in the service and construction industries in Phnom Penh have been less successful. Work in these industries is casual and seasonal, and dispersed among small-scale concerns, resulting in fluid relationships among workers and between workers and employers.

A further distinction can be drawn between the situation of garment workers and public servants. A teachers' union, the Cambodian Independent Teachers' Association, created in March 2000, has also pursued pay increases on behalf of its members through strikes and demonstrations. A national strike in January 2001, seeking a flat rate of teachers' pay of $100 a month, brought an increase in teachers' basic pay of only 10 per cent per month – raising their salary from 30,000 riel to 33,000 riel, or from about $8.50 to about $9.40. The president of the association, Rong Chhun posited three significant differences between the teachers' unions and the garment unions. Firstly, an alleged lack of concern on the part of the government for standards in education resulted in teachers lacking meaningful bargaining chips. Secondly, the organization of the Cambodian state around personal relations of protection and assistance is threatened by strike action on the part of entire sectors of public servants. The assertion of demands for a living wage undermines the selectivity of such relations, and offers opportunities for horizontal alliances that can prompt the breakdown of vertical relations of loyalty. Rong Chhun commented:

> They don't want to pay high salaries because then we become difficult to control. When the government provides teachers with a low salary, teachers don't care about the nation or the country. They have to go and do other jobs, such as farming or moto driving ... It is easy for the government to control them. When government officials, and especially teachers on very low salaries, they are very poor, so when they meet high ranking officials, they feel very afraid to talk to them. Especially officials with landcruisers. Now the government doesn't want to increase salaries, because if they do so they'll lose the means for corruption.[27]

The link between low wages and control is significant, given the importance of low wages and transformed relations of patronage in underpinning the cohesion of the state. However, the teaching profession represents a group of state workers that has benefited little from the political economy of the state. Teachers are caught between professional aspirations for a living wage and improving standards of education, and the political economy of the state sector. For teachers, the transformed patronage of the state sector offers limited rewards and operates in direct opposition to professional concerns, as teachers are forced to prey upon students to supplement their salaries. For rural teachers, in particular, this produces scant pickings. As public servants, teachers are subject to the same meagre wages of the whole state sector, and pay claims are invariably resisted on the grounds that the government lacks the budget to increase pay for state employees across the board.

A further, significant problem for the teachers' pay claim was the practical difficulties faced by the union in organizing nationwide strike action, given problems of transport and communication. Rong Chhun claimed that teachers had been threatened by local authorities in rural areas and prevented from joining the strike, and that a lack of organizational capacity on the part of the union in organizing across the entire country entailed poor co-ordination of the action, resulting in an inability to challenge the government's stance on public sector pay. He commented, 'If all the teachers went on strike, the government would give the pay rise demanded. The most important thing is the number of participants. If all the teachers in all the schools walked out, we would get our demands'.[28]

These factors combined to render the teachers poorly placed to take on a government whose resistance was based upon political as well as economic concerns. While the strike in 2001 brought a minimal pay rise, it did not achieve any form of legal or de facto recognition of the teaching union as a negotiating partner. Rong Chhun described the situation:

> When we held demonstrations this year, the association waited for representatives from the Ministry of Education and the government, but no one came to talk to us. We wrote a petition to the Ministry of Education, but they didn't invite us to talk to them. We held demonstrations at the schools and we asked the government to nominate a contact person to come and talk to us, but they didn't do this ... So throughout the whole strike, we had no official discussions with the government at all. The government just announced their position through newspapers and radio ... This is not the way to solve the problem. If the government had any good will towards the teachers, they would have asked a representative of the union to talk to them.[29]

The weakness of the teaching unions, the difficulty of organizing scattered employees, and the politicization of the relationship between teachers and their employers contrasts sharply with the situation in the garment factories.

Building on early successes in individual factories, the factory-based unions affiliated at an early stage into trade union federations, which pursued industry-wide campaigns to promote legislation to protect workers, particularly vis-à-vis minimum wage and overtime rates. Again, the clustering of the garment industry around Phnom Penh, in contrast to the teaching profession that is spread across the country, facilitates industry-wide action. The president of one of the earliest federations, the Free Trade Union of Workers of the Kingdom of Cambodia (FTUWKC), Chea Vichea, commented that the extent to which employers respect an agreement obtained by the unions over minimum wages declined with distance from Phnom Penh:

> About 80 per cent of the employers respect this agreement, but not all factories. If factories are far away from Phnom Penh, for example, in the provinces, far away from the trade unions. For example, Sihanoukville, Kompong Cham, Kandal, Kompong Speu – we don't yet have a trade union office in any other province.[30]

The trade union federations also tie the factory-based unions into a range of broader relationships, using their Phnom Penh headquarters as bases for national and international networking and advocacy. Victories in co-ordinated action over pay and a proactive stance in recruiting, training and supporting factory-level union representatives has permitted the trade union federations to build upon the momentum initiated by the militancy of ordinary workers in the factories.

Furthermore, the trade union federations have operated to link the factory-based unions with national and international sources of support. National sources of support include newspapers, parliamentary representatives, human rights monitors and legal representation. International support includes financial support from trade union associations in the US and France, training and assistance in establishing official negotiating channels from the International Labour Organization (ILO) and monitoring by international consumer groups, such as the Clean Clothes Campaign, and by brand names such as Gap, which have established codes for working conditions in response to consumer concerns. While violence against demonstrating workers was common in the early days of the movement, as evidenced in particular by the grenade attack of 30 March 1997 and everyday incidents of violence between police and strikers outside factories, the frequency and degree of such violence has declined as international organizations have shown increased interest in workers' movements and campaigns.

A bilateral trade agreement signed between the US and Cambodia in 1999 incorporated provisions which explicitly link expanding US quotas for the import of Cambodian garments to improving working conditions in Cambodian factories. This led to the development of an ILO monitoring project, which in turn has prompted the establishment of a formal mechanism for dialogue between Cambodian workers, employers and government officials. The mechanism takes the form of a Labour Advisory Committee, comprising one representative each from the five largest trade union federations, five representatives from employers' organizations and ten representatives from the Ministry of Labour.

The establishment of such codes and mechanisms on a wider level has had a double-edged effect on Cambodian garment unions as protest movements which contribute to democratization by permitting the engagement of ordinary people in the setting of political agendas. On the one hand, a sympathetic international response has helped to protect the movement from devastating attacks, such as the 30 March grenade attack. Furthermore, input from external agencies, including international organizations such as the ILO and national political parties such as the SRP, has brought organizational skills to the workers themselves. FTUWKC president Chea Vichea commented on the input of Sam Rainsy into the formation of the union: 'Sam Rainsy formed this trade union, because at that time [1996] the workers didn't know what a trade union was'.[31]

Equally, some trade union federations and international organizations such as the ILO have focused upon attempting to provide resources to factory level union leaders. These can increase opportunities for participation in discussions with government representatives at the factory level. For example, training in the Cambodian Labour Law can offer a focus for workplace action. A strike over forced overtime by workers at the Independence Garment Factory in Tuol Kok, observed in August 2000, resulted in the formation of a union at the factory and the election (by acclamation rather than by ballot) of a representative from among the workers to lead it. Subsequently, the elected representative was issued with a copy of the Labour Law by the trade union federation. The representative declared his intention to take time off work to study the law, the better to assist his fellow workers in their struggle for improved working conditions:

> Some of the workers are not well-educated, so they just do what the supervisor tells them to do. But now the trade union federation has provided us with the book about the Labour Law. I just got it today – I'm going home to learn about it. Then I'll know what people have been talking about. Before, we didn't have any information, but now I'm going to start telling my other colleagues about the Labour Law, because I'm the only worker in the factory who has the book. [32]

On the other hand, the importance of representation, advocacy and networking, particularly at international level, leads to a privileging of the trade union federation over the factory-level union. The trade union federation gains the initiative in negotiation and mediation, while also accruing greater financial and organizational resources from international donors and supporters. Formalization of the role of the union encourages the usurpation of the leading role of the shop floor militant by the trained professional. This usurpation is evident in the description of one trade union federation president of his role:

> After unions are registered, employers recognize the union as a negotiating party ... Unfortunately the union leaders don't speak English, so I have to go myself to communicate with the employers ... We don't use the strike weapon too much. All the employers know me – I enforce the law. I don't want to do things that are irrelevant to what I have learned – the US Government spent a lot of money for me to study in the US, so I have to use what I learned. If we make an agreement with the factory employer, and if they don't follow the agreement, then I write a detailed report, and send a copy to the US Embassy, International Labour Organization, Ministry of Labour, Gap, Nike. And then the employers write a reply, and said they have changed their policy. Then I ask the workers, and they confirm that this has been changed. So there are positive responses, the United

> States is happy, Gap are happy and everyone wins. The employers are very interested in this approach.[33]

The professionalization of labour relations is evident in this interviewee's view that the need for foreign language skills, legal knowledge, the ability to write reports and a facility for international networking render the professional trade unionist a more appropriate bargaining partner than the workers themselves. It suggests a regimentation of the movement, whereby the professional attributes of the trade union federation, rather than the militancy and relations of solidarity between workers in the factories, become the key attribute of power.

This regimentation extends further with the establishment of the Labour Advisory Committee. This was organized under an ILO initiative to provide channels of dialogue between federation representatives and employers' representatives as a means to reduce the frequency of spontaneous walkouts and demonstrations at the factory level. However, a certain distance exists between the rank and file union members and their shop stewards at the factory level, on the one hand, and the trade union federations represented on the committee, on the other. An ILO officer pointed out, 'if you ask the worker in the factory which federation they belong to, they can't give the name, they just point to the union representative'. At the level of the trade union federations, leaders are less likely to be former garment workers themselves (only one out of six federation leaders is a former garment worker) and more likely to be politically engaged with various political parties. While the committee is intended to provide opportunities to discuss improvements in working conditions for the workers in the factories, it has the coincidental effect of taking negotiations and decision-making further away from those workers.

Formalizing representation in this way is also detrimental to the more militant sections of the labour movement, which find themselves in a minority, outvoted by the combined weight of employers, government officials and moderate unions. Distinct attitudes towards labour relations have emerged within the trade union movement, and these reflect different party political orientations. On the one hand, moderate trade unions echo government concerns that strike action is detrimental to Cambodia's industrialization in an increasingly competitive regional environment.[34] The Cambodia Union Federation, for example, is reluctant to pursue improved working conditions aggressively, and has rejected calls for a campaign for a 40-hour week. Such unions focus on mediating over individual grievances in the factories, but view problems with working conditions as the pertaining only to a few fly-by-night employers, rather than as endemic to the industry. The purpose of the union is to provide a channel for dialogue so as to identify common problems and interests shared by employers and workers. Chuon Momthol, the union's president, described a change in the attitude of most employers towards unions – 'they come to realize the union is like a family rather than a strange animal'.[35] Furthermore, he regarded strike action as more detrimental to workers than to employers, both because of the ability of employers to lock workers out in the short term and because of fears of flight of the industry to take advantage of more disciplined workforces in China and Vietnam over the long term. Thus Chuon Momthol commented on the question of strike action:

> If I meet the employers – they love me. I don't cause any problems for them – I give them prosperity, because I don't call the workers out on strike. You can ask at GMAC. I criticize and ask for correction – sometimes I send them an email. They really respond. I put it on the table, and they say we will resolve this. And if they can't resolve it, we go on strike ... I say if you can't give me a positive response in one week, I will go on strike, but I don't want to strike. I don't want to play politics.[36]

Some trade union federations are specifically created in order to defuse the threat of militancy in the factories. An ILO official commented:

> Pro-government unions are also on the side of the government – they don't want to make trouble for the employers. But that is not the job of the union, the union should represent interests of the workers. Some workers don't know about their rights and are afraid to lose their job, so they try to link with a safer union. They do a good job vis-à-vis individual grievances.[37]

This stance contrasts sharply with the stance of the pro-opposition FTU, which has promoted strike action as a means of specifically promoting the position of the worker in the factory. This pits the FTU, not only against pro-government unions, but also, to an extent, against the professionalizing philosophy of the ILO. Chea Vichea commented:

> The idea from the ILO is that they don't like the workers to strike, they like to negotiate. But in Cambodia, the employers look down on the workers, they cannot negotiate with the workers. If they don't see the workers are strong, they don't negotiate. When there is a strike, they worry about production, and then they negotiate. In France and the US, employers are afraid of the trade unions already, the trade unions are strong, they have a strong financial base. So the employers respect the law.

The FTU views strike action as a political weapon and a necessary step in the evolution of a new, more egalitarian relationship between employers and workers. The present inequality between employers and workers is regarded as a result of the complicity of the employers and the Cambodian government, who conspire to maintain the subjugation of Cambodia's poor. For the FTU, problems in the investment climate emerge primarily from the poverty of Cambodia's infrastructure and the corruption of its bureaucracy, rather than from the militancy of the workers. Consequently, unionization and strike action is an important strand of a broader political strategy to defend the poor against the attacks of the government, as well as the exploitation of employers. Chea Vichea explained the FTU's philosophy as follows:

> If the government doesn't respect the law, then rich men don't respect the law and who is the victim? The workers. If we have a strike, I go to the factory, I take a megaphone. I tell them, if we are afraid every day, they will pay a small salary and use us very hard. But if we start to fight we can have better conditions … The employers and the government have a good alliance – one has money and the other has power. They co-operate and abuse the poor … So we must break the alliance, by paying dues to the trade union and organizing a strike.[38]

Here, the strike is used specifically as a weapon to be wielded by the workers as a means to gaining power vis-à-vis the government and employers. This view is strongly influenced by the political platform of the SRP which has been heavily involved with the FTUWKC, although under ILO pressure, the FTU has begun to distance itself from the party since 1999, and Sam Rainsy himself is less frequently seen on picket lines than previously.[39] The framing of workers' struggles as a matter of law, in which government is intimately involved, renders the FTUWKC a specifically political entity, and transposes conditions in the factories into an issue for the national political agenda, and brings it directly into the sphere of party political competition.

The ILO project of internationalization of issues regarding working conditions in Cambodian factories and formalization of union–employer relations within the framework of the Labour Advisory Committee, and the ILO's efforts to remove the issue of labour relations from the highly charged sphere of party politics has the opposite effect. It delinks the workers' movement from broader issues of government accountability via party political competition. Equally significant is the difference in political strategies. Whereas the ILO's project promotes demobilization and professional representation in the interests of Cambodia's regional economic competitiveness and further industrial development, the FTUWKC project promotes the direct input of the workers in mobilizing, demonstrating and demanding responses from ministries and employers.

In terms of Cambodia's broader political trajectory, these two projects have different implications. The use of workers' struggles as a platform for the SRP in the early years of the movement, from 1996, were undoubtedly significant in creating a new understanding of opposition and possibilities for political participation and protest in 1990s Cambodia. The demonstrations of factory workers revived the spirit of popular anti-government protest that had been so severely dampened by the shooting of student demonstrators in 1991. The 1997 grenade attack against a workers' demonstration threatened to crush the new spirit of opposition once again, but the constant renewal of momentum behind the protests, provided by the continued militant responses of workers to ongoing abuses in the factories from 1997 to 1999 entailed a continued bubbling up of protest over this period. Continued spontaneous outbreaks of demonstrations represented the defiance, by workers, of the oppressive political atmosphere that pertained in rural areas between the July fighting of 1997 and the formation of a new government at the end of 1998. In a context in which the participation of ordinary people in setting political agendas is far from established, such activities represent a powerful force for further political change in the direction of greater democracy.

While recognizing the status of the workers' movement as a 'very important civil force in Cambodia', the ILO regards any contribution of the trade unions to political reform, in terms of setting precedents for public action and pluralizing forms of opposition to government in Cambodia, as beyond the scope of its project.[40] Rather, the ILO has pursued a narrower objective, designed to institutionalize labour relations in a form that encourages bureaucratic solutions attained by professional negotiators, to decrease the likelihood of disputes spilling over onto the streets and disrupting industrial production. While the ILO mechanism institutionalizes a channel for raising labour concerns with management and government, the opportunities for ordinary workers, as opposed to trade union professionals, to engage directly in public debate, to challenge the power of employers and government and to experience political participation, are arguably more limited. This is particularly the case given the economic stratification of Cambodian society, which renders bureaucratic channels difficult to access for the poor and illiterate. The sense of empowerment arising from public actions of solidarity is lost.

Furthermore, the Labour Advisory Committee, which comprises fifteen representatives of government and the employers and only five labour representatives, ties the more militant sections of the labour movement into an institutional structure that confines the scope of labour's agenda, and insulates labour activism from wider political issues. To the extent that the ILO represents a link between the trade union federations and international supporters donors, the FTUWKC has been encouraged to accept the constraints of engagement in the mechanism.

The ILO regards its efforts to persuade unions to distance themselves from political parties as promoting trade union independence. Consequently, the ILO emphasizes the importance of collecting dues from members, and of training and educating members in issues pertaining to trade unionism and in ILO conventions regarding working conditions. However, this may be more accurately seen as the substitution of co-optation by Cambodian political parties for co-optation to an international agenda of professionalization, which, arguably, is equally disempowering to the average workers in an impoverished country. To this extent, the treatment of the labour movement is similar to the treatment of Cambodian human rights NGOs, with the important distinction that the labour movement, unlike the human rights movement, originated from grassroots activism. Thus the professionalization of the labour movement represents an attempt to transform a pre-existing situation, removing it from local control and dampening its vitality. For example, the ILO's effort to promote the concept of a seven-day 'cooling off period' between an issue arising and the calling of strike action reflects the imposition of international standards at the expense of local militancy, which operates to encourage the resolution of disputes by committee rather than the exercise of popular power via popular protest.

The activities of the SRP have also sought to co-opt the struggles of workers, in support of the party's political agenda. Sam Rainsy's use of anti-Vietnamese rhetoric, much criticized by international observers, on picket lines is an example of this.[41] Chea Vichea, however, argues that the union's support of the SRP is not absolute, but contingent on the party's specific policies towards the workers. He commented in 2000:

> Sam Rainsy made a promise to the workers before the election – he said, if he becomes prime minister, he will increase the minimum wage to $60 a month ... I think he spoke the truth. But if he becomes prime minister and doesn't increase the minimum wage, then we will strike again.[42]

The preservation of the vitality of a labour movement that can retain its independence from both political parties and international organizations offers, arguably, wider opportunities for political participation by the poor, and for the contribution of the poor to further democratization in Cambodia, than the constraining of the movement within an institutional structure designed to professionalize, bureaucratize and limit its political agenda according to international norms.

Democracy Square

The Democracy Square movement can be regarded as a direct descendent, or culmination, of previous demonstrations by workers in a number of ways. Firstly, the site of the Democracy Square protests – a park in front of the National Assembly Building in Phnom Penh – is the same site upon which the 30 March grenade attack took place. The SRP has actively attempted to preserve the site as a memorial to the attack by naming the site 'Democracy Square' as a testament to the aspirations of the 30 March demonstrators, by holding anniversary vigils on the spot, and, more recently, by engaging in protracted conflict with the government over the question of a memorial stupa raised on the site in memory of the dead.

By these activities, the SRP has linked the 30 March demonstration and the post-election demonstrations in a determined effort to open and preserve a space for protest, situated in the heart of constitutional government. The park is bordered to the north by the Royal Palace, offering both continuity with traditional petitions to the king for assistance by the poor and oppressed and the shadow of the king's protection to demonstrators. To the east, it faces the National Assembly Building, the repository of representative democracy. To the west, it is bordered by Wat Botum-Vadei, one of the foremost pagodas in the capital. To the south, the park faces the Hun Sen gardens, containing the Cambodian–Vietnamese friendship monument – symbolic of the origins and continuation of CPP power. A broad lawn situated in the middle of these four buildings, which represent different branches of power in Cambodian state and society, Democracy Square represents an important symbolic space. By conducting demonstrations on this site, the SRP symbolically places the struggles of poor workers, farmers and others at the centre of power in Cambodia.

Furthermore, the site of Democracy Square close to many of Phnom Penh's main tourist attractions, and just a few blocks away from the Foreign Correspondents' Club of Cambodia, the Office of the United Nations Secretary-General's Personal Representative in Cambodia, the headquarters of the Joint International Observers Group and a host of other international agencies, rendered it particularly visible. During the weeks of the sit-in on the site, journalists gathered in the top floor bar of the Regent Hotel, across the street from the park, to observe the protests and, perhaps, to witness any violence that might be perpetrated against the demonstrators.

Secondly, in terms of the motivations of the participants, Democracy Square resembled workers' struggles more closely than is often imagined. Like strike action in the garment factories, Democracy Square also emerged spontaneously from the actions of a grassroots constituency uprooted from their customary place in Cambodia's villages. This reading of the protests is at odds with the views of many observers, but is the interpretation most consonant with the statements of demonstrators themselves, interviewed on the site in August and September 1998.

The Democracy Square movement began with attempts by leaders to call off a demonstration on 23 August which had attracted a crowd of 10,000 protesters. Commenting, 'I didn't expect you to come in large numbers like this', Rainsy suggested a 'sit in' at the National Assembly as an alternative to an illegal march through the Phnom Penh streets, largely, perhaps, in response to the evident high feeling in the crowd.[43] Arguably, in part the sit-in took off because it met the practical, as well as the political, needs of demonstrators. Many of the full-time demonstrators were refugees from the provinces who had left their homes in the wake of rumours of retaliations by the CPP against opposition voters. For these marginalized individuals, mass protest in front of national and international observers in Phnom Penh was preferable to a return to the insecurity of anonymous village life. The

Democracy Square movement grew out of the coincidence between the angry mood in Phnom Penh and the desperation of opposition supporters and other marginalized people in the countryside, who feared they had been identified as anti-CPP and had fled to Phnom Penh after the results were announced. Once arrived in the city, these people had no income, no shelter and were fearful of returning home.

The circumstances of these people and the mood of the city combined to make the Democracy Square movement a significantly more impressive demonstration than any seen in Phnom Penh since the early 1970s. After opposition party and UN officials negotiated a guarantee from the Ministry of the Interior, late on 26 August, that force would not be used to oust the demonstrators, the numbers 'sitting in' full time in the square grew to around a thousand. Each evening this number was swelled by the arrival of Phnom Penh residents on motorbikes, who came to hear Rainsy and Ranariddh address the crowds, to show their support, to see and be seen.

The demands of the sit-in, as portrayed by Rainsy and Ranariddh, related to aspects of election procedure. However, interviews with demonstrators in the early days of the movement found that most had attended due to economic concerns. Many interviewees declared themselves to be farmers from the provinces, some of whom had left home because of drought, their presence at the demonstrations coinciding with a more general drift towards Phnom Penh at the time of economic refugees fleeing rural hunger. Around a quarter of those interviewed were unemployed, while others were members of the urban poor. Fewer than a quarter of interviewees claimed to be an activist for any party at this time.[44]

In later days, more district activists from the provinces arrived, having travelled with the purpose of joining the demonstration. There were some reports of harassment along the roads of people coming to join, which further increased concern among district activists to get into Phnom Penh to join their party for protection. A number of interviewees, asked if they felt concerned about the potential for violence against the sit-in, claimed to feel safer there than elsewhere. For some, the move from a village subject to strict CPP surveillance, in which opposition supporters kept their views secret, to a place where opposition supporters stood together in open relations of solidarity was empowering:

> At home, I'm scared, but in Phnom Penh I'm not scared. *Why are you scared at home?* I'm scared because at home, very few people support the Sam Rainsy Party. But here there are a lot of people living together.[45]

> At home I was afraid but here I'm not afraid. Because in the provinces the people who share our ideas are very few, but here there are many and we support each other.[46]

> I'm concerned that they might try to oppress us but I'm not afraid, because we came here in a big crowd so we can protect each other.[47]

These comments suggest that for poor farmers, as for garment workers, public political action was valuable in itself, in promoting a sense of personal security in the expression of political dissent, perhaps for the first time. To this degree, the demonstrations contributed significantly to democratic aspiration in Cambodia.

Concerns about local authority oppression were intensified by the reaction of CPP authorities in the provinces to the demonstration, underlining the distinction between the village and the city in terms of opportunities for freedom of expression. One interviewee claimed the commune chief in her area had gone from house to house at night asking for thumbprints 'to support Hun Sen'. She reported that she had fled her village to join the demonstration in order to avoid having to comply with this requirement, and commented: 'if I go back I will be pressured and ill-treated'.[48] This account suggests that for the first time the movement offered voters an opportunity to defy, publicly, CPP control in the countryside. During the election opposition leaders had encouraged supporters to co-operate with the thumbprint campaign and to hide their resistance until safe in the secrecy of the polling booth. Democracy Square offered voters an opportunity to resist en masse, gaining strength from solidarity and relief from the burden of isolated, secret defiance. Fears that 'in the countryside ... they may come and arrest me'[49] were a direct result of the atmosphere of threat and surveillance generated by CPP officials in the countryside.

In terms of their demands, demonstrators interviewed also suggested that economic and political marginalization by 'local authorities' in the villages was the key factor propelling the demonstrations. One demonstrator told the story of her own family's exclusion in this way:

> Before the election ... they were accusing people of belonging to other parties, and then you can't do business freely ... Also my husband was killed by A3 soldiers in 1988. He used to do business and they asked him for [protection] money, but he didn't pay so he was killed. Now my children have no jobs and no chance to go to school.[50]

Another demonstrator claimed that he had been hounded out of the police force by threats from colleagues, because he supported FUNCINPEC:

> I supported the opposition party in Kompong Cham, but, because there was a lot of intimidation, I escaped from Kompong Cham to Kompong Chhnang, otherwise I would have been killed. *Why would you have been killed?* Because I used to be a policeman in Kompong Cham. They accused me of being Pol Pot, or of being an enemy. They just used me

> as a dogsbody and didn't include me. And finally they threatened to shoot me. Because at that time I supported FUNCINPEC.[51]

A third demonstrator, from Kraingyov Commune, the home of Hun Sen's Development Zone, said she had come to the demonstration because of her economic marginalization within the commune:

> *Why did you want to come here?* Because Hun Sen has given the land to the *yuon* and the people suffer and have no food. *Didn't Hun Sen help the people in Kraingyov?* Hun Sen just helped the commune chief and the military chief. The people were not allowed to use the things that Hun Sen gave.[52]

In this account, and in others, the distinction between those profiting from the transformed patronage of the CPP and those excluded from it was couched in terms of an ethnic distinction between Khmer and Vietnamese, in line with the rhetoric of the leaders of FUNCINPEC and the SRP. For example:

> In the rubber plantations in Kompong Cham, all the Vietnamese have come to work there. Even if Cambodians pick just one branch for firewood they have to pay 1000 riel to the Vietnamese owners. Cambodians are slaves to the Vietnamese.[53]

The overall picture offered was one of marginalization to the extent where livings became impossible to earn.

However, complaints about alleged Vietnamese interference in Cambodian affairs increased within Democracy Square as time went on, an indicator of the increasing co-optation of protesters' concerns regarding exclusion in the countryside by political leaders, who made frequent speeches to demonstrators denouncing the CPP as '*yuon* puppets' and 'barbarians'.[54] This increasing influence of political parties over the ideas of protesters resulted, as in the trade union movement, from efforts by the SRP, in particular, to exercise control over the demonstrations. For example, party full-timers, mainly from the Sam Rainsy Party, organized security patrols and distributed coupons for food, via activists from either FUNCINPEC or the SRP, based on lists of names of people who had joined the demonstration from the different districts. Thus the top-down network structure of district activists was maintained and empowered vis-à-vis other protesters.

Central tents collected donations from Phnom Penh market traders and other sympathizers, while a central loudspeaker system kept up a constant stream of announcements and read out letters sent by supporters. Demonstrators submitted poems to be read out over loudspeakers to the assembled crowds – yet these were read by party officials, rather than by the poets themselves, in order to promote control over their content and to avoid the use of 'inflammatory language'.[55] Sam Rainsy and Prince Norodom Ranariddh arrived at the site twice a day to make speeches to the demonstrators but spent little time talking to demonstrators themselves because of security concerns. The movement was thus not a representative movement, with the result that few observers picked up on the many economic grievances of most of the demonstrators, and viewed the demonstrations as primarily concerned with election fraud.

As a result of the power of the political parties to represent the demonstrations to external observers, the demands emerging from Democracy Square differed little from those regularly presented by the SRP and FUNCINPEC. Tactically, the focus of the movement, as determined by the political leadership, was on persuading individuals and organizations already perceived as powerful to lend support, rather than attempting to empower subordinate groups in society. Key CPP leaders were asked to withdraw support from Hun Sen, and decisive intervention was requested from the international community.

This was significant in that it undermined the demonstrations as an opportunity for ordinary people to voice their own concerns publicly and to assert their own rights to hold their government accountable, rather than petitioning international actors to hold the government to account on their behalf. The input of ordinary people was not facilitated in terms of the movement's rhetoric, and the question of accountability, with regard to the issue of the electoral process and other 'crimes' of which Hun Sen was accused, was routed via the international community. Rainsy told demonstrators that each individual who added to the number of demonstrators in the square was 'invaluable' because 'each person gathers to show the international community how much we love democracy'.[56]

Mass participation in the Democracy Square movement was portrayed as an illustration of the illegitimacy of Hun Sen's power and the rightfulness of the opposition challenge, but not as an expression of the power of the sovereign people themselves. The lack of emphasis within the movement upon providing opportunities for ordinary demonstrators to express their views also reflected this orientation. In a significant remark made in one speech to Democracy Square, Sam Rainsy commented:

> In the history of Cambodia, no Khmer people have ever stood up and protested like this. The people never stand in a group ... This gives victory to the democratic movement. *What is more important, is that we have support from the international community.*[57]

Rainsy claimed that as a result of their observance of the demonstrations, 'now the international community pressures Hun Sen and pressures the NEC'.[58] Equally, in criticizing Hun Sen to demonstrators, Rainsy obliquely presented his own more international profile, as a returnee from France, as an essential attribute of successful leadership of Cambodia:

> All Hun Sen's group are uneducated people ... they speak foreign languages like a cat in a coconut shell[59] so nobody can understand. When he tries to speak English or French, nobody understands, and they say, you are crazy.[60]

While the importance of international communication was thus emphasized, the issue of direct accountability owed by the government to the people was not addressed, reflecting a long-standing belief within the opposition movement that reform is most likely to be successful if it is internationally-sponsored and top-down, implemented on behalf of, but not by, the Cambodian people.

Yet the support of the international community fell far short of what was anticipated. On one occasion when Rainsy spelled out the extent of international intervention hoped for, he met a critical response from international media and diplomats. On this occasion, Rainsy alleged that Hun Sen was a 'murderer', a 'drug dealer' and 'the boss of the terrorists', and asked:

> What are the Americans are waiting for? Send the special air forces and remove Tuol Krasang [Hun Sen's military base in Ta Khmau]. When the Americans waged war in Iraq, they didn't have to send their armed forces in on foot. They just sent their air forces, aircraft which can fly very fast, they are invisible because they fly very high, equipped with laser missiles ... Hun Sen is a terrorist, so there is no point in America waiting any longer. Please fly in the planes to attack Tuol Krasang.[61]

Demonstrators representing a newly formed organization named 'Students for Democracy', which led students around Phnom Penh to various embassies and international agencies, pursued a similar line of argument:

> We want the international community to take Hun Sen from power and use the international court to judge Hun Sen and the coup d'état and we want the EU to deny the result of the elections and to show the evidence ... Especially the US, we students want to thank Senator Dana Rohrabacher – he understands well about the situation in Cambodia.[62]

> Only the US can give us an answer. The US said they support our demonstration. The EU said they went to the polling but they didn't see with their own eyes. If the EU do not reveal the facts we will go every day.[63]

There was little discussion of what precisely the international community might do to assist the demonstrators aside from sending in troops. Few demonstrators asked about this issue had a clear idea of practical steps the international community might take. Those that did offer specific suggestions generally viewed international input as useful to the extent that it could offer access to economic, rather than political, resources, independently of the CPP:

> The international community should help Cambodia by all means. For example, the farmers have no job and construction workers cannot find work. The international community must help to solve the problem of work.[64]

> I want to ask the UN to help ... To help Khmers to find jobs. I want my fatherless children to have a chance to go to school and get a job.[65]

The 'Students for Democracy' movement, that developed as an outgrowth of the Democracy Square movement, and organized marches around the city, also looked to the international community to deliver Cambodia from Hun Sen, citing the absence of authoritative institutions in Cambodia for mediating political conflict:

> We come here because the students have no other place to go to file a complaint – only the embassies. Because the NEC is a puppet of Hun Sen and the Constitutional Council also serves Hun Sen.[66]

Consequently, while the Democracy Square represented an unprecedented mobilization of the people in a public show of political and economic grievance, the rhetoric of its leaders continued to emphasize the lack of power of the people taking part. The response of the CPP was also designed to deny a duty of accountability that the sheer scale of the movement was making increasingly apparent. Hun Sen repeatedly claimed that he had no intention of breaking up the protest, declaring:

> if they have the capacity to continue for three months, six months or a year more, that is up to them and they can get married and have children there too, without any problem.[67]

Hun Sen expressed the view that 'Democracy Square' would soon become a 'very everyday matter' if it was simply left to its own devices, and could safely be ignored by a continuing Ung Huot–Hun Sen government.[68]

Eventually, arguably, the xenophobic rhetoric promoted by the political leaders of the movement undermined the movement's status, particularly vis-à-vis the international monitors who provided the movement with a considerable degree of protection. Increasingly inflammatory anti-Vietnamese speeches coincided with an outbreak of food poisoning in Phnom Penh, which pro-opposition newspapers claimed were a Vietnamese response to the demonstrations. At the same time, attacks against ethnic Vietnamese began in Phnom Penh; the government reported that eleven individuals were attacked, and four killed. Human rights workers reportedly blamed opposition party protesters for at least two of these attacks.[69] Soon afterwards police cleared the site.

Democracy Square represented the coalescence of a mixture of social groups, motivated by socio-economic exclusion, insecurity and discontent arising from a variety of sources. While attendance at the demonstrations boosted feelings of security among the protesters, the leaders of the movement finally operated to restrain the protesters, putting faith in international actors rather than 'people power'.

Despite these limitations, just as the protests of the trade union movement paved the way for Democracy Square, so Democracy Square itself made the concept of the 'sit-in' a familiar one in Cambodian politics in the late 1990s. From 1998 onwards, the Democracy Square site was host to a series of sit-ins by mainly rural protesters, who journeyed to Phnom Penh to express grievances by this means. Frequently comprising villagers who had been expelled from their farmland, the 'sit-in', accompanied by attention from the media and donations of rice and other necessities organized by NGOs and the SRP, offered a preferable alternative to the anonymous homelessness that would otherwise have been their lot. Democracy Square has become a site in which the government, represented by the National Assembly building across the road, is daily confronted by its own inadequacies and injustices, both in the form of makeshift camps of the poor and dispossessed and in the form of the memorial stupa raised by the SRP to commemorate the victims of the 30 March 1997 grenade attack. As such, the movement and memories of it reflected an important strand contributing to the entrenchment and deepening of democracy in Cambodia.

The O'Russei market traders' campaign

A third urban campaign seeking accountability from government was conducted by the traders of one of Phnom Penh's major markets, the Psaa O'Russei. This campaign differed from the industrial militancy of the garment workers and the political protest of Democracy Square in that it drew heavily on organizational structures and understandings of entitlements emerging from the State of Cambodia era. As such, it represented a movement by former regime insiders, who had found themselves newly disadvantaged by the new political economy of 1990s Cambodia.

The O'Russei traders held protests in the year 2000, following the redevelopment of the O'Russei market building by a private company. The company demanded payments of between $1980 and $3300 from traders for stalls in the reopening market. It is important to note that the traders from whom these payments were demanded had already purchased stalls in the market when it reopened after the DK era, in the early 1980s, and possessed ownership certificates validating their rights to stalls in the markets. The thousands of dollars demanded by the developers thus represented a charge for the redevelopment of stalls that the traders were already entitled to own.

The traders' protested a number of aspects of the redevelopment project. Firstly, they protested that the redeveloped stalls were not adequate to their needs. They were too small, reflecting a concern by the developers to squeeze in extra stalls, to make more money, at the expense of existing traders who would lose space for storing and displaying their wares as well as suffering from increased competition. Secondly, the redeveloped market was a multi-storey building and positions within were allocated by lot. The traders argued that those with existing ownership rights should have first call on the ground-floor stalls, considered to be the most profitable. Thirdly, and crucially, the traders asked for time to pay the charges, rather than having to hand over a lump sum before taking possession of their stalls.

Like the garment workers, the market traders viewed government as an actor in their dispute with the private developers. The traders had purchased their stalls from the government in the 1980s, and the municipality of Phnom Penh had been responsible for awarding the contract to privatize and redevelop the market to the private developers. Most market traders were unaware of the name of the company that now owned the market, as the contract had changed hands in the ten years since the initial removal of the market into temporary premises in preparation for the redevelopment of the O'Russei site. Many traders interviewed did not distinguish between the municipality and the development company. One traders' representative commented that the municipality had made a promise to the traders to provide them with a better market and had broken this promise in order to 'exploit the people'.

Disappointed by their treatment, the traders held several demonstrations outside Phnom Penh City Hall to demand that the municipality intervene in the situation. Failing to gain any response from City Governor, Chea Sophara, the traders then marched to the National Assembly. However, they were told by National Assembly representatives that this was a matter for the city authorities and, consequently, they went back to City Hall, again with no result. Finally, the traders demonstrated for two days outside the house of Prime Minister Hun Sen near the Independence Monument. Although they failed to meet the prime minister himself, they were able to meet with one of his senior advisers to discuss their grievances. Eventually, however, the movement collapsed as the traders were informed that anyone who did not pay to secure their stall by a certain date would lose their right to trade in the market and their stall would be auctioned off. This threat was decisive in destroying the traders' resistance, as those who could afford it, or who could borrow sufficient money, paid to maintain their place in the market.

The traders' campaign is interesting in that it is an example of a campaign by a group who had previously viewed themselves as insiders in the political economy of the city, but had recently come to see themselves as exploited. Interviews with traders in the O'Russei Market in July 2000 revealed that many of them had links to the state. Most traders with ownership rights had acquired these in the early 1980s from the People's Republic of Kampuchea government. All the traders interviewed had had family members who worked for the state at the time, and many continued to do so. Similarly, all the traders interviewed owned houses in Phnom Penh that had been allocated to them in the 1980s as a result of their connection with the state apparatus. The ownership rights granted to traders in the 1980s was at the heart of their grievance in the year 2000. A number of traders complained that they had already purchased ownership rights to market stalls, and objected to having to pay for these again. An even more pressing concern was the plan to widen ownership rights, through the building and sale of excess stalls. Traders were concerned that long-standing owners should retain a privileged position, for example, on the ground floor as opposed to the first floor of the market. Reflecting this, the traders' movement was limited to those with ownership rights and excluded those traders working on the temporary market site who had acquired stalls unofficially in the 1990s by bribing security guards.[70]

The nature of the campaign organized by the traders reflected their status vis-à-vis the state. The campaign was organized by long-standing section representatives, appointed in the 1980s to represent the market traders. The attitude of some of the market traders towards their campaign also indicated a perception of themselves as insiders vis-à-vis the municipality. For example, one trader, asked if she was angry at the lack of response from the various government agencies approached, commented:

> We were not angry that there was no result – we asked rather than insisted. The municipality or government is like a father, and the sellers are like children. When the child asks for something from the father and the father doesn't give it, then the children feel disappointed.[71]

This portrayal of the relationship between the market traders and the government reflects a belief, on the part of the interviewee, in the continued inclusion of the traders in a patrimonial relationship with government. As such, it is sharply at odds with the view of their own exclusion, espoused by factory workers and Democracy Square protesters, and indicates the different status of the market traders within the political economy of Phnom Penh. However, this view was not shared by all the traders. Another trader directly linked the failure of the protest to the failure of democracy in Cambodia:

> We went to the municipality, to the National Assembly and to Hun Sen's house. But Hun Sen didn't come to meet us – didn't agree to help us. They think about us only during the elections – after they win they don't know the people. The people get nothing. Nobody helped us.[72]

Although attitudes of interviewees were mixed, some clearly viewed the protests as an effort to insert their grievances onto an elite agenda which, to the extent that it failed, reflected a deficiency in Cambodia's democratization process. The use of both street protests and demands for accountability from supposedly representative institutions such as the National Assembly also suggest that the legacy of trade unionism and the Democracy Square movement has prompted a new attitude to public expression of grievances in Cambodia over the course of the 1990s.

The market traders' campaign, like the teachers' strikes of 1999 and 2001, indicate that the transformation of the state, which emerged from the transition to the free market in the late 1980s and early 1990s, caused the alienation of groups that had previously been broadly aligned with the PRK regime in the 1980s. Free market relations privileged large property developers and high-ranking officials to a greater degree than small property owners and low ranking public employees. The attempts by these groups to gain a hearing from the government went disregarded to a remarkable degree, suggesting a lack of concern on the part of the CPP-led municipal and national government for the votes and allegiances of these newly marginalized groups. This lack of attention coincides with the CPP's realignment in the 1990s as the party of the countryside, where the vast majority of the electorate is located.

Central and municipal government response

The responses of the government to the increased frequency and intensity of urban protest have been muted. Since the clearance of the Democracy Square movement of 1998 by riot police, there have been few overt attacks on protest movements. The stance of the government has instead been twofold. Firstly, the government has as far as possible ignored protests, retreating behind the walls and guardhouses of official buildings and denying assertions of government accountability made by protesters by simply failing to respond. The refusal to negotiate with striking teachers and protesting market traders, and Hun Sen's assertion that the sit-in at Democracy Square would become an 'everyday matter' if left alone, exemplify this response. However, this dissociation of the government from protest movements is belied by behind the scenes manoeuvring against protesters. In the aftermath of the Democracy Square protests, 24 bodies were found around the city, floating in rivers or buried in shallow graves, apparently the victims of extrajudicial killing. The identities of all but two of the victims could not be established, but they were mainly young people, men and women, and included Buddhist monks, fitting the profile of many of the most active demonstrators.[73] These finds heightened tensions in the capital in the immediate aftermath of the demonstrations. The university remained closed for some months and temples were empty as monks returned to their home villages following police searches of pagodas, looking for monks who had been involved in the demonstrations. The refusal to negotiate with striking teachers was followed, according to union officials, by attempts to penalize union leaders by excluding them from extra paid work such as examinations administration.[74] The use of covert methods of suppression, combined with an overt pose of non-response, suggests an attempt by the government to deny legitimacy to these protests, even while attempting to suppress them secretly.

These tactics have combined with a longer-term strategy to reappropriate the space of the city, both materially and symbolically, for the CPP and its leaders. This strategy is particularly associated with CPP municipal governor Chea Sophara – a self-styled reformer on a mission to modernize and beautify the city, by means of a series of radical redevelopment schemes. These schemes are significant, both as illustrations of the ways in which the transformed patronage networks within the government conflict and compete in the complex political environment of the city and as representing a new reorganization of political space in the city, with a concomitant impact upon urban social movements.

The reorganization of political space envisaged includes both the exiling of unruly elements of the population from the city altogether, and the replacement of unregulated areas of squatter development with monuments to CPP power. Interviewed in August 2001, Chea Sophara stated that his aim was to manage urbanization so as 'to keep a high standard of living ... by not encouraging the poor to live in the city'.[75] While the presence of garment workers was unavoidable, because of the concentration of factories around Phnom Penh, Chea Sophara suggested that the relocation of squatters out of the city was an urgent priority. He claimed this would contribute to raising living standards by improving the city environment as an aid to attracting tourists and foreign investors and to promoting public health. It would also contribute to a reduction in crime.

Thus, the beautification plan associates a reappropriation of public space by the municipality with greater security and safety in the city. In a manifesto published in 2000 outlining the scope and rationale behind the beautification plan, Sophara comments that squatter settlements 'are difficult to control and get access to. The area is like a barrier preventing fresh air from blowing into the city, instead of a foul stink'.[76] The replacement of such settlements by 'parks full of flowers' will represent a 'symbol of peace, brotherhood, love, harmony, inhostility, no violence and none of the harm that has created insecurity and turmoil in Cambodia for three decades'.[77] Earlier, the clearance of a floating village of ethnic Vietnamese from the area of the river near the Monivong Bridge was described in similar terms. Chea Sophara told reporters that the village was an eyesore and a pollutant of the water, and that removing it would improve 'the security of the bridge and the reform of the city scene'.[78]

In Chea Sophara's manifesto, squatters are decried as 'opportunists', bribing local officials to gain ownership of lands, and the spread of squatter settlements is viewed as 'badly damag[ing] the beauty and well-managed social order of the capital'.[79] This association of squatter settlements with disorder and an inability to manage the city is indicative of the ways in which the unregulated free market of the 1990s led to a situation in which political control was eventually undermined by the commodification of relations. The opening of the city to the anonymous poor, whose status was contingent upon cash transactions which largely replaced, rather than supplemented political loyalties, permitted the emergence of an unsurveyed and unruly population. This contrasted with the maintenance of tight surveillance in the internally transparent world of the village.

Dealing with this situation has led to a number of controversial policies, such as the clearance of squatter settlements. An example of this occurred in May 2001, when a squatter community was removed from the Tonle Bassac area of the city. This community, ironically, has long been viewed as a power base of the CPP, and in the 1998 elections reports were frequently heard that people from the community had been paid to mobilize counter-protests against demonstrators or campaigners from FUNCINPEC and the SRP. Yet in May 2001, the outbreak of a fire which razed hundreds of houses prompted a police operation to bulldoze the rest of the site and move squatters to a new village, named 'Solidarity Village', outside Phnom Penh.

The operation was not only illustrative of the heavy-handed imposition of beautification schemes at the expense of an impoverished population. It also exemplified the operations of city government. Local and international NGOs, such as the Urban Sector Group and Action Nord-Sud, and international organizations, prominently the United Nations Centre for Housing, offered assistance to the municipal government in providing building materials for the former squatters to build homes on their new land, and in providing basic infrastructure, such as water and sanitation to the site. However, interviews with squatters living on the site in August 2001 found that little had been achieved in this regard, and squatters complained that they had been the victim of widespread corruption at the hands of district and borough authorities. Many of the squatters had paid local authorities for documents acknowledging their residence in the Bassac community, and regarded this as evidence of ownership rights. One former resident's complaint was typical:

> In Bassac, we owned our house. We bought it. We didn't know we could be moved. When we bought it, the local authorities processed the sale and issued us with a family book. So we didn't think we would be moved. After the fire we found out ... We protested but it wasn't effective. It was useless in fact. The fire was in the afternoon and the very next morning they brought bulldozers and pulled down the rest of the house.[80]

Exploitation of the position of the former Bassac residents by local authorities continued after the fire as material for rebuilding houses in the new village, donated by international agencies and distributed by the municipal government, offered opportunities for local officials to cash in. Residents were asked to pay fees of up to $25 for the cost of transporting donated materials such as corrugated iron and pipes to the site of their new homes – costs that UN officials said had already been paid by the donating agencies. Furthermore, the allocation of plots of land offered great scope for official skulduggery, particularly given a dearth of records regarding the number and identity of households in the Bassac area. One resident of Solidarity Village commented:

> When we moved here, the people who worked for the government got more than one piece of land, so they could sell some. They are the people who work in the community – I don't know who they are. But some got two or three pieces of land.[81]

In addition to providing opportunities for local officials to cash in on allocations of land and materials, the removal of the residents of the Bassac area also rendered helpless and dependent a community that previously had been impervious to surveillance and control. In the new village, employment was scarce and the trip to Phnom Penh too costly for casual workers. Consequently, the inhabitants of the new village were dependent upon government officials for receiving a share of any aid that was bestowed by international or Cambodian organizations. Residents scrambled to register themselves with the authorities and were reluctant to act in any manner that might be construed as unsupportive. One resident described the impact of this upon the relationship between residents and officials:

> [Officials from] the city hall, district and borough came – they helped to arrange for the ownership of the land. We didn't dare tell them about our problems. We couldn't approach them. We could only watch from a distance. We were afraid that we might be thought rebellious … We were afraid that if they thought we were rebellious, then there'll be some problem. For example, a group of villagers whose houses were burned in the Tonle Bassac haven't got a house yet because they don't know anyone working in the government. So they've got no land yet. Some complained to the SRP for help. Those who have relatives working in the government have no difficulty getting land.[82]

The removal of one illegal community is likely to have little far-reaching impact on the overall governability of the city. However, in the context of a sustained development drive which systematically extends private property relations, particularly in the hands of private developers, and which increasingly excludes the poor from public land, the long-term effect on the city could be far-reaching. The policy is unlikely to reverse the alienation of the middle classes and workers; nor can it restore the level of control over living space in the city enjoyed by the government before 1989. However, it does offer the government the chance to assert symbolic control over the space of the city.

Chea Sophara's manifesto for the city is entitled, 'Phnom Penh Before and After 1997'. The notion of 1997 as a turning point is significant – not only is it the date of Chea Sophara's personal rise to power within the municipal administration at the expense of the former FUNCINPEC mayor, but it is also the date of the CPP's military victory over FUNCINPEC.

On his rise to power in the city, Chea Sophara adopted a plan to reorganize public space which complemented Hun Sen's post-1997 security drive in providing the basis for greater stability and progress within the city. The implementation of this plan represented not only a consolidation of CPP power, but also a consolidation of power within the CPP. For example, it included a limited purge of elements of the city's government, prominently including the municipal court. The Chief Judge of the Municipal Court was sacked on the grounds that he had taken bribes to release criminals, leading to a controversial order from Prime Minister Hun Sen to rearrest and retry a number of acquitted defendants. It is important to note, however, that this anti-corruption purge did not extend to the district and commune officials who profited from the relocation of squatters from the Tonle Bassac area in 2001.

However, the more profound impact of the beautification scheme is the reassertion of governmental control over public space vis-à-vis the more radical political challenge offered by the urban protest movements of the late 1990s. An example of this is the Chruoy Changvar development across the river from Phnom Penh, which incorporates as a centrepiece a large conference centre. The municipality's Chief Architect, Chhay Rithisen, explained that a major feature of the new development will be a new public space, intended to replace Democracy Square:

> The mayor plans at the same time we construct the convention centre, we will also create a big space for recreation. This is a democratic idea. In the street, people protest and make demonstrations, which causes traffic jams and affects social order. So maybe we can reserve some place in Chruoy Changvar for demonstrations. There is not enough space for demonstrations in front of the palace, and also the King is not pleased with all these demonstrations. But Chruoy Changvar is in front of the palace also.[83]

The removal of demonstrations to a point in front of the palace and the National Assembly Building, but distanced from them by the width of the Mekong River, is likely to significantly reduce the impact of such demonstrations. Furthermore, this severs future protest movements from the growing historical associations surrounding 'Democracy Square' as the site of the 30 March 1997 grenade attack and the post-election demonstrations of 1998. Attempts by the SRP to preserve these historical associations by the raising of a memorial stupa commemorating the victims of the grenade attack on the Democracy Square site were resisted by the government for many months, suggesting a sensitivity to these growing associations of the square with popular challenges to executive power. Removal of protests to a remote site limits the perception of demonstrations as part of a pro-democratic trajectory, as opposed to sporadic incidents that can be contained within a framework of transformed patronage. A plan to move the National Assembly, from its present site opposite 'Democracy Square' to a new building opposite the Hun Sen Gardens, will also contribute to severing the emerging connection between protest and constitutional democracy that was embedded in the spatial relations of protest in Phnom Penh in the late 1990s.

Conclusion

The late 1990s saw the spontaneous emergence of urban protest movements in the city which sought to use the new public spaces and constitutional forms of government to press their own, primarily economic, grievances onto an elite political agenda. The most successful of these movements, arguably, was the trade union movement, which succeeded in gaining an increase in the minimum wage from $27 a month in 1996 to $42 a month in 2001, and locally negotiated improvements in working conditions in certain factories. While the gains achieved fell far short of the workers' demands, they nevertheless presaged the emergence of the trade union movement as an internationally and nationally recognized movement in Cambodian civil society, if not Cambodian politics.

By contrast, the Democracy Square movement failed to gain a positive response from the election authorities in 1998 regarding investigations into allegations of election fraud, or significant concessions from the CPP on the composition of the new government. The O'Russei Market traders' protests similarly failed in evoking any substantive response from municipal or national government. Furthermore, like the NGO sector, these movements exhibit a sharp awareness of the contingent nature of political space, even in Phnom Penh. For those movements associated with opposition political parties, in particular, there was a strong tendency to view the sphere of international politics, rather than national politics, as the most appropriate sphere in which to demand accountability from the Cambodian government, since this awarded protection as well as material and organizational resources to the movements. There is a danger here that over-emphasis of international action on behalf of Cambodian constituencies leads to a professionalization of protest movements that distances them from grass-roots activism, and inadvertently reiterates, rather than reduces, the sense of disempowerment of the Cambodian poor.

However, all these movements represented the emergence of a precedent for demonstrations and the marking out of public space upon which protests could be staged, and, to this degree, they forged new ground in terms of asserting political freedoms, creating public political arenas and promoting the engagement of the ordinary Cambodian in a spirited contestation of government agendas. Individual responses to the failure of these movements varied, but there are indications that protesters viewed their protests as legitimate efforts to demand accountability from the Cambodian government. Thus, while some interviewees regarded a refusal to negotiate as within the rights of a patrimonial government, others expressed their disgust and disillusionment at the refusal of supposedly representative government agencies, such as the National Assembly or the prime minister, to negotiate with them or press their demands.

The emergence of the view that public protest is possible and legitimate, and an apparently widespread perception of government as obligated to respond, represents an emerging consensus that government has a duty to be accountable to the people. This emerging political ethic contrasts sharply with the political economy of power that sustained the state in 1990s Cambodia, in which accountability was precluded by the networks of transformed patronage and protection that pervaded the state apparatus. Rejection of this extends to public servants themselves, as the teachers' strikes of 1999 and 2001 indicated.

In the context of Phnom Penh, the response of the government has been, firstly, to deny the principle of accountability by failing to respond to these movements in public, even while frequently acting covertly against them. A second response is encapsulated within an ambitious plan to transform the contours of the urban environment itself, imposing social order through the wholesale eviction of unruly elements of the urban population and the replacement of uncontrolled and uncontrollable housing developments with parks and squares designed as monuments to CPP power. This attempt to reconstitute control through the co-optation of public space represents an attempt to impose the kind of control over land and resources, both material and symbolic, that has also been used across rural Cambodia. The logic of the new political economy of power in Cambodia turns on the ability to gain and defend control of land and the landscape, both as the basis of the subsistence economy in the countryside and as the space for conducting protests that will be visible nationally and internationally in the cities.

9 Conclusion

Manipulating Cambodia's transitions

Cambodia's political trajectory in the 1990s moved the country away from war and towards a formal peace between the warring armies of the 1980s. It installed elections at local and national level, and various other formations of democracy, such as a multi-party political sphere and a 'civil society' comprising, prominently, a vibrant community of NGOs based in Phnom Penh and a plethora of urban protest movements.

However, Western commentators on Cambodian politics have frequently expressed a degree of unease about the significance of these achievements. Elections have returned to power an individual – Prime Minister Hun Sen – who styles himself a 'strongman', and a party – the Cambodian People's Party – that is perceived internationally as corrupt, authoritarian and violent, and as using personal networks of power and patronage to undermine the constitutional state. Equally, the capacities and orientation of Cambodian opposition political parties and NGOs have also been viewed with suspicion. The former are undeniably xenophobic and have failed to establish a clear relationship of representation with voters, particularly in rural areas. The latter are hierarchical and heavily dependent upon international aid and agendas.

These asserted problems of contemporary Cambodian politics are frequently viewed as emerging from one of two sources. A commonly cited problem is the supposedly reactionary nature of Khmer culture, which is alleged to have consistently worked against international efforts at democracy promotion. Alternatively, problems have been viewed as issuing from the insufficiently zealous application of liberal doctrine by international democracy promoters, who have been undermined by cynics in their own state departments, and have consequently failed to implement policies in Cambodia with a sufficiently firm hand.

This study has adopted a different stance by examining the way in which different actors in Cambodian politics have manipulated new opportunities, arising from the opening of the Cambodian economy and from interventionary policies of international democracy promotion. This offers an understanding of the trajectory of Cambodian politics as determined by both changing opportunities, political actors' perceptions of those opportunities and the different ways in which political actors have taken advantage of them. The most successful actor – the Cambodian People's Party – has consolidated power since the late 1980s through a strategy which permitted the near monopolization of political arenas in rural Cambodia, through the use of violence, to take control of economic resources and thereby strengthen a state that in the 1980s was observably weak.

Having recognized the failure of the state to achieve its major policy goals in the 1980s in the face of military insurgency, diplomatic isolation and, no less significantly, significant resistance from the rural population, the CPP pursued policies from 1989 intended to transform necessity into virtue. The transformation of the economy to a free market system recognized the creeping privatization of the 1980s, and harnessed this to the service of state consolidation. The dissemination of ideology and policy from the centre had failed. Allowing local officials to use their positions of political power, backed by local militarization, to enrich themselves at the expense of the broader population around them strengthened loyalties within the state apparatus without requiring renewed efforts at promoting central control or building new institutions.

For the CPP, this strategy of state consolidation had the advantageous by-product of entrenching the entanglement between party and state. This permitted the selective co-optation or exclusion of other political actors returning to Cambodian politics under the UN-sponsored peace plan of the early 1990s, according to their willingness to participate in the new system of decentralized exploitation of resources and appropriation of wealth. FUNCINPEC has been partially co-opted into the system at the cost of losing its rural network of political and military supporters; the PDK has been integrated more fully. The SRP has been consistently excluded because of its insistence upon a different, more liberal, model of governance.

Two points are worth noting in regard to the analysis of these events. Firstly, viewing these practices as traditional expressions of Khmer culture mistakes the specifically modern tactics of political power to which the form of gift exchange and dyadic relations has been harnessed. Patronage relations have been manipulated and transposed out of the village sphere: in fact, the village population has become the exploitable resource underpinning patronage within a commodified state. Relations between patrons and clients remain personal and particular, but these relationships, under the umbrella of the party organization, have been organized into a coordinated, systematic and nation-wide policy of exclusion of both rival members of the elite and marginalized sections of the poor from engagement in political and economic life. The result is not merely the circulation of wealth and power between rich and poor within the village, as in 'traditional' models of patron–clientism, but the harnessing of these local relationships into a national system of effective and symbolic power, encompassing the military and the government, with the 'strongman', Hun Sen, at the head.

The linking of foreign investors and cross-border trade in precious commodities such as timber and gems into this system releases funds upon a scale unthinkable in traditional village-based systems of patronage. These permit the dominance through personal sponsorship, by individuals such as Hun Sen, not only of a local village landscape, but of the national landscape. This, in turn, is harnessed into nation-wide co-optation of villagers into mass acclamations of legitimacy at election time. While the cloaking of these relationships in traditional terminology may be a useful legitimizing device, the political operations these references refer to operate in the service of a modern, rationalized system of economic exploitation and political surveillance.

Secondly, analyses of this system which simply point out its divergence from a liberal free market democracy fail to consider the problems associated with implementing a process of political change, permitting movement from the current system to a posited ideal. For example, commentators have frequently pointed out that the system of exploitation and surveillance operating in 1990s Cambodia works because of the absence of the rule of law in the country. While this is certainly the case, it is worth asking whether movement to a rule-of-law state was a viable alternative, in the context of the late 1980s, where the ability of the central state to impose policies on villagers, local authorities and the military had been proven to be extremely limited. Centralized attempts by the party to promote such liberal democratic institutionalization would have pitted the weak party and state against powerful and embedded vested interests, much as the attempts to promote socialist collectivist institutions had done. The significant advantage of the way that economic transition was implemented was that it turned local vested interests to the benefit of the centre, rather than attempting to confront them. This is the basis of Cambodia's current political stability, and was the dynamic that permitted the successful conclusion of the second transition – the ending of the civil war.

This success must be qualified by the fact that the system of exploitation into which the National Army of Democratic Kampuchea was integrated requires continued militarization for its operation. The strategy of co-opting a decentralized, entrepreneurial and exploitative military has posed great difficulties for post-war demobilization. Not only is state power dependent upon the ability to coerce opponents and intimidate outsiders, but the military itself represents a powerful vested interest that can be cut loose from the system of co-optation only with great danger. For these reasons, progress on demobilization has been slow, despite significant donor pressure on the issue. Society has remained militarized and violent as a result, calling into question the nature of the peace achieved. However, while alternative strategies, such as reining in the military, disciplining local authorities into a culture of public service and promoting the power of the judiciary at an early stage, may have aimed at a nobler ideal, such strategies would have flown in the face of actually existing distributions of power in the early 1990s. Consequently, they would have been much more likely to founder in chaos at an early stage, intensifying rather than ameliorating the civil war.

An approach to the study of democratization which views political change as a series of perceptions and manipulations of expanding opportunities by a variety of actors offers a better basis from which to analyse the question of democracy. This is because it permits the identification of newly emerging and disappearing opportunities for widespread and empowering participation in the process of democratization itself. Thus the entrenchment of state and party by virtue of their co-optation of the transition to the free market can be seen to have closed down opportunities for internationally supported and promoted non-state organizations – intended to furnish the institutional basis for democracy in Cambodia – to establish a strong representative relationship with villagers in rural Cambodia.

In an environment of severe poverty, the concentration of economic power and resources in the hands of local officials problematized the emergence of strong grassroots political movements in the context of an internationally funded and promoted democratization effort in the 1990s. The transition to the free market thus strengthened the Cambodian elite at the expense of the ordinary farmer, who lacked significant resources to promote to the advance of his or her political and economic position vis-à-vis local authorities. The use of coercion to dispossess the poor and politically untrustworthy, and the lack of alternative sources of protection or economic assistance beyond the local authorities, was a significant disincentive to participation newly emerging organizations beyond the state and the CPP. Consequently, the emergence of public debate around government sponsored political processes such as elections, or the pursuit of alternative forms of open political contestation, has been limited in Cambodia's rural villages. Similarly, the co-optation of state employees into networks of rent-seeking and transformed patronage has problematized the emergence of horizontal ties of professionalism and solidarity, even amongst those public servants who view themselves as poorly served by the system.

This has rendered the promotion of democracy in Cambodia difficult. While democratic processes – in particular, elections – and proto-institutions – such as a 'civil society' of NGOs and a multi-party sphere – have been supported internationally, they are undermined by two features of the context. Firstly, the power of the CPP over rural political arenas has entailed that there has been little emergence of the public debate necessary to strengthen connections of representation between the masses and the political elite. While election results since 1993 show that the majority of the population has not voted for the CPP, voting against them has been rendered a covert activity. This has caused great problems for the development of meaningful political competition between parties in Cambodia. The CPP's opponents – and indeed, the CPP themselves – have found themselves cut off from any qualitative understanding of local political and economic concerns. Elite agendas are thus insulated from popular input, and the representative function of political parties is undermined.

This exacerbates the second feature of the context – an inevitable elitism in the formation of non-state organizations, emerging from the fact that the resources for launching new political parties have generally come from outside Cambodia or from Phnom Penh, from the pockets of wealthy individuals, many of whom are returnees from abroad. While the strategies of the CPP have made the engagement of these individuals with local political realities difficult, it is also the case that the CPP's opponents have not themselves prioritized the forging of such links. All parties have concurred in urging their followers to refrain from openly confronting CPP surveillance and mobilization in the villages, in effect conceding the public sphere of village life to the CPP. The party system that has emerged, consequently, is poorly linked to the mass of the rural electorate, and the quality of party programmes and debates is poor as a result.

Rather than mobilizing locally, the CPP's major political opponents have paid great attention to mobilizing and manipulating international resources instead. This course of action is often prompted by a greater familiarity with the concerns and operations of 'the international community' as a result of the emergence of the CPP's opponents as diplomatic organizations in the 1980s. It closes down opportunities for greater empowered participation by the masses in three major respects. Firstly, it removes political debate and political solutions from the purview of the Cambodian electorate, displacing them into a different sphere entirely. Such displacement is anti-democratic – if democracy is viewed as appropriately involving political participation on a day-to-day level through a certain degree of informed engagement in agenda-setting and opinion formation. Secondly, it has tended to result in inconsistencies of position for political parties, which adopt different rhetorics for international, as opposed to local, audiences, and which vary their stances according to international and local contingencies. This is costly in terms of the maintenance of political resources. The increasingly unenthusiastic response of voters to FUNCINPEC's wavering strategies vis-à-vis the CPP, and the SRP's loss of international sympathy in the light of a xenophobic election campaign in 1998, are prominent examples. Thirdly, this is a strategy with which the 'international community' surrounding Cambodia is increasingly uncomfortable, and to which it is increasingly unresponsive, rendering the manipulation of international resources to great effect locally an increasingly difficult business.

By contrast, international input has been forthcoming to a much greater extent with regard to the building of 'civil society' in Cambodia. This term is frequently used loosely to refer to the emergence of an NGO sector, headquartered in Phnom Penh but with branches across Cambodia. However, the very closeness of this relationship has placed great strains upon organizations in terms of their ability to exploit and create political opportunities locally. The suspension of these organizations between a sympathetic and resource-rich international sphere and a sphere of rural politics that is dominated by often unsympathetic local authorities has compromised the ability of these NGOs to develop a representative relationship vis-à-vis the 'grassroots'. While these organizations have grown into impressive professional establishments in Phnom Penh, this development has intensified dependence upon international funding and, consequently, orientation to international agendas, as increasing professionalism requires increased resources. This removes the organizations ever further from their rural constituents. Consequently, NGOs have emerged as didactic, hierarchical organizations, which continue to wrestle, ten years after their emergence, with the problems of their connections with the 'people'.

In the urban areas, however, the past ten years have seen a significantly different trajectory. The opening of the Cambodian polity and economy have attracted an influx of foreign aid and investment, which have been heavily concentrated in the urban sector. Economic resources are distributed beyond the monopolizing abilities of the state; this has made economic resources available to non-state actors, including workers and traders, who consequently have a much greater potential for political organization than farmers in the countryside. Equally, the fluid nature of economic, political and personal relations in the city prevent the exertion of surveillance to the same degree as in the countryside. The ability to flee from patrons, or to play patrons off against one another, awards a greater freedom than is available in the rural village. Relations between state officials and citizens are impersonal and more frequently mediated by cash payments than by ongoing dyadic ties of patronage. While this is financially burdensome on the ordinary citizen, it permits much greater political freedom to determine the nature and extent of one's own relationship with the state.

Furthermore, the city of Phnom Penh offers a greater variety of state actors with which to engage, and these actors are constrained by an ostensible commitment to international norms and standards of civil and political rights, and to their own asserted commitment to the 1993 constitution. While members of the National Assembly, although elected to represent different provinces, are almost unreachable by their own constituents, they are manifestly present in the National Assembly Building in Phnom Penh, which is the frequent target of protests and demonstrations. The headquarters of the various ministries are similarly public symbols of political power.

The organizational capacities of political parties and NGOs are also at their height in the urban centres, close to international funders and protectors.

In the urban areas, parties and NGOs have formed closer and more representative links with political constituencies, and their activities have provided an exemplar for other groups of aggrieved citizens to adopt. The result has been the emergence of a lively street culture of protest, incorporating strikes, marches, sit-ins, public petitions and rallies. Protesters participating in these frequently express two different rationale for their protest – the failure of patrons to live up to the expectations of clients is still a commonly expressed grievance; however, alongside this protesters frequently refer to a duty of representation and accountability emerging from the establishment of electoral democracy.

The emergence of these forms of political activism in the urban areas represents, arguably, the most secure footing for the future of democracy in Cambodia, emerging, as it does, from the local capacities and enthusiasms of Cambodian citizens. There remains a significant international dimension to these protests. Frequently, demonstrators choose to address the international community when demanding action or redress of grievances. Furthermore, it is the greater international scrutiny of Phnom Penh that facilitates the emergence of public spaces within which protesters feel secure in enacting public resistance. However, the international dimension is supplementary to movements securely embedded in local concerns and frames of reference. The concern for international democracy promoters must be to find a way of engaging with protest leaders without removing them from their local constituency, and replacing a relationship of representation with a relationship of internationally-sponsored didacticism.

Broadly speaking, co-optation and monopolization of local political economies by the partisan state in the 1990s has led to a substitution of internationalization for democratization in Cambodian society. This is problematic in that the consequence importance of skill manipulating international frames of reference has exacerbated elitism in Cambodian society, and has prompted the emergence of new hierarchies in which those most able to operate in an internationalized sphere are increasingly distanced from the 'grassroots'. This conclusion has major implications for the ability to promote short cuts to democracy in an environment of severe material dearth. The experience of Cambodia suggests that the contribution of international resources specifically dedicated to the enabling of political participation does widen opportunities for political participation beyond the narrow sphere of the partisan state.

However, these opportunities are mostly limited to an internationalized elite, and are much less observable in rural areas. This is not because of a lack of interest among rural voters in political participation. Primarily it is because international intervention has rarely penetrated far into rural Cambodia, where political terrain remains monopolized by partisan state authorities. Stepping out of this political terrain and into a more plural, internationally sponsored, sphere of political action requires the confidence to reject co-optation into state structures, access to resources independent of such co-optation, and, crucially, a sophisticated understanding of how to operate in relation to the international community. While, in Cambodia's cities, these conditions are increasingly met, in the countryside the majority of voters remain in thrall to the monopolization of public activities by the partisan state. The moment in the polling booth offers a rare opportunity to transform resistance into political action; yet it is an isolated moment, with limited implications for the ability to participate in the setting of elite agendas, and, consequently, the consolidation of substantive democracy.

Notes

Introduction: points of departure

1 This goal was spelt out in a key policy document by United Nations Secretary General Boutros Boutros-Ghali entitled 'An agenda for peace', and published in *An Agenda for Peace 1995*, (New York: UN Publications Dept, 1995), pp. 39–72. The implications of this document for Cambodia are discussed in detail in Chapter 5.

2 A comparable case is discussed in Paul B. Henze, 'Is Ethiopia democratic? A political success story', *Journal of Democracy* 9.4 (1998): 40–54.

3 See Atul Kohli, 'On Sources of Social and Political Conflicts in Follower Democracies', in *Democracy's Victory and Crisis*, ed. Axel Hadenius (Cambridge: CUP, 1997), pp. 71–80.

4 Robert A. Dahl, *Polyarchy: Participation and Opposition* (New Haven: Yale UP, 1971).

5 This is reflected in increasing attention to democratic consolidation, as opposed to democratic transition, and in accounts of the problems associated with illiberal democracy. With regard to the former, see, for example, Guillermo O'Donnell, 'Illusions about democratic consolidation', *Journal of Democracy* 7.2 (1996): 34–51; Andreas Schedler, 'What is democratic consolidation?' *Journal of Democracy* 9.2 (1998): 91–107. With regard to the latter, see, for example, Samuel P. Huntington, 'Democracy for the long haul', *Journal of Democracy* 7.2 (1996): 3–13; Charles Taylor, 'The dynamics of democratic exclusion', *Journal of Democracy* 9.4 (1998): 143–156; Fareed Zakaria, 'The rise of illiberal democracy', *Foreign Affairs*, 76.6 (1997): 22–43.

6 Dietrich Rueschemeyer, Evelyne Huber Stephens and John D. Stephens, *Capitalist Development and Democracy* (Cambridge: Polity, 1992), p. 4.

7 John Girling, 'Development and democracy in SE Asia', *Pacific Review* 1.4 (1988): 332.

8 Atul Kohli, 'On sources of social and political conflicts in follower democracies', in *Democracy's Victory and Crisis*, ed. Axel Hadenius (Cambridge: CUP, 1997), p. 71.

9 Benedict R. Anderson, 'Elections and participation in three Southeast Asian countries', in R.H. Taylor (ed.) *The Politics of Elections in Southeast Asia* (Cambridge: CUP, 1996), p. 14.

10 Control of agendas is regarded by Stephen Lukes as one of the three dimensions of power, see Lukes, *Power: A Radical View*, (London: Macmillan, 1974).

11 The Kantian connection between democracy and international peace is discussed in Daniele Archibugi, 'Immanuel Kant, Cosmopolitan Law and Peace', *European Journal of International Relations* 1 (1995): 429–56; and Michael Doyle, 'Liberalism and world politics', *American Political Science Review* 80 (1986):

1151–63. The role of transitions to democracy in conflict resolution is posited in Juan Linz, 'Some thoughts on the victory and future of democracy', in Axel Hadenius (ed.) *Democracy's Victory and Crisis* (Cambridge: CUP, 1997), p. 418.
12 Theodore Sorensen, 'Rethinking national security', *Foreign Affairs* 69.3 (1990): 17.
13 See discussion in Chapter 5.
14 An account of a Khmer psychology that is predisposed towards either passivity or violence is found in Seanglim Bit, *The Warrior Heritage: A Psychological Perspective of Cambodian Trauma*, (El Cerrito: Seanglim Bit, 1991). The clearest account of how this may have undermined Cambodia's political transitions is put forward by David Roberts, *Political Transition in Cambodia, 1991–99* (Richmond: Curzon, 2001).
15 Guillermo O'Donnell and Philippe Schmitter, *Transfers from Authoritarian Rule: Tentative Conclusions about Uncertain Democracies*, (London: Johns Hopkins UP, 1986), p. 66.
16 Larry Diamond, 'Introduction: political culture and democracy', in *Political Culture and Democracy in Developing Countries*, Larry Diamond (ed.), textbook edition (London: Lynne Rienner, 1994), p. 7.
17 Frederick Brown and David Timberman (eds), *Cambodia and the International Community: The Quest for Peace, Development and Democracy* (New York: Asia Society, 1998), p. 15.
18 Stephen Solarz, press conference, Phnom Penh, 28 July 1998, recorded by Caroline Hughes.
19 Stephen Haggard and Robert R. Kaufman, *The Political Economy of Democratic Transitions* (Princeton: Princeton UP, 1995), pp. 6–7
20 Alberto Melucci, *Nomads of the Present, Social Movements and Individual Needs in Contemporary Society*, eds John Keane and Paul Mier (London: Hutchinson Radius, 1989), p. 26.
21 *Ibid.*, p. 35.
22 Jean-Francois Bayart, 'Finishing with the idea of the Third World: the concept of the political trajectory', in James Manor (ed.) *Rethinking Third World Politics* (London: Longman, 1991), p. 56.
23 James Mayall, 'Introduction', in James Mayall (ed.) *The New Interventionism 1991–4: United Nations Experience in Cambodia, Former Yugoslavia, Somalia* (Cambridge: CUP, 1996), p. 22.

2 Economy and state–society relations

1 Georg Sørensen, *Democracy and Democratization, Processes and Prospects in a Changing World*, 2nd edn (Boulder: Westview, 1998), p. 103.
2 James C. Scott, 'The erosion of patron–client bonds and social change in rural Southeast Asia', *Journal of Asian Studies* 32 (1972): 8.
3 See James C. Scott, *Weapons of the Weak: The Everyday Forms of Peasant Resistance*, (London: Yale UP, 1985), pp. 34–5.
4 Sorpong Peou, *Intervention and Change in Cambodia, Towards Democracy?* (New York: St Martin's Press, 2000), p. 62.
5 Eva Mysliwiec, *Punishing the Poor: The International Isolation of Kampuchea*, (Oxford: Oxfam, 1988), pp. 10–11.
6 Peou (2000), pp. 93–101.
7 Nicolas Regaud, *Le Cambodge dans la Tourmente: Le Troisième Conflit Indochinois 1978–1991*, (Paris: FEDN-L'Harmattan, 1992), p. 63.
8 Nayan Chanda, *Brother Enemy, the War after the War: A History of Indochina Since the Fall of Saigon*, (New York: Collier, 1986), pp. 371–2.

9 Judge (J3), personal interview, Kampot, April 1996.
10 Journalist (N3), personal interview, Phnom Penh, March 1996.
11 Martin Stuart-Fox and Bunheang Ung, *The Murderous Revolution*, (Bangkok: Orchid Press, 1998), p. 178.
12 Journalist (N3), personal interview, Phnom Penh, March 1996.
13 Mysliwiec (1988), *Punishing the Poor*, p. 85.
14 Grant Curtis, 'Cambodia: a country profile', report (Stockholm: SIDA, 1990), p. 27.
15 Economist Intelligence Unit (EIU), *Country report: Indochina – Vietnam, Laos, Cambodia*, 3 (1986): 23.
16 *Ibid.*
17 Curtis (1990), 'Country Profile', p. 40.
18 *Ibid.*
19 Eva L. Mysliwiec, 'Cambodia: NGOS in Transition', paper presented to the Workshop on the Social Consequences of the Peace Process in Cambodia, Geneva, 29–30 April 1993, p. 8.
20 Regaud (1992), pp. 69–70.
21 Roberts (2001), p. 51.
22 David Chandler, *The Tragedy of Cambodian History*, (New Haven: Yale UP, 1991), p. 313.
23 Michael Vickery, *Cambodia 1975–82* (Boston: South End Press, 1984), p. 250.
24 Serge Thion, *Watching Cambodia*, (Bangkok: White Lotus, 1993), pp. 106–7.
25 *Ibid.*, p. 107.
26 Economist Intelligence Unit, *Quarterly Economic Review of Indochina – Vietnam, Laos, Cambodia*, Annual Supplement (1985): 41–3.
27 Economist Intelligence Unit, *Country Report: Indochina – Vietnam, Laos, Cambodia*, 1 (1986): 22.
28 Economist Intelligence Unit, *Quarterly Economic Review of Indochina: Vietnam, Laos, Cambodia* 2 (1996): 26.
29 EIU 1 (1986): 22.
30 Curtis, 'Country Profile', p. 32.
31 EIU 3 (1986): 25.
32 Curtis, 'Country Profile', p. 64. Inflation between 1980 and 1988 ran at less than 10 per cent per year, indicating that the price rises were real rather than nominal.
33 Economist Intelligence Unit, 'Country Profile: Indochina – Vietnam, Laos, Cambodia', (1989–90): 55.
34 Viviane Frings, 'Cambodia after decollectivization (1989–1992)', *Journal of Contemporary Asia* 24.1 (1994): 49.
35 World Bank, East Asia and Pacific Region, Country Dept. 1, 'Cambodia: Agenda for Rehabilitation and Reconstration', report, Bangkok, June 1992.
36 EIU (1989–90): 53.
37 Vickery (1984), p. 222.
38 Thion (1993), p. 116.
39 Chanda (1986), p. 372; Thion (1993), p. 114.
40 Chang Pao-min, 'Kampuchean Conflict: the Continuing Stalemate', *Asian Survey* 17.7 (1987): 750.
41 EIU 3 (1986): 23.
42 Economist Intelligence Unit, 'Country Report: Indochina – Vietnam, Laos, Cambodia', 2 (1986): 24.
43 *Ibid.*: 25.
44 Economist Intelligence Unit, *Quarterly Economic Review of Indochina: Vietnam, Laos, Cambodia* 3 (1985): 19.

45 Economist Intelligence Unit, *Quarterly Economic Review of Indochina: Vietnam, Laos, Cambodia*, 2 (1986): 25.
46 Raoul Jennar, Cambodia Mission Report 19 April–10 May 1990, 3. Quoted in Carlyle A. Thayer, 'The Soviet Union and Indochina', paper presented to the IV World Congress for Soviet and East European Studies, Harrogate, 21–26 July 1990, p. 8, available online at ftp://coombs.anu.edu/coombspapers/.
47 Thayer (1990), p. 8.
48 World Bank, 'Agenda for Rehabilitation', p. 20.
49 'Proclamation on the Political Goal of Practicing Agricultural Exploitation According to the Method of Mutual Aid', *Kampuchea*, 25 May 1989, 3. Quoted in Frings (1994), p. 52.
50 Thayer (1990), p. 7.
51 Frings (1994), p. 56.
52 Gavin Shatkin, 'Claiming a piece of the city: squatting as a response to changing property relations in Phnom Penh's transitional economy', Masters dissertation, University of Hawai'i, August 1996, p. 39.
53 *Ibid.*, p. 54.
54 Interviews with the author, Samaki Village, Phnom Penh, July–August 2001.
55 Shatkin (1996), p. 40.
56 Frings (1994), p. 57.
57 Sik Boreak, 'Land ownership, sales and concentration in Cambodia: a preliminary review of secondary data and primary data from four recent surveys', Working Paper No. 16 (Phnom Penh: CDRI, 2000), p. 21.
58 Villagers, Khmer Citizens Party campaign rally, Stung District, Kompong Thom, 20 June 1998, recorded and transcribed by the author and Sok Ty.
59 Sam Rainsy, campaign rally, Kraceh Provincial Town, 4 July 1998, recorded and transcribed by the author and Sok Ty.
60 Student, male, Faculty of Medicine, from Kampot Province (DEM30), personal interview, 'Students for Democracy' demonstration, Phnom Penh, 2 September 1998.
61 Frings (1994), p. 50.
62 Royal Government of Cambodia, 'First draft of the Second Five-Year Socio-Economic Development Plan 2001–5', paper for discussion at the High Level Forum, Cambodiana Hotel, Phnom Penh, 22 March 2001, p. 5.
63 International Institute of Rural Reconstruction, 'Participatory rural appraisal output in Thlork, Chrok Motes, and Toul Ampil Villages, Svay Teap District, Svay Rieng Province, Kingdom of Cambodia, 27 February–16 March 1996', report, Catholic Relief Services Cambodia, Phnom Penh, 1996, p. 15.
64 World Food Program and Food and Agriculture Organization, 'Statistical Supplement: WFP/FAO Crop and Food Supply Assessment Mission, 1996/7, Cambodia', report, Phnom Penh, 1997.
65 Huw Watkin, '200,000 facing food crisis in Southeast', *Phnom Penh Post*, 3–16 July 1998, p. 1.
66 Bou Saroeun, 'Government to streamline food aid as hunger hits the provinces', *Phnom Penh Post*, 30 October–12 November 1998, p. 1.
67 US Agency for International Development, 'South and South East Asia Floods Fact Sheet #2', 14 November 2000, accessed online at www.reliefweb.int.
68 Ministry of Planning, 'Demographic survey of Cambodia, summary results', report, Phnom Penh, 1996.
69 Ministry of Planning, 'Cambodia human development report 1998: women's contribution to development', report, Phnom Penh, 1998, p. 50.
70 Ministry of Planning, 'Report on the Cambodian Socio-Economic Survey 1997', report, Phnom Penh, 1997, p. 2.

71 United Nations Population Fund, 'Report on the Cambodian Socio-Economic Survey 1997', report, Phnom Penh, 1998, p. 8.
72 Ministry of Planning 1998, p. 38.
73 Royal Government of Cambodia (2000), First Draft, p. 12.
74 *Ibid.*, p. 15.
75 *Ibid.*, p. 16.
76 *Ibid.*, pp. 17–18, and p. 1.
77 *Ibid.*, p.18.
78 *Ibid.*, p. 17.
79 *Ibid.*, p. 39.

3 Economic reform and state-making in the 1990s

1 Laura Summers, 'Cambodia: the prospects for a UN-controlled solution', *Asian Review,* 5 (1991): 52.
2 Michael Ward, 'Constraints on re-building Cambodia's economy', paper delivered at Conference on Cambodia's Economy, University of Washington, Seattle, 3–5 November 1994, p. 5.
3 UNTAC Office of Rehabilitation and Economic Affairs, 'Short term economic management and stabilization strategies for Cambodia', background draft prepared for the meeting of the Extended Permanent Five, Phnom Penh, 17 June 1993, p. 9.
4 Ward (1994: 3).
5 World Bank, East Asia and Pacific Region, Country Dept. 1, 'Cambodia: agenda for rehabilitation and reconstruction', report, Bangkok, June 1992, pp. 20–1.
6 Asian Development Bank (ADB), International Monetary Fund, United Nations Development Programme, United Nations Transitional Authority in Cambodia, and World Bank, 'Cambodia: short term needs', paper prepared for International Conference on the Reconstruction of Cambodia, Paris, 8–9 September 1993, p. 10.
7 *Ibid.*: 9, 10.
8 H.S. Greve, *Land Tenure and Property Rights in Cambodia*, (Phnom Penh: H.S. Greve, 1993), p. 52, quoted in Sik Boreak, 'Land ownership, sales and concentration in Cambodia: a preliminary review of secondary data and primary data from four recent surveys', Working Paper No. 16 (Phnom Penh: CDRI, 2000), p. 17.
9 World Bank (1992), 'Agenda for rehabilitation', p. 30.
10 Human rights lawyer, personal interview, Phnom Penh, January 1996 (L1).
11 World Bank (1992), 'Agenda for rehabilitation', p. 18.
12 World Bank, 'Background note: Cambodia, a vision for forestry sector development', paper prepared for Consultative Group Meeting on Cambodia, Tokyo, February 1999, accessed online at www.worldbank.org, p. 1.
13 Sam Rainsy, 'The logging issue, its impact on public finance, environment, and the food situation', documents for International Conference on the Reconstruction of Cambodia (ICORC), Paris, 14–15 March 1995.
14 Sam Rainsy, 'A condition for further international assistance should be greater transparency in public decision making', documents for ICORC, pp. 4, 6.
15 World Bank (1999), 'Background note', p. 4.
16 Hurley Scroggins, 'Bout of pre-CG lobbying', *Phnom Penh Post*, 27 June–10 July 1997, p. 15.
17 Global Witness, 'Putting Cambodia's forests on the international agenda: Global Witness and the transnational campaign against the logging trade', paper delivered at conference on 'Cambodia: Building a Better Future', Oxford, July 1999.

18 Global Witness, 'Chainsaws speak louder than words', report, London, May 2000, p. 8.
19 *Ibid.*, p. 11.
20 Environment Working Group of NGO Forum on Cambodia, 'Review of fishery conflict in Stung Treng' report, Phnom Penh, January 2000, pp. 6/7.
21 *Ibid.*, p. 5.
22 *Ibid.*, p. 5.
23 The term interest – *pruyaoch* – refers to profit or advantage; it is often pecuniary.
24 Human rights lawyer (L1), personal interview, Phnom Penh, January 1996.
25 Human rights NGO activist (H7), personal interview, Kompong Cham, July 1996.
26 Human rights NGO activist (H2), personal interview, Kompong Cham, July 1996.
27 Human rights NGO activist (H11), personal interview, Kompong Cham province, July 1996.
28 Gavin Shatkin, 'Claiming a piece of the city: squatting as a response to changing property relations in Phnom Penh's transitional economy', Masters dissertation, University of Hawai'i, August 1996, p. 39.
29 Human rights NGO worker (H5), personal interview, Phnom Penh, January 1996.
30 Human rights lawyer (L4), personal interview, Phnom Penh, January 1996.
31 'Stronger than a tiger!' A reader's view, *Moneaksekar Khmer*, 28–9 June 1996, p. 1.
32 Amnesty International, 'Update on human rights concerns', report, London, October 1992, p. 5.
33 Pin Sisovann, 'Land protesters return to Poipet defeated', *Cambodia Daily*,14 May 2001, p. 12.
34 Shaun Williams, 'Where has all the land gone?', *Cambodia Land Study Project*, vol. 2, Phnom Penh, Oxfam (GB), 1999, accessed online at http://www.camnet.com.kh/ngoforum/
35 'Please Mr Tol Lah, tell Hun Sen!', letter to editor, *Moneaksekar Khmer* (Khmer Conscience), 3–4 July 1996, pp. 1–3.
36 University professor (U1), personal interview, Phnom Penh, May 1996.
37 Judge (J1), personal interview, Kampot, April 1996.
38 Judge (J5), personal interview, Phnom Penh, May 1996.
39 Ker Munthit and Mathew Grainger, 'Snguon gets tough in support of courts', *Phnom Penh Post*, 23 February–7 March 1996, p. 1.
40 Judge (J1), personal interview, Kampot, April 1996.
41 University lecturer (U3), personal interview, Phnom Penh, June 1996.
42 Royal Government of Cambodia, 'Cambodia: supplementary memorandum of economic and financial policies for 2000', Phnom Penh, 31 August 2000, accessed online at www.imf.org.
43 Phelim Kyne, 'Investors question PM's anti-corruption initiative', *Phnom Penh Post*, 18 February–2 March 2000, online edition accessed at www.phnompenhpost.com.
44 Phelim Kyne, 'RAC booted, RCAF boosted, by Hun Sen', *Phnom Penh Post*, 7–20 July 2000, online edition accessed at www.phnompenhpost.com.
45 Report of the Special Representative, 'Situation of human rights in Cambodia', UN Economic and Social Council, 28 December 2001, Sect. II, § B (l). This has been repeated a theme in the reports of the United Nations Special Representative for Human Rights in Cambodia; see also, for example, Report of the Special Representative, 'Situation of human rights in Cambodia', UN Economic and Social Council, 26 February 1999, pp. 12–17; Report of the

Special Representative, 'Situation of human rights in Cambodia', UN Economic and Social Council, 13 January 2000, pp. 13–17.

46 Dylan Hendrickson, 'Cambodia's security sector reforms: limits of a downsizing strategy', *Conflict Security Development* 1.1 (2001): 72.

47 *Ibid.*: 80.

48 John Vijghen, 'Decision making in a Cambodian village: a study of decision making processes in a development project in Cambodia, Takeo', Report No. 15, Phnom Penh: Cambodian Researchers for Development , 1996, pp.17–20.

49 Judy Ledgerwood and John Vijghen, 'Decision making in rural Khmer villages', in Judy Ledgerwood (ed.) *Cambodia Emerges from the Past: Eight Essays*, (DeKalb: Southeast Asia Publications, Center for Southeast Asian Studies, 2002).

50 Human rights NGO activist (H6), personal interview, Kampot, April 1996.

51 John Girling, 'Development and democracy in SE Asia', *Pacific Review* 1.4 (1988).

52 See, for example, Nick Lenaghan, 'Officials implicated in Koh Kong sex trade', *CD*, 19–21 April 1996, p. 1; Lenaghan, 'Pimps up for hefty sentences, but reservations about new law', *Phnom Penh Post*, 8–21 March 1996, p. 13. In the latter article, Lenaghan cites Kien Serey Phal, president of the Cambodian Women's Development Association, who says of a new Law on Suppression of Trafficking of Humans, 'We are afraid this law will not be effective because the people enforcing it already have their hands in the business'.

53 Thomas Hammerberg, press conference, Phnom Penh, 30 July 1998; Neb Sinthay and Janet Ashby, 'Possibilities to reduce the number of weapons and the practice of using weapons to solve problems in Cambodia', report, Peace Partnership, Phnom Penh, 28 July 1998; Amnesty International, 'Kingdom of Cambodia. The children of Krang Kontroul: waiting for justice', London, March 1997.

54 Yem Sam Oeun and Rebecca F. Catalla, *'I Live in Fear': Consequences of Small Arms and Light Weapons on Women and Children in Cambodia,* Research Series on Small Arms and Light Weapons Issues in Cambodia, Report No. 2, Working Group on Weapons Reduction, Phnom Penh, 2001, p. 19.

55 *Ibid.*

4 State and party in the 1990s

1 See John Girling, *Cambodia and the Sihanouk Myths,* Occasional Paper No. 7 (Singapore: ISEAS, 1971); Milton Osborne, *Politics and Power in Cambodia: The Sihanouk Years* (Camberwell: Longman, 1973).

2 James Scott, 'The erosion of patron–client bonds and social change in rural Southeast Asia', *Journal of Asian Studies* 32 (1972): 7–8.

3 Amnesty International, 'Cambodia: human rights developments, 1 October 1991 to 31 January 1992', report, London, April 1992, p. 37.

4 *Ibid.*

5 Judge (J1), personal interview, Kampot, April 1996.

6 Nate Thayer, 'Unsettled land', *Far Eastern Economic Review* 27 February 1992, p. 26.

7 Amnesty International, 'State of Cambodia: update on human rights concerns, Oct. 1992', London, 1992, pp. 8–9.

8 UNTAC, Information and Education Division, 'Report on public perceptions of UNTAC in the City of Phnom Penh', Phnom Penh, September 1992, p. 4.

9 Michael Doyle, *UN Peacekeeping in Cambodia: UNTAC's Civil Mandate*, (New York: International Peace Academy Occasional Paper, 1995), p. 16.

10 US Department of State, 'Cambodia: Human Rights Abuses, 1993', report, Washington DC, 1994, p. 4.
11 *Phnom Penh Post*, 18–31 December 1992, p. 12, quoted in Caroline Hughes, *UNTAC in Cambodia, the Impact on Human Rights*, Occasional Paper No. 92 (Singapore: ISEAS, 1996), p. 47.
12 *Phnom Penh Post*, 18–31 December 1992, p. 12.
13 Amnesty International, 'Cambodia. human rights concerns: July to December 1992', report, London, February 1993, p. 10.
14 Boutros Boutros-Ghali, 'Report of the Secretary-General on the implementation of Security Council Resolution 7883 (1992) on the Cambodia Peace Process', in United Nations, *The United Nations and Cambodia, 1991–1995*, (New York: United Nations, 1995), Doc. 54, § 7.
15 Oum Mean, Chief of Secretariat, Central Committee Cabinet of the CPP, personal interview, May 1998.
16 The CPP's use of these resources in 1993 is described by Judy Ledgerwood, 'Patterns of CPP political repression and violence during the UNTAC period', in Steve Heder and Judy Ledgerwood (eds) *Propaganda, Politics, and Violence in Cambodia, Democratic Transition under United Nations Peace-keeping*, (London: M.E. Sharpe, 1996), pp. 114–33.
17 CPP 'Party group book', Phnom Penh, 19 May 1998.
18 Memorandum, Cambodian Office of the High Commissioner for Human Rights, Phnom Penh, 19 May 1998. With reference to the last point, membership of the 'Khmer Rouge' is illegal in Cambodia.
19 Neang Sovath, Director, COMFREL, Kompong Cham, personal interview, Kompong Cham Provincial Town, 6 July 1998.
20 Keat Sokhun, Grandfather Son Sann Party Candidate for Kompong Speu Province, press conference, Phnom Penh, 29 June 1998, recorded by the author.
21 Lucien M. Hanks, Jr, 'Merit and power in the Thai social order', *American Anthropologist* 64 (1962): 1247–61.
22 Oum Mean, Chief of Secretariat, Central Committee Cabinet, Cambodian People's Party, personal interview, Phnom Penh, 22 May 1998.
23 FUNCINPEC commune activist (SK2), personal interview, S'aang District, Kandal, May 1998.
24 FUNCINPEC supporter (LA2), personal communication, Lvea Aem District, Kandal, 11 June 1998; commune FUNCINPEC activist (LA4), conversation with FUNCINPEC MP observed by the author, Lvea Aem District, Kandal, 11 June 1998.
25 FUNCINPEC District Activist (SK1), personal interview, S'aang District, Kandal, 10 July 1998; FUNCINPEC Commune Activist (SK2), personal interview, S'aang District, Kandal, 19 July 1998; FUNCINPEC District Activist (SK3), personal interview, S'aang District, Kandal, 13 July 1998; FUNCINPEC Commune Activist (LA1), personal communication, Lvea Aem District, Kandal, 11 June 1998; Villager (LA5), personal communication, Lvea Aem District, Kandal, 19 June 1998.
26 Woman (DEM9), vegetable trader, 45 years, from Tboung Kmum District, Kompong Cham, personal interview, 'Democracy Square', Phnom Penh, 26 August 1998.
27 Man (DEM11), SRP activist, small businessman, 41 years, from Kompong Chhnang provincial town, personal interview, 'Democracy Square', Phnom Penh, 26 August 1998.
28 Villager (LA5), personal communication, Lvea Aem District, Kandal, 19 June 1998.

29 FUNCINPEC District Activist (SK1), personal interview, S'aang District, Kandal, 10 July 1998 (author's question in italics).
30 FUNCINPEC Commune Activist (SK2), personal interview, S'aang District, Kandal, 19 July 1998 (author's question in italics).
31 Judy Ledgerwood and John Vijghen, 'Decision-making in rural Khmer villages', in Judy Ledgerwood (ed.) *Cambodia Emerges from the Past: Eight Essays*, (DeKalb: Southeast Asia Publications, Center for Southeast Asian Studies, 2002), p. 41.
32 *Ibid.*, p. 42.
33 John Vijghen, *Decision-making in a Cambodian Village: A Study of Decision-making Processes in a Development Project in Cambodia, Takeo*, report No. 15 (Phnom Penh: Cambodian Researchers for Development, 1996), p. 18.
34 Vijghen, *Decision-making*, p. 18.
35 Thomas Hammarberg, 'Monitoring of election related intimidation and violence', report, 19 August–23 September 1998', Phnom Penh, 23 September 1998, p. 5.
36 Sam Rainsy Members of Parliament, 'The rule of terror', press release, Phnom Penh, 18 January 2002, accessed online at www.samrainsyparty.org.
37 Sam Rainsy Members of Parliament, 'A state of anarchy', press release, Phnom Penh, 14 January 2002, accessed online at www.samrainsyparty.org.
38 Oeur Hunly, FUNCINPEC candidate for Kandal, personal communication, Phnom Penh, 7 August 1998.
39 Yim Sokha, Sam Rainsy Party Secretary General and candidate for Siem Reap, personal interview, Phnom Penh, 20 May 1998.
40 Sam Rainsy Party Provincial Co-ordinator (name withheld on request), personal interview, Kompong Cham, July 1998.
41 Sam Rainsy Party Provincial Co-ordinator, personal interview, Kompong Cham, July 1998.
42 Man (W1), 62 years old, from Kampot Province, press conference, Sam Rainsy Party Office, Phnom Penh, 30 July 1998, recorded by the author.
43 NGO election observer (EO2), quoted in Caroline Hughes and Real Sopheap *The Nature and Causes of Conflict in the 1998 National Elections*, (Phnom Penh: Cambodian Centre for Conflict Resolution, 1999), p. 58.
44 Hammarberg, 'Election related intimidation', pp. 2–6.
45 Koul Panha, 'The 1993 Cambodian election – experiences and lessons: a Cambodian view', *National Elections: Cambodia's Experiences and Expectations* Kao Kim Hourn and Norbert von Hoffman (eds) (Phnom Penh: Cambodian Institute for Cooperation and Peace, 1998), p. 37.
46 Figures for April 1993, NGO Resource Project, Daily Report, report, Phnom Penh, 11 May 1993.
47 Cambodia Office of the United Nations Centre for Human Rights, 'Memorandum to the Royal Government of Cambodia, Evidence of Summary Executions, Torture and Missing Persons Since 2–7 July 1997', Phnom Penh, 21 August 1997.
48 Campaign leaflet, distributed by Cambodian People's Party, Phnom Penh, 1 July 1998.
49 FUNCINPEC District Activist (SK1), personal interview, S'aang District, Kandal, 10 July 1998.
50 FUNCINPEC District Activist (SK1), personal interview, S'aang District, Kandal, 10 July 1998.
51 Author's observations, visit to Kraingyov Commune, S'aang District, Kandal, 13 July 1998.

52 This story was mentioned by a variety of sources, including FUNCINPEC activists in S'aang District, demonstrators from Kraingyov who joined the post-electoral demonstrations and opposition party supporters in Phnom Penh.
53 This is described in more detail in Chapter 6.
54 Woman (DEM13), 63 years old, servant, from Kraingyov Commune, Kandal, personal interview, Democracy Square, 26 August 1998.
55 Woman (DEM20), 40 years old, farmer, from Kraingyov Commune, Kandal, personal interview, Democracy Square, 27 August 1998.
56 Chan Kheang, Committee Member, CPP France, conversation with the author, Dangkao, Phnom Penh, 1 July 1998.
57 Author's observations, CPP parade, 7 January District to Dangkao District, Phnom Penh, 1 July 1998. These crowds may have been mustered using the group system, but the enthusiasm appeared genuine.
58 News Report, FM95 MHz, 1–1.45 p.m., Phnom Penh, 5 February 1998, recorded and translated by the Office of the United Nations Secretary General's Special Representative in Cambodia.
59 Hun Sen, speech to Ministry of Transport workers, Phnom Penh, 29 June 1996, reported in 'Hun Sen: exhorting the party workers', *Phnom Penh Post*, 26 July –8 Aug. 1996, p. 5.
60 Hun Sen, 'Exhorting the party workers', p. 5.
61 Hun Sen, speech to party members, Kompong Cham, June 1996, quoted in 'Create a political crisis in order to find political scapegoats', *Reasmei Kampuchea (Light of Cambodia)* 12 June 1996, p. 1.
62 Hun Sen, speech, Kandal Province, 25 Nov. 1997, quoted in Ker Munthit, 'Hun Sen; the 'Worms' that Must Die', *Phnom Penh Post*, 1–14 Dec. 1995, 3.
63 Hun Sen, speech, Kompong Speu, n.d., quoted in 'Mr Hun Sen deploys his own bodyguards because he doesn't trust the activities of the national police?', *Udam Kate Khmer (Khmer Ideal)*, 26 June 1996, p. 1.
64 Hun Sen, speech, Medical Training School, Phnom Penh, 27 Apr. 1996, quoted. in 'Hun Sen: live and die with the people', *Phnom Penh Post*, 3–16 May 1996, p. 3.
65 Associated Press, 'Government creates National Election Commission', Phnom Penh, 26 January 1998, *Camnews*, at camnews@lists.best.com, 27 January 1998.
66 Associated Press, 'Hun Sen says no need for him to actively campaign for vote', Kompong Speu, 26 June 1998, *Camnews* at camnews@lists.best.com, 27 June 1998.
67 'Legislative and physical security are of paramount and guaranteed', *Cambodian Business*, June 1998, pp. 5–13.
68 'Hun Sen: 20 minutes with VOA by telephone', *Reasmei Kampuchea (Light of Cambodia)*, 14 August 1998, pp. 1–11, author's own translation.
69 This is discussed in greater detail in Chapter 6.

5 International intervention and 'international community'

1 Sam Rainsy, 'A call for international standards in Cambodia', address to National Press Club, Washington DC, 10 April 2002, posted to camnews
2 Chang Pao Min, 'Kampuchean conflict: the continuing stalemate', *Asian Survey* 27 (1987): 748–64.
3 The classic statement of this view is found in William Shawcross, *Sideshow: Kissinger, Nixon and the destruction of Cambodia*, (London: Fontana, 1980).
4 International Secretariat of Amnesty International, 'Cambodia: escaping the killing fields?', news release, 23 October 1997, posted on Camnews

5 George Bush, State of the Union Address, 29 January 1991, Washington DC, quoted. in Jack Nelson-Pallmeyer, *Brave New World Order: Must We Pledge Allegiance?* (New York: Orbis, 1992), p. ix.
6 Francis Fukuyama, *The End of History and the Last Man*, (London: Penguin, 1992).
7 Boutros Boutros-Ghali, *An Agenda for Peace 1995* (New York: UN Publications Dept., 1995), p. 39.
8 Accounts of these are offered, respectively, in David Held, 'Democracy: from city states to a cosmopolitan order?', *Political Studies* 15 (1992), Special Issue: 10–39; and Stanley Hoffman, 'The crisis of liberal internationalism', *Foreign Policy* 98 (1995): 159–77.
9 Nikhil Aziz, 'The human rights debate in an era of globalization: hegemony of discourse', *Bulletin of Concerned Asian Scholars* 27.4 (1995): 9–18.
10 Oliver Ramsbotham and Tom Woodhouse, *Humanitarian Intervention in Contemporary Conflict: A Reconceptualization*, (Cambridge: Polity, 1996), p. 30.
11 Chris Brown, 'International political theory and the idea of world community', in Ken Booth and Steve Smith (eds) *International Relations Theory Today*, (Cambridge: Polity, 1995), p. 93.
12 David Held, 'The transformation of political community', in Ian Shapiro and Casiano Hacker-Cordón (eds) *Democracy's Edges*, (Cambridge: CUP, 1999), p. 99.
13 *Ibid.* p. 102.
14 Richard Falk, *Human Rights Horizons: the Pursuit of Justice in a Globalizing World*, (London: Routledge, 2000), p. 13.
15 *Ibid.* p. 14.
16 Ramsbotham and Woodhouse (1996) p. 224.
17 Boutros-Ghali, *Agenda* (1995) p. 44.
18 Boutros Boutros-Ghali, 'Foreword', in Thomas G. Weiss and Leon Gordenker (eds) *NGOs, the UN and Global Governance*, (Boulder: Lynne Rienner, 1996), pp. 7, 10.
19 Surin Maisrikrod, 'Thailand's policy dilemmas towards Indochina', *Contemporary South East Asia* 14.3 (1992): 296.
20 Kusuma Snitwongse, 'Thai foreign policy in the global age: principle or profit?', *Contemporary South East Asia* 23.2 (2001): 194.
21 *Ibid.* pp. 199, 209.
22 Gareth Evans, 'Co-operative security and intra-state conflict', *Foreign Policy* 96 (1994): 111.
23 In 1991, these comprised Brunei, Indonesia, Malaysia, Singapore, Thailand and the Philippines.
24 Aside from the State of Cambodia, the Lao People's Democratic Republic and the Socialist Republic of Vietnam also attended.
25 The Soviet Union, China, the United States, France and the United Kingdom.
26 James A. Baker III, 'America in Asia: emerging architecture for a Pacific community', *Foreign Affairs* 70.5 (1991): 18.
27 Stephen J. Solarz, 'Cambodia and the international community', *Foreign Affairs* 69.2 (1990): 115.
28 'Agreement concerning the sovereignty, independence, territorial integrity and inviolability, neutrality and national unity of Cambodia', 30 October 1991, Articles 2.2 (b), 3.2(b), published in *The United Nations and Cambodia, 1991–1995*, (New York: UN, 1995), Doc. 19.
29 *Ibid.*, Article 5.

30 'Agreement on a comprehensive political settlement of the Cambodia conflict', 30 October 1991, Annex 5, § 2, published in *The United Nations and Cambodia, 1991–1995*, (New York: UN, 1995), Doc. 19.
31 *Ibid.* §§ 4/5.
32 'Final act of the Paris Conference on Cambodia', 30 October 1991, § 15, published in *The United Nations and Cambodia, 1991–1995*, (New York: UN, 1995), Doc. 19.
33 'Declaration on the rehabilitation and reconstruction of Cambodia', 30 October 1991, § 2, published in *The United Nations and Cambodia, 1991–1995*, (New York: UN, 1995), Doc. 19.
34 *Ibid.* §§ 3, 13.
35 *Ibid.* § 7.
36 *Ibid.* § 12.
37 *Ibid.* § 12.
38 Yasushi Akashi, 'To build a new country: the task of the UN Transitional Authority in Cambodia', *Harvard International Review* (Winter 1992/3): 69.
39 Boutros-Ghali, *Agenda*, (1995) p. 61.
40 *Ibid.* p. 62.
41 Human Rights Component, 'Final report', Phnom Penh, 1993, pp. 9–10.
42 Steve Heder and Judy Ledgerwood (eds), 'The politics of violence: an introduction', *Propaganda, Politics and Violence in Cambodia, Democratic Transition under United Nations Peace-Keeping*, (London: M.E. Sharpe, 1996), p. 15.
43 Yasushi Akashi, 'To build a new country, the task of the UN Transitional Authority in Cambodia', *Harvard International Review* 15 (1992/3): 69.
44 Lakhan Mehrotra, personal interview, Phnom Penh, April 1999.
45 United Nations Secretary General, 'Human rights questions: technical cooperation in the field of human rights', United Nations General Assembly Document A/50/68 Add. 1, September 1995, p. 5.
46 Grant Curtis, *Cambodia Reborn? The Transition to Democracy and Development*, (Washington: Brookings Institute, 1998), pp. 74/5.
47 *Ibid.* p. 75.
48 Extract from a speech made by Hun Sen, Kandal Province, 5 December 1996, quoted in Barber and Munthit, 'Hun Sen talks tough to the West', *PPP* 15–28 December 1995: 3.
49 Susumo Awanohara, 'Full circle', *FEER* 9 June 1997: 14.
50 Leaflet distributed at student demonstrations, Phnom Penh, 8–12 September 1998.
51 Kingdom of Cambodia, *Constitution of the Kingdom of Cambodia*, Phnom Penh, September 1993, Article 33.
52 Extracts from a speech made by Hun Sen, Kandal Province, 5 December 1995, quoted in 'Hun Sen talks tough to the West', *PPP* 15–28 December 1995. Referring to this speech, one human rights NGO director commented:

> He said that before the election we worked without the international community. But it's not true! Cambodia was aided completely by the former Soviet Union. Why has he forgotten that? But now … the Communist countries have fallen and now we need international aid … Can we live with only businessmen from Malaysia, Indonesia and Taiwan? I doubt it. Because these businessmen, when they give $100, they plan to take out $300 [H14].

53 Extract from a speech made by Hun Sen, Kandal Province, 9 Dec. 1995, quoted in 'Hun Sen talks tough to the West', *PPP* 15–28 December 1995.

54 Robin McDowell, 'Lord to push for "unconditional" MFN', *Cambodia Daily* 17 January 1996, p. 1.
55 Extract from a speech made by Hun Sen, Kong Pisey District, Kompong Speu Province, 12 February 1996, quoted in Chheang Sopheng, 'Hun Sen blasts opposition efforts abroad', *Cambodia Daily* 13 February 1996, p. 6.
56 Human rights NGO activist (H5), personal interview, Phnom Penh, January 1996.
57 Human rights NGO activist (H14), personal interview, Phnom Penh, January 1996.
58 COHCHR official (I4), personal interview, Phnom Penh, April 1996.
59 Global Witness, 'Putting Cambodia's forests on the international agenda: Global Witness and the transnational campaign against the logging trade', unpublished paper, delivered at the conference on *Cambodia: Towards a Better Future*, Oxford, June 1999.
60 Cambodian government, confidential letters to the Thai Prime Minister from Cambodia's co-Prime Ministers, leaked to Global Witness in April 1996, January and February 1996, quoted in Global Witness, 'Putting Cambodia's forests on the international agenda: Global Witness and the transnational campaign against the logging trade', unpublished paper, delivered at the conference on *Cambodia: Towards a Better Future*, Oxford, June 1999.
61 Global Witness, 'Putting Cambodia's forests on the international agenda: Global Witness and the transnational campaign against the logging trade', unpublished paper, delivered at the conference on *Cambodia: Towards a Better Future*, Oxford, June 1999.
62 Grant Curtis, *Cambodia Reborn?* (1998), p. 72.
63 For example, a speech in 1996, in which Ranariddh espoused an 'Asian values' argument to counter human rights concerns, caused a stir in international NGO circles in Phnom Penh. (Office of Prince Norodom Ranariddh, 'Vital Issues Addressed by HRH Samdech Krom Preah Norodom Ranariddh, First Prime Minister of the Royal Government of the Kingdom of Cambodia vis-à-vis the Current Situation in the Country', text of speech, Phnom Penh, 3 August 1995.) In the sphere of economic reform, the prince was also involved in a number of money-making deals, such as the 'million meter' logging deal, which aroused the ire of donors.
64 'Ta Mok: Ranariddh should believe in me', *Koh Santepheap* (Island of Peace), (11 March 1998), p. 1.
65 'ASEAN backs off as Hun Sen digs in', *Phnom Penh Post*, 25 July–7 August 1997, p. 3.
66 *Ibid*. p. 3.
67 Alexander Downer, media release, FA73, Canberra, 15 July 1997, posted on camnews
68 Michael Hayes, 'CPP takes Siem Reap, FUNCINPEC back to the jungle', *Phnom Penh Post*, 12–24 July 1997, p. 8.
69 *Ibid.*
70 Vicheth S. Tuon, 'Rally against violence in Cambodia', email, Vicheth.Tuon
71 Sam Rainsy, 'Paris Accords still hold key to peace in Cambodia', statement, 30 October 1997, posted on camnews
72 COHCHR official (I4), personal interview, Phnom Penh, 19 May 1998.
73 Spokesman's Office of the Royal Government of Cambodia, 'Memorandum', Phnom Penh, 3 April 1998, posted on camnews
74 Electoral observer (EO1), personal interview, Phnom Penh, March 1999.

75 Caroline Hughes and Real Sopheap, *Nature and Causes of Conflict Escalation in the 1998 National Election*, (Phnom Penh: Cambodia Development Resource Institute/Cambodian Centre for Conflict Resolution, 2000), p. 89.
76 UNDP, statement to the 2001 Consultative Group Meeting for Cambodia, Tokyo, June 2001.
77 Royal Government of Cambodia, 'Cambodia: Supplementary Memorandum of Economic and Financial Policies for 2000', Phnom Penh, 31 August 2000, available online at www.imf.org
78 Keat Chhon, Senior Minister, Ministry of Economics and Finance, 'Foreword: advances in implementing a new partnership paradigm in Cambodia', prepared for the 2001 Consultative Group Meeting for Cambodia, Tokyo, June 2001.
79 *Ibid.*
80 *Ibid.*
81 Thomas Risse-Kappen, 'Bringing transnational relations back in: introduction', Risse-Kappen (ed.) *Bringing Transnational Relations Back In: Non-State Actors, Domestic Structures and International Institutions*, (Cambridge: CUP, 1995), p. 32.
82 Margaret Keck and Kathryn Sikkink, *Activists Beyond Borders: Advocacy Networks in International Politics*, (Ithaca: Cornell UP, 1997), p. 13.

6 Multi-party politics in the 1990s

1 Sam Rainsy, 'Analysis of election result', 11 February 2002, online at www.samrainsyparty.org
2 Figures reflect provisional counting and are taken from Sam Rainsy, 'Analysis of election result' 11 February 2002, online at www.samrainsyparty.org
3 David Chandler, *A History of Cambodia*, 2nd ed. (Chiang Mai: Silkworm, 1993), p. 234.
4 Oeur Hunly, 'FUNCINPEC candidate for Kandal', personal communication, Lvea Aem District, Kandal, June 1998.
5 FUNCINPEC party bulletin, 15 July 1992, p. 1, quoted in Kate Frieson, 'The politics of getting the vote in Cambodia', in Heder and Ledgerwood (eds) *Propaganda, Politics and Violence in Cambodia: Democratic Transitions under United Nations Peacekeeping*, (London: M.E. Sharpe, 1996), p. 201.
6 Prince Norodom Ranariddh, speech to FUNCINPEC members, Ta Khmau District, Kandal Province, May 1998. Recorded and translated by Caroline Hughes and Sok Ty.
7 Former FUNCINPEC MP, currently Sam Rainsy Party activist (name withheld), personal communication, Sam Rainsy Party Rally, Kraceh Provincial Town, July 1998.
8 'Editorial: If you want to defeat the people's party', *Reasmei Kampuchea*, 29 June 1996, p. 2.
9 Hun Sen, speech to party workers at the Ministry of Transport and Public Works, Phnom Penh, 29 June 1996, quoted in 'Hun Sen: exhorting the party workers', *Phnom Penh Post*, 26 July–8 August 1996, pp. 4–5.
10 Tricia Fitzgerald and Sok Pov, 'Factional fighting jolts the Northwest', *Phnom Penh Post*, 21 February–6 March 1997, p. 1.
11 Claudia Rizzi, 'Power, money and the politics of peace', *Phnom Penh Post*, 21 March–3 April 1997, p. 6.
12 Jason Barber and Ker Munthit, 'Battambang is a lesson' *Phnom Penh Post*, 7–20 March 1998, p. 6.
13 Hurley Scroggins, 'Bun Chhay: loved, feared, admired, hated', *Phnom Penh Post*, 27 June–10 July 1997, p. 5.

14 Ministry of Foreign Affairs and International Co-operation, *Crisis in July, Report on the Armed Insurrection: Its Origins, History and Aftermath*, Phnom Penh, 22 September 1997, endnote 2.
15 The 21 August Report was the 'Memorandum to the Royal Government of Cambodia on Cases of Summary Execution, Torture and Persons Missing since 2–7 July 1997', submitted by the Special Representative of the United Nations Secretary-General for Human Rights in Cambodia, Phnom Penh, 21 August 1997.
16 COHCHR official (I4), personal interview, Phnom Penh, 19 May 1998.
17 May Sam Oeun, Executive Chairman, FUNCINPEC Election Campaign Committee, personal interview, Phnom Penh, May 1998.
18 Svay Sitha, quoted in 'Hun Sen dwells in development as CPP campaigns', *Phnom Penh Post*, 17–23 July 1998, p. 8.
19 May Sam Oeun, personal interview, May 1998.
20 This is an indication of the high level of militarization in Cambodian society, but militarization in Cambodia has served civilian-controlled political parties. The political parties led by these leaders are not parties representing specifically military interests.
21 Author's conversations with candidates, 1998.
22 Ouk Phourrik, President, Khmer Democratic Party, personal interview, May 1998.
23 Chhim Oum Yun, President, Liberal Democratic Party, personal interview, Phnom Penh, June 1998.
24 Ouk Phourrik, personal interview, May 1998.
25 Commune activist (SRP1), Sam Rainsy Party, personal interview, Kompong Chhnang, June 1998.
26 Liv An, President, Khmer Improvement Party, personal interview, Phnom Penh, May 1998.
27 Bit Seanglim, President, Liberal Republican Party, personal interview, Phnom Penh, June 1998.
28 The policy statements offered to voters in the campaign materials of thirteen political parties were compared. Three of these parties had participated in the National United Front alliance: FUNCINPEC, the SRP, and the Cambodia Neutral Party; four were CPP alliance parties: the CPP, the Khmer Citizen's Party, the Free Republican Development Party, and the Liberal Republican Party. The remaining six described themselves as neutral, although three of them – the Beehive Social Democracy Party, the Party for National Rebuilding and the Cambodia National Sustaining Party were viewed as pro-opposition, while the National Unity Party was a FUNCINPEC breakaway party and the Cambodia Woman Party and the National Development Party were parties specifically dedicated to furthering the position of women. In the campaign materials of these parties, nine of the thirteen included 'protection of territorial integrity' as a principle; nine promised respect for 'human rights' and 'multiparty democracy', and nine promised to 'fight corruption', while eight included commitments to 'national reconciliation', 'reduction of poverty' or 'helping the poor' and 'solving the problem of immigration'. Seven called for a 'state of law' while four indicated their support for 'constitutional monarchy' and 'separation of powers'.
29 Slogan of the Beehive Social Democracy Party.
30 Slogan of the Nokor Chum Party.
31 Conversations with villagers attending party rallies in Kandal , Svay Rieng, Kompong Speu and Kompong Thom provinces, June–July 1998.
32 Chea Chansarin, FUNCINPEC candidate for Kandal Province, conversation with voters, Lvea Aem District, Kandal, June 1998.

33 Sam Rainsy Party organizer (SRP2), interview with the author, Kien Svay District, Kandal, June 1998.
34 Sam Rainsy, campaign speech, Chhlang District, Kraceh Province, July 1998. Recorded and translated by the author and Sok Ty.
35 Sam Rainsy Party Provincial Co-ordinator (SRP3), personal interview, Kompong Cham, July 1998.
36 FUNCINPEC voter education trainer (F1), personal communication, Koh Thom District, Kandal, July 1998.
37 FUNCINPEC commune activist (SK2), personal interview, S'aang District, Kandal, July 1998.
38 FUNCINPEC commune activist (SK5), personal interview, S'aang District, Kandal, July 1998.
39 'Agreement on a comprehensive political settlement of the Cambodia conflict', 30 October 1991, Article 29, published in *The United Nations and Cambodia, 1991–1995*, (New York: UN, 1995), Doc. 19.
40 SRP Secretary-General Khieu Rada, personal interview, Phnom Penh, July 1996.
41 Journalist (N9), personal interview, Phnom Penh, June 1996.
42 Sam Rainsy, 'To the Friends of Cambodia: Elections Must be Postponed to Ensure Fairness', letter, Bangkok, 14 June 1998, posted to *Camnews* at camnews
43 Woman (DEM 10), rice farmer, 47 years, from Lvea Aem District, Kandal Province, personal interview, 'Democracy Square', Phnom Penh, 26 August 1998.
44 Student (DEM31), National Institute of Management, personal interview, Phnom Penh, 2 September 1998.
45 Woman (DEM2), former vegetable trader now unemployed, 58 years old, Tuol Kok District, Phnom Penh, personal interview, Democracy Square, Phnom Penh, 25 August 1998.
46 Man (DEM23), wounded soldier, 35 years, attended from hospital in Phnom Penh, originally from Kampot, personal interview, 'Democracy Square', Phnom Penh, 27 August 1998.
47 Prince Norodom Ranariddh, speech to supporters, FUNCINPEC headquarters, Phnom Penh, 8 August 1998; Sam Rainsy, speech to protesters, 'Democracy Square', Phnom Penh, 26 August 1998; both recorded and translated by Caroline Hughes and Sok Ty.
48 Sam Rainsy, 'Press conference by Sam Rainsy, Leader of the Parliamentary Opposition of Cambodia', press release, 24 May 2000.
49 Tik Ngoy, campaign speech, Boursedth District, Kompong Speu, 17 July 1998, recorded and translated by the author and Sok Ty.
50 Kingdom of Cambodia, Constitution of the Kingdom of Cambodia, Phnom Penh, September 1993, Article 51.
51 Oeur Hunly, personal communication, S'aang District, Kandal, July 1998.
52 Ahmed Yahya, FUNCINPEC Party Candidate for Phnom Penh, personal communication, FUNCINPEC Headquarters, Phnom Penh, 27 July 1998.
53 Pen Dareth, Vice-President, Cambodia Neutral Party, personal interview, Phnom Penh, August 1998.
54 Virath Ngin, Campaign Manager, Khmer Citizens Party, personal interview, Phnom Penh, June 1998.

7 Promoting democracy: NGOs and 'civil society'

1 The argument in this chapter has benefited greatly from the insightful comments of Dr Vanessa Pupavac.

2 Boutros Boutros-Ghali, 'Report of the Secretary-General on Cambodia containing his proposed implementation plan for UNTC including administrative and financial aspects', UN Document s/23613, 19 February 1992, §13, §19.
3 Human Rights Component, 'Final Report', Phnom Penh, 1993, p. 7.
4 *Ibid.* p. 68.
5 Definition offered by Laura Roper Renshaw, 'Strengthening civil society: the role of NGOs'. *Development* (1994): 46.
6 Gordon White, 'Civil society, democratization and development (1): Clearing the analytical ground', *Democratization* 1 (1994): 375–90.
7 See for example, Larry Diamond, 'Rethinking civil society, toward democratic consolidation', *Journal of Democracy* 5.3 (1995): 4–14.
8 Michael Bratton, 'The politics of government–NGO relations in Africa', *World Development* 17 (1989): 570.
9 Diamond (1995), 'Rethinking Civil Society'.
10 Data on the modes of operation and perceptions of Cambodian NGOs, discussed in the present chapter, is drawn primarily from four sources: interviews conducted by the author with sixty directors and staff members of human rights, democracy promoting, academic and media organizations in 1996, presented in Caroline Hughes, 'Human rights in Cambodia: international intervention and the national response', PhD dissertation, University of Hull, 1998; Yukiko Yonekura's survey of forty 'civil associations', including democracy promoting organizations and development NGOs in Cambodia in 1995/6, presented in Yukiko Yonekura, 'The emergence of civil society in Cambodia: its role in the democratization process', PhD dissertation, University of Sussex, 1999; the Cambodian Institute for Cooperation and Peace's survey of seventy governmental and non-governmental representatives, undertaken in 1999 and published as Kao Kim Hourn, *Grassroots Democracy in Cambodia, Opportunities, Challenges and Prospects* (Phnom Penh: CICP and Forum Syd, 1999); and evaluations of ten human rights and democracy promotion NGOs, commissioned by SIDA, Diakonia and Forum Syd in 2000, and published as the 'Capacity building through participatory evaluation of human rights NGOs in Cambodia reports' (Phnom Penh: SIDA, 2001). Particular emphasis is placed here upon the activities of human rights and democracy-promoting NGOs, which international donors regarded as spearheading the contribution of 'civil society' to Cambodia's democratization.
11 John Girling, 'Development and democracy in South East Asia', *Pacific Review* 1.4 (1988): 332.
12 John Girling, 'Thailand in Gramscian perspective', *Pacific Affairs* 57.3 (1984): 385.
13 CCC Agency Personnel Listing, Phnom Penh, December 1995, pp.1–6; survey conducted by Yukiko Yonekura, 'The emergence of civil society in Cambodia', p. 71.
14 PONLOK, *1999 Cambodian NGO Resource Directory: Grants, Services, Volunteers, Networks, Local Fundraising Case Studies*, (Phnom Penh: PONLOK, 1999), quoted in Yukiko Yonekura, 'Partnership for whom? Cambodian NGOs' supporting schemes', *IDS Bulletin* 31.3 (2000): 36. Throughout the 1990s, NGOs were not required to register with the government in order to operate, although plans to bring in a regulatory regime were frequently mooted. Consequently, surveys of Cambodian NGOs existing in the 1990s tend to be restricted to those organizations that made themselves visible to international interveners by networking internationally and opening offices in Phnom Penh, and which consequently appeared in the various published directories and attended the workshops and discussion forums organized with international assistance.

15 Steve Heder and Judy Ledgerwood, 'Introduction', in S. Heder and J. Ledgerwood (eds) *Propaganda, Politics and Violence in Cambodia: Democratic Transition under United Nations Peace-Keeping* (London: M.E Sharpe, 1996), p. 18.
16 Yukiko Yonekura (2002), 'The Emergence of Civil Society', pp. 173/4.
17 John Vijghen, *Understanding Human Rights and Democracy NGOs in Cambodia*, Capacity Building through Participatory Evaluation of Human Rights NGOs in Cambodia Report No. 35 (Phnom Penh: SIDA, 2001), pp. 11, 18.
18 Norman Uphoff, 'Grassroots organisations and NGOs in rural development: opportunities with diminishing states and expanding markets', *World Development* 24 (1993): 607–22.
19 *Ibid.*: 609.
20 *Ibid.*: 608.
21 *Ibid.*: 610
22 *Ibid.*
23 'Action plan for 1996', CCC Newsletter, Phnom Penh, Nov. 1995, p. 1.
24 Grant Curtis, *Cambodia Reborn? The Transition to Democracy and Development*, (Washington DC: Brookings Institute, 1998), p. 72.
25 *Ibid.* pp. 110–19.
26 Human rights NGO activist (H17), personal interview, Phnom Penh, January 1996.
27 COHCHR official (I5), personal interview, Phnom Penh, August 1996, Phnom Penh.
28 International human rights NGO activist (I1), personal interview, Washington DC, August 1995.
29 Former UNTAC official (I7), personal interview, Phnom Penh, July 1996.
30 COHCHR official (I5), personal interview, Phnom Penh, August 1996, Phnom Penh.
31 Heder and Ledgerwood (1996), 'Introduction', pp. 30–1.
32 See, for example, Curtis (1998), *Cambodia Reborn?*, pp. 112–13.
33 Michael Kirby, 'Oral statement', delivered to Third Committee of the General Assembly, 27 November 1995, p. 2.
34 Yukiko (2000), 'Partnership', p. 42.
35 Larry Diamond, 'Promoting democracy in the 1990s: actors, instruments and issues', in Axel Hadenius (ed.) *Democracy's Victory and Crisis*, (Cambridge: CUP, 1997), pp. 340–1.
36 *Ibid.*, p. 341.
37 National Assembly Deputy (D3), personal interview, Phnom Penh, July 1996.
38 Subsequently renamed the Cambodia Office of the High Commissioner for Human Rights.
39 Human rights NGO activist (H4), personal interview, Kompong Cham, July 1996.
40 Human rights NGO activist (H15), personal interview, Phnom Penh, March 1996.
41 Human rights NGO activist (H1), personal interview, Kampot, April 1996.
42 Kao Kim Hourn (1999), p. 31.
43 *Ibid.*, pp. 42/3.
44 *Ibid.*, pp. 40–1.
45 Human rights NGO activist, (H14), personal interview, Phnom Penh, January 1996.
46 Human rights NGO activist (H5), personal interview, Phnom Penh, January 1996.

47 Cecilia Karlstedt, *Relationship between Cambodian and Swedish Partner Organizations*, Capacity Building through Participatory Evaluation of Human Rights NGOS in Cambodia Report No. 39, (Phnom Penh: SIDA, 2001), p. 24.
48 Human rights NGO activist, (H18), personal interview, Phnom Penh, Mar. 1996. This NGO, in common with some other smaller NGOs, did not pay salaried staff but sought funding to pay professional staff in the future.
49 John Vijghen (ed). *Impact of Human Rights Activities in Cambodia*, Capacity Building through Participatory Evaluation of Human Rights NGOs in Cambodia, Report No. 36 (Phnom Penh: SIDA, 2001), Annex B, p. 1.
50 Royal Government of Cambodia, 'Analysis of NGO activity in Cambodia', (Phnom Penh: NGO Coordination Unit, Council for the Development of Cambodia, 1996), p. 8; quoted in Grant Curtis, *Cambodia Reborn? The Transition to Democracy and Development*, (Washington DC: Brookings Institute, 1998), p. 143.
51 International human rights NGO activist (I8), personal interview, Phnom Penh, July 1996.
52 Yukiko (2000), 'Partnership', p. 36.
53 International NGO human rights activist (I3), personal interview, Phnom Penh, January 1996.
54 International NGO human rights activist (I1), personal interview, Washington DC, August 1995.
55 Former UNTAC official (I2), personal interview, Washington DC, August 1995.
56 Karlstedt (2001), p. 29. The Swedish agencies funding Cambodian human rights NGOs did, however, state that they did not plan to force internal democracy onto Cambodian NGOs, preferring gentle persuasion and leadership by example.
57 National Democratic Institute Representative, interview with the author, Phnom Penh, August 2000.
58 Caroline Hughes, *Strategies and Impact of Election Observer Coalitions in Cambodia*, Capacity Building through Participatory Evaluation of Human Rights NGOs in Cambodia Report No. 38 (Phnom Penh: SIDA, 2001), p. 13. This was a period in which actual electoral monitoring was not required as there were no elections scheduled in Cambodia. However, all three networks remained in operation during this period, with COMFREL and COFFEL choosing to devote most of their expenditure to the functioning of their headquarters, rather than their provincial networks.
59 Kao Kim Hourn (1999), p. 52.
60 *Ibid*.
61 *Ibid*., p. 43.
62 Thida Kus, 'Proceedings NGO-donor workshop', in John Vijghen (ed.) *Project Document*, Capacity Building Through Participatory Evaluation of Human Rights NGOs in Cambodia Report No. 23, (Phnom Penh: SIDA, 2001), p. 72.
63 Human rights NGO activist (H6), personal interview, Kampot, April 1996.
64 Human rights NGO activist (H7), personal interview, Kompong Cham, July 1996.
65 Human rights NGO activist (H2), personal interview, Kompong Cham, July 1996.
66 Human rights NGO activist (H11), personal interview, Kompong Cham, July 1996.
67 Kus (2001), p. 72.
68 Human rights NGO activist (H5), personal interview, Phnom Penh, January 1996.
69 Human rights lawyer (L4), personal interview, Phnom Penh, January 1996.
70 Human rights NGO activist (H19), personal interview, Phnom Penh, May 1996.

71 Human rights NGO activist (H5), personal interview, Phnom Penh, January 1996.
72 COHCHR official (I15), interview with the author, Phnom Penh, April 1999.
73 Human rights NGO activist (H14), personal interview, Phnom Penh, January 1996.
74 Human rights lawyer (L3), personal interview, Phnom Penh, Mar. 1996.
75 Kao Kim Hourn (1999), p. 32.
76 *Ibid.*, p. 33.
77 Center for Social Development, cover illustration, Capacity Building through Participatory Evaluation of Human Rights NGOs in Cambodia reports, (Phnom Penh: SIDA, 2001).
78 Human rights NGO activist (H17), personal interview, Phnom Penh, January 1996.
79 Kao Kim Hourn (1999), p. 32.
80 Monk involved in human rights activism, (V3), personal interview, Phnom Penh, June 1996.
81 Human rights NGO activist (H20), personal interview, Siem Reap, January 1996.
82 Supreme Patriarch of Monks (Mohannikay), personal interview, Phnom Penh, June 1996.
83 Boutros-Ghali (1992), 'Implementation' §12
84 Student leader (S2), personal interview, Phnom Penh, June 1996.
85 Human rights lawyer (L1), personal interview, Phnom Penh, January 1996.
86 Kus (2001), p. 72.
87 *Ibid.*, p. 73.
88 University professor (U1), personal interview, Phnom Penh, May 1996.
89 Human rights NGO activist (H5), personal interview, Phnom Penh, January 1996.
90 Kao Kim Hourn (1999), pp. 52/3.
91 This orientation was noted in the views of human rights NGO directors in 1996, and also noted by John Marston, conducting an evaluation of advocacy by NGOs in human rights and democracy promotion in 1999 for SIDA: John Marston, *Impact of Human Rights Advocacy in Cambodia*, Capacity Building through Participatory Evaluation of Human Rights NGOs in Cambodia Report No. 37 (Phnom Penh: SIDA, 2001), p. 25.
92 Human rights lawyer (L4), personal interview, Phnom Penh, January 1996.
93 William Collins, 'Grassroots civil society in Cambodia', discussion paper, presented at Forum Syd and Diakonia Workshop, Phnom Penh, November 1998.
94 The Ven. Maha Ghosananda, personal interview, Phnom Penh, May 1996.
95 Van Sivon, personal interview, Phnom Penh, July 2000.
96 Leaflet distributed by *Dhammayietra* marchers, Phnom Penh, May 1996.
97 Human rights NGO activist (H10), personal interview, Phnom Penh, January 1996.

8 Urban protest movements: the future of Cambodian democracy?

1 Interviews with evicted squatters, 'Solidarity Village', July 2001.
2 Royal Government of Cambodia, *First Draft of the Second Five-Year Socio-Economic Development Plan, 2001–5*, Discussion Paper, Phnom Penh, 5 March 2001, p. 39.
3 *Ibid.*, pp. 34, 38.
4 Interviews with evicted squatters, 'Solidarity Village', August 2001.

5 Interviews with market traders and cyclo-drivers, Phnom Penh, August 2000 and August 2001; see also Suzanna Stout Banwell, 'Vendors' voices: the story of women micro-vendors in Phnom Penh markets and an innovative program designed to enhance their lives and livelihoods', *Asia Foundation*, Phnom Penh, 2001.
6 Banwell (2001), p. 25.
7 Interviews with cyclo-drivers, Phnom Penh, August 2000 and August 2001.
8 Banwell (2001), pp. 46/7.
9 *Ibid.*, pp. 36/7.
10 Amnesty International, 'State of Cambodia: human rights developments, 1 October 1991–31 January 1992', report, London, April 1992, p. 37.
11 University professor (U4), interview with the author, Phnom Penh, July 1998.
12 Chan Ratana (aka Yim Sokha), 'Cambodia: assassinations, terrorism, warnings, judiciary pursuits ... against freedom of press', address to the Foreign Correspondents Club of Cambodia, Phnom Penh, 31 July 1996.
13 Christine Chaumeau, 'Motive still unknown in shooting of radio star', *Phnom Penh Post*, 23 February–7 March 1996, p. 4.
14 Extract from a speech by Hun Sen in Kraingyov Commune, S'aang District, Kandal Province, 30 October. 1995, quoted in Jason Barber and Ker Munthit, 'PM says attackers defended their honor', *Phnom Penh Post*, 3–16 November 1995, p. 1.
15 Extract from a speech made by Hun Sen to villagers in Kraingyov Commune, S'aang District, Kandal Province, 25 November 1997, quoted in Ker Munthit, 'Hun Sen: the "worms" that must die', *Phnom Penh Post*, 1–14 December 1995, p. 3.
16 Hun Sen, speech to Ministry of Transport workers, Phnom Penh, 29 June 1996, reported in 'Hun Sen: exhorting the party workers', *Phnom Penh Post*, 26 July–8 August 1996, p. 5.
17 Since 1997, Hun Sen has taken to referring to himself as the 'referee' in Cambodian politics, as opposed to a contender. For example, explaining a decision not to participate personally in CPP campaigning in the 1998 elections, Hun Sen commented: 'I don't look down on my competitors. But they are not fit enough to draw me into a face-to-face competition ... If I campaign, it would look no different from a football player who also blows the whistle. And it would not look good even if I win'. [Associated Press, 'Hun Sen says no need for him to actively campaign to vote', *Kompong Speu*, 26 June 1998, posted on camnews
18 See Jason Barber and Ker Munthit, 'Hun Sen talks tough to the West', *Phnom Penh Post*, 15–28 December 1995, p. 3.
19 John A. Hall, 'Human rights and the garment industry in contemporary Cambodia', unpublished manuscript, Phnom Penh, 1999, p. 10.
20 'Cambodia: garment industry wins export boost from USA', internet posting, 3 January 2002, available online at www.bharattextile.com/news
21 Export boost.
22 Chea Huot and Sok Hach, 'The Cambodian garment industry', *Cambodia Development Review* 5.3 (2001): 1, 3.
23 *Ibid.*: 3.
24 Hall (1999), pp. 7, 12.
25 Garment worker (GW1), personal interview, Tak Fat Garment Factory, Phnom Penh, August 2000.
26 Garment worker (GW2), personal interview, Tak Fat Garment Factory, Phnom Penh, August 2000.
27 Rong Chhun, personal interview, Phnom Penh, August 2001.
28 *Ibid.*

29 *Ibid.*
30 Chea Vichea, personal interview, Phnom Penh, August 2001.
31 *Ibid.*, July 2000.
32 Garment worker (GW3), personal interview, Independence Garment Factory, Tuol Kok, August 2000.
33 Chuon Momthol, President, Cambodia Union Federation, personal interview, Phnom Penh, August 2001.
34 *Ibid.*; see also comments by Minister of Commerce Cham Prasidh, in 'Government says strikers hurt garment industry', news report, 30 November 1999, BharatTextile.Com, available online at www.bharattextile.com.
35 Chuon Momthol, personal interview, Phnom Penh, August 2001.
36 *Ibid.*
37 Nuon Rithy, ILO trainer, personal interview, Phnom Penh, August 2001.
38 Chea Vichea, personal interview, Phnom Penh, August 2001.
39 *Ibid.*
40 Lejo Sibbel, Chief Technical Advisor, ILO Working Conditions Improvement Project, personal interview, Phnom Penh, August 2001.
41 Sam Rainsy was taken to task over this by UN monitors monitoring his security after his return to Phnom Penh in late 1997. UN officer, UNSGPRC's Office, personal communication, Phnom Penh, April 1998.
42 Chea Vichea, personal interview, Phnom Penh, July 2000.
43 Authors' observations, demonstration, Olympic Stadium, Phnom Penh, 24 August 1998.
44 Due to the amorphous nature of the protest in its earliest days, representative samples could not be obtained with any confidence. These figures are offered as impressions only.
45 Woman (DEM8), casual labourer, 40 years, from S'aang District, Kandal Province, personal interview, 'Democracy Square', Phnom Penh, 26 August 1998.
46 Woman (DEM6), not economically active, 21 years, from Kampot Province, personal interview, 'Democracy Square', Phnom Penh, 25 August 1998.
47 Man (DEM11), Sam Rainsy activist, former policeman currently small businessman, 41 years, from Kompong Chhnang provincial town, personal interview, 'Democracy Square', Phnom Penh, 26 August 1998.
48 Woman (DEM10), rice farmer, 47 years, from Lvea Aem District, Kandal Province, personal interview, 'Democracy Square', Phnom Penh, 26 August 1998.
49 Woman (DEM9), vegetable trader, 45 years, from Tboung Kmum District, Kompong Cham, personal interview, 'Democracy Square', Phnom Penh, 26 August 1998.
50 *Ibid.*
51 Man (DEM11), Sam Rainsy activist, former policeman currently small businessman, 41 years, from Kompong Chhnang provincial town, personal interview, 'Democracy Square', Phnom Penh, 26 August 1998.
52 Woman (DEM13), 63 years old, servant, from Kraingyov Commune, S'aang District, Kandal Province, personal interview, 'Democracy Square', Phnom Penh, 26 August 1998.
53 Man (DEM22), former police officer, 40 years old, from Kompong Cham province, personal interview, 'Democracy Square', Phnom Penh, 27 August 1998.
54 '*Tmil*' – this derogatory term was used by Sam Rainsy in a speech to demonstrators, 'Democracy Square', Phnom Penh, 28 August 1998, recorded and translated by Caroline Hughes and Sok Ty.
55 Lor Chandara and Kay Johnson, 'Demonstrators protest through poetry, song', *CD* 1 September1998, 9.

56 Sam Rainsy, speech to demonstrators, 'Democracy Square', Phnom Penh, 28 August 1998, recorded and translated by the author and Sok Ty.
57 Sam Rainsy, 28 August 1998 (author's emphasis).
58 Sam Rainsy, 28 August 1998.
59 '*chmaa choul tralouk*' –, jumbled or disordered.
60 Sam Rainsy, speech to demonstrators, 'Democracy Square', Phnom Penh, 26 August 1998, recorded and translated by Caroline Hughes and Sok Ty.
61 *Ibid.*
62 Student (DEM25), male, third year, Institute of National Management, personal communication, Phnom Penh, 2 September1998.
63 Student (DEM31), female, National Institute of Management, personal communication, Students for Democracy Demonstration, Phnom Penh, 2 September1998.
64 Woman (DEM10), rice farmer, 47 years, from Lvea Aem District, Kandal Province, personal interview, 'Democracy Square', Phnom Penh, 26 August 1998.
65 Woman (DEM6), not economically active, 21 years, from Kampot Province, personal interview, 'Democracy Square', Phnom Penh, 25 August 1998.
66 Pharmacy student (DEM27), male, Faculty of Medicine, personal communication, Students for Democracy Demonstration, Phnom Penh, 2 September1998.
67 Hun Sen, press conference, Phnom Penh, 31 August 1998, quoted in 'You can hold non violent, illegal demonstrations for three or six months more', *Reasmei Kampuchea*, 2 September 1998, p. 3.
68 *Ibid.*
69 'Gov't condemns murder of ethnic Vietnamese', *Cambodia Daily*, 2 September 1998, 2.
70 This characterization of the movement is drawn from personal interviews with thirty market traders, O'Russei Market, July 2000.
71 Dye seller (OR1), personal interview, O'Russei Market, Phnom Penh, July 2000.
72 Monks' presents seller (OR2), O'Russei Market, personal interview, July 2000.
73 Thomas Hammarburg, 'Situation of human rights in Cambodia', report of the Special Representative of the Secretary-General for Human Rights in Cambodia to the UN Commission on Human Rights, Economic and Social Council, Geneva, 26 February 1999, p. 6.
74 Rong Chhun, personal interview, Phnom Penh, August 2001.
75 Chea Sophara, personal interview, Phnom Penh, August 2001.
76 Pen Khou, *Phnom Penh Before and After 1997* (Phnom Penh: Reasmei Kampuchea, 2000). pp. 62/3.
77 Chea Sophara, quoted in Pen Khou (2000), p. 60.
78 Chea Sophara quoted in Saing Soenthrith, 'Floating village residents get boot today', *Cambodia Daily*, 3 November 1999, p. 1.
79 Pen Khou (2000), p. 91.
80 Former Bassac resident (SQU1), personal interview, 'Solidarity Village', August 2001.
81 Former Bassac resident (SQU2), personal interview, 'Solidarity Village', August 2001.
82 Former Bassac Resident (SQU3), personal interview, 'Solidarity Village', August 2001.
83 Chhay Rithisen, Chief Architect and Director of Bureau of Urban Affairs, Municipality of Phnom Penh, personal interview, August 2001.

Sources

Speeches recorded

Lu Lay Sreng and Ahmed Yahya. Speech to demonstrators, Olympic Stadium, Phnom Penh, 23 August 1998.

Nguon Soeur, President, Khmer Citizens' Party. Speech to supporters, Koh Ondeth District, Takeo, 10 June 1998.

—— Speech to supporters, Stung District, Kompong Thom, 20 June 1998

—— Speech to supporters, Baray District, Kompong Thom, 20 June 1998.

—— Speech to party activists, KCP Headquarters, Phnom Penh, 8 July 1998.

—— Campaign speech, Olympic Stadium, Phnom Penh, 20 July 1998.

—— Speech to party activists, Party Headquarters, Phnom Penh, 24 July 1998.

Norodom Ranariddh, President, FUNCINPEC Party. Speech to supporters, Ta Khmau District, Kandal, 27 May 1998.

—— Speech to supporters, Kompong Tralach District, Kompong Chhnang, 8 June 1998.

—— Speech to Cham Islam FUNCINPEC members. FUNCINPEC Headquarters, Phnom Penh, 11 June 1998.

—— Speech to supporters, Pursat Provincial Town, 22 June 1998.

—— Campaign speech, Oudong District, Kompong Speu, 30 June 1998.

—— Campaign speech, Ta Kmau District, Kandal, 18 July 1998.

—— Campaign speech, Olympic Stadium, Phnom Penh, 19 July 1998.

—— Speech to supporters, FUNCINPEC Headquarters, Phnom Penh, 8 August 1998.

—— Speech to demonstrators, 'Democracy Square', Phnom Penh, 26 August 1998, am.

—— Speech to demonstrators, 'Democracy Square', Phnom Penh, 26 August 1998, pm.

Pen Dareth, First Vice-President, Khmer Neutral Party. Speech to supporters, Pursat Provincial Town, 26 May 1998.

—— Speech to supporters, Kompong Chhnang Provincial Town, 23 June 1998.

Sam Rainsy, President, Sam Rainsy Party. Speech to demonstrators, Olympic Stadium, Phnom Penh, 21 June 1998.

—— Speech to Party Members. Sam Rainsy Party Headquarters, Phnom Penh, 21 June 1998.

—— Campaign speech, Svay Tiep District, Svay Rieng, 27 June 1998.

—— Campaign speech, Kompong Trabek District, Prey Veng, 27 June 1998.

—— Campaign speech, Kien Svay District, Kandal, 27 June 1998.
—— Campaign speech, Pursat Provincial Town, 3 July 1998.
—— Campaign speech, Prey Prasath District, Kraceh, 4 July 1998.
—— Campaign speech, Kraceh District, Kraceh, 4 July 1998.
—— Campaign speech, Chhlong District, Kraceh, 5 July 1998.
—— Campaign speech, Stung Trang District, Kompong Cham, 5 July 1998.
—— Campaign speech, Koh Thom District, Kandal, 22 July 1998.
—— Campaign speech, Kien Svaay District, Kandal, 22 July 1998.
—— Campaign speech, Memot District, Kompong Cham, 23 July 1998.
—— Campaign speech, Phumi Krek District, Kompong Cham, 23 July 1998.
—— Campaign speech, Tboung Kmum District, Kompong Cham, 23 July 1998.
—— Campaign speech, Koh Souten District, Kompong Cham, 24 July 1998.
—— Campaign speech, Kompong Cham Provincial Town, 24 July 1998.
—— Campaign speech, opposite National Assembly, Phnom Penh, 24 July 1998.
—— Speech to supporters, outside Royal Phnom Penh Hotel, Phnom Penh, 29 July 1998.
—— Speech to demonstrators, 'Democracy Square', Phnom Penh, 26 August 1998, am.
—— Speech to demonstrators, 'Democracy Square', Phnom Penh, 26 August 1998, pm.
—— Speech to demonstrators, 'Democracy Square', Phnom Penh, 27 August 1998, am.
—— Speech to demonstrators, 'Democracy Square', Phnom Penh, 28 August 1998, am.
—— Statement, press conference. Sam Rainsy Party Headquarters, Phnom Penh, 18 Sept 1998.
—— Speeches to demonstrators, Olympic Stadium, Phnom Penh, 23 August 1998.
Tik Ngoy, President, Free Republican Development Party. Campaign speech, Boursedth District, Kompong Speu, 17 July 1998.
—— Campaign speech, Samraong Tong District, Kompong Speu, 21 July 1998.

Books and articles

Akashi, Yakushi, 'To build a new country: the task of the UN transitional authority in Cambodia', *Harvard International Review* 15 (1992/3): 34–5, 68–9.
Anderson, Benedict, *Imagined Communities, Reflections on the Origin and Spread of Nationalism*, revised edn, London: Verso, 1991.
—— 'Elections and participation in three Southeast Asian countries', R.H. Taylor (ed.) *The Politics of Elections in Southeast Asia*, Cambridge: CUP, 1996, pp. 12–33.
Archibugi, Daniele, 'Immanuel Kant: cosmopolitan law and peace', *European Journal of International Relations* 1 (1995): 429–56.
Aziz, Nikhil, 'The human rights debate in an era of globalization: hegemony of discourse', *Bulletin of Concerned Asian Scholars* 27.4 (1995): 9–18.
Baker, James A. III., 'America in Asia: emerging architecture for a pacific community', Foreign Affairs 70.5 (1991): 1–18.

Bayart, Jean-Francois, 'Finishing with the idea of the Third World: the concept of the political trajectory', James Manor (ed.) *Rethinking Third World Politics*, London: Longman, 1991, pp. 51–71.

Bit, Seanglim, *The Warrior Heritage: A Psychological Perspective of Cambodian Trauma*, El Cerrito: Seanglim Bit, 1991.

Boutros-Ghali, Boutros, *An Agenda for Peace 1995*, New York: UN Publications Dept., 1995.

—— 'Foreword', in Thomas G. Weiss and Leon Gordenker (eds) *NGOs, the UN and Global Governance*, Boulder: Lynne Rienner, 1996.

Bratton, Michael, 'The politics of government–NGO relations in Africa', *World Development* 17 (1989): 569–87.

Brown, Chris, *International Relations Theory, New Normative Approaches*, New York: Columbia UP, 1992.

—— 'International political theory and the idea of world community', in Ken Booth and Steve Smith (eds) *International Relations Theory Today*, Cambridge: Polity, 1995, 90–109.

Brown, Frederick Z. and David G. Timberman (eds), *Cambodia and the International Community: The Quest for Peace, Development and Democracy*, New York: Asia Society, 1998.

Brown , McAllister and Joseph J. Zasloff, *Cambodia Confounds the Peacemakers, 1979–1998*, Ithaca: Cornell UP, 1998.

Chai-Anan Samudavanija, 'The three-dimensional state', in James Manor (ed.) *Rethinking Third World Politics*, London: Longman, 1991, pp. 15–23.

Chanda, Nayan, *Brother Enemy, the War after the War: A History of Indochina Since the Fall of Saigon*, New York: Collier, 1986.

Chandler, David, *The Tragedy of Cambodian History*, New Haven: Yale UP, 1991.

—— *A History of Cambodia*, 2nd edn, Chiang Mai: Silkworm, 1993.

—— 'The Burden of Cambodia's Past', in Frederick Z. Brown and David G. Timberman (eds) *Cambodia and the International Community: The Quest for Peace, Development and Democracy*, New York: Asia Society, 1998, pp. 33–47.

Chang Pao-min, 'Kampuchean conflict: the continuing stalemate', *Asian Survey* 17.7 (1987): 748–64

Chea Huot and Sok Hach, 'The Cambodian garment industry', *Cambodia Development Review* 5.3 (2001): 1, 3.

Curtis, Grant, *Cambodia Reborn? The Transition to Democracy and Development*, Washington: Brookings Institute, 1998.

Dahl, Robert A, *Polyarchy: Participation and Opposition*, New Haven: Yale UP, 1971.

Diamond, Larry (ed), *Political Culture and Democracy in Developing Countries*, text-book edn, London: Lynne Rienner, 1994.

—— 'Rethinking Civil Society: Toward Democratic Consolidation', *Journal of Democracy*, 5.3 (1995): 4–14.

—— 'Promoting democracy in the 1990s: actors, instruments and issues', in Axel Hadenius (ed.) *Democracy's Victory and Crisis*, Cambridge: CUP, 1997, pp. 311–70.

Doyle, Michael, 'Liberalism and world politics', *American Political Science Review* 80 (1986): 1151–63.

—— *UN Peacekeeping in Cambodia: UNTAC's Civil Mandate*, New York: International Peace Academy Occasional Paper, 1995.

Evans, Gareth, 'Co-operative security and intra-state conflict', *Foreign Policy* 96 (1994): 3–20.

Fairbanks, Charles H, Jr, 'What went wrong in Russia? The feudalization of the state', *Journal of Democracy* 10.2 (1999): 47–53.

Falk, Richard, *Human Rights Horizons, the Pursuit of Justice in a Globalizing World*, London: Routledge, 2000.

Fitzgerald, E.V.K, 'The economic dimension of social development and the peace process in Cambodia', in Peter Utting (ed.) *Between Hope and Insecurity: The Social Consequences of the Cambodian Peace Process*, UNRISD Report 94.1. Geneva: UNRISD, 1994, pp. 48–60.

Frings, Viviane, 'Cambodia after decollectivization (1989–1992)', *Journal of Contemporary Asia*, 24.1 (1994): 49–66.

Fukuyama, Francis, *The End of History and The Last Man*, London: Penguin, 1992.

Girling, John, *Cambodia and the Sihanouk Myths*, Occasional Paper No. 7, Singapore: ISEAS, 1971.

—— 'Development and democracy in South East Asia', *Pacific Review* 1.4 (1988): 332–40.

—— 'Thailand in Gramscian perspective', *Pacific Affairs* 57.3 (1984): 385–403.

Hadenius, Axel (ed.), *Democracy's Victory and Crisis*, Cambridge: CUP, 1997.

Haggard, Stephen and Robert R. Kaufman, *The Political Economy of Democratic Transitions*, Princeton: Princeton UP, 1995.

Hanks, Lucien M, Jr, 'Merit and power in the Thai social order', *American Anthropologist* 64 (1962): 1247– 61

Haynes, Jeff, *Democracy and Civil Society in the Third World: Politics and New Political Movements*, Cambridge: Polity, 1997.

Heder, Steve and Judy Ledgerwood (eds) *Propaganda, Politics and Violence in Cambodia: Democratic Transition under United Nations Peace-Keeping*, London: M.E Sharpe, 1996.

Held, David, 'Democracy: from city states to a cosmopolitan order?' *Political Studies* 40 (1992), Special Issue: 10–39.

—— 'The transformation of political community: rethinking democracy in the context of globalization', in Ian Shapiro and Casiano Hacker-Cordón (eds) *Democracy's Edges*, Cambridge: CUP, 1999, pp. 84–111.

Helman, Gerald B. and Steven R. Ratner, 'Saving failed states', *Foreign Policy* (Winter 1992/3): 3–14.

Hendrickson, Dylan, 'Cambodia's security sector reforms: limits of a downsizing strategy', *Conflict Security Development* 1.1 (2001): 67–82.

Henze, Paul B, 'Is Ethiopia democratic? A political success story', *Journal of Democracy* 9.4 (1998): 40–54.

Hoffman, Stanley, 'The crisis of liberal internationalism', *Foreign Policy* 98 (1995): 159–77.

Hughes, Caroline, *UNTAC in Cambodia: The Impact on Human Rights*, Occasional Paper No. 92, Singapore: ISEAS, 1996.

Huntington, Samuel P, 'Democracy for the long haul', *Journal of Democracy* 7.2 (1996): 3–13.

Kao Kim Hourn, *Grass Roots Democracy in Cambodia: Opportunities, Challenges and Prospects*, Phnom Penh: CICP and Forum Syd, 1999.

Keck, Margaret and Kathryn Sikkink, *Activists Beyond Borders: Advocacy Networks in International Politics*, Ithaca: Cornell UP, 1997.

Kohli, Atul, 'On sources of social and political conflicts in follower democracies', in Axel Hadenius (ed.) *Democracy's Victory and Crisis*, Cambridge: CUP, 1997, pp. 71–80.

Koul Panha, 'The 1993 Cambodian election – experiences and lessons: a Cambodian view', in Kao Kim Hourn and Norbert von Hoffman (eds) *National Elections: Cambodia's Experiences and Expectations*, Phnom Penh: Cambodian Institute for Cooperation and Peace, 1998, pp. 36–9.

Ledgerwood, Judy, 'Patterns of CPP political repression and violence during the UNTAC period', in Steve Heder and Judy Ledgerwood (eds) *Propaganda, Politics and Violence in Cambodia: Democratic Transition under United Nations Peace-keeping*, London: M.E. Sharpe, 1996, pp. 114–33.

Ledgerwood, Judy and John Vijghen 'Decision-making in rural Khmer villages', in Judy Ledgerwood (ed.) *Cambodia Emerges from the Past: Eight Essays*, (DeKalb: Southeast Asia Publications, Center for Southeast Asian Studies, 2002).

Linz, Juan, 'Some thoughts on the victory and future of democracy', in Axel Hadenius (ed.) *Democracy's Victory and Crisis*, Cambridge: CUP, 1997, pp. 404–26.

Lukes, Stephen, *Power: A Radical View*, London: Macmillan, 1974.

Maisrikrod, Surin, 'Thailand's policy dilemmas towards Indochina', *Contemporary South East Asia* 14.3 (1992): 296

Mayall, James (ed.), *The New Interventionism 1991–4: United Nations Experience in Cambodia, Former Yugoslavia, Somalia*, Cambridge: CUP, 1996.

Meas Nee, *Toward Restoring Life, Cambodian Villages*, translated and transcribed by Joan Healy, Phnom Penh: *Krom Akphiwat Phum*, 1995.

Melucci, Alberto, *Nomads of the Present: Social Movements and Individual Needs in Contemporary Society*, John Keane and Paul Mier (eds), London: Hutchinson Radius, 1989.

Mysliwiec, Eva, *Punishing the Poor: The International Isolation of Kampuchea*, Oxford: Oxfam, 1988.

Neher, Clark D., 'Asian-style democracy', *Asian Survey* 34.11 (1994): 949–61

Nelson-Pallmeyer, Jack, *Brave New World Order: Must We Pledge Allegiance?*, New York: Orbis, 1992.

O'Donnell, Guillermo, 'Illusions about democratic consolidation', *Journal of Democracy* 7.2 (1996): 34–51.

O'Donnell, Guillermo and Philippe Schmitter, *Transfers from Authoritarian Rule: Tentative Conclusions about Uncertain Democracies*, London: Johns Hopkins UP, 1986.

Osborne, Milton, *Politics and Power in Cambodia: The Sihanouk Years*, Camberwell: Longman, 1973.

Pen Khou, *Phnom Penh Before and After 1997*, Phnom Penh: Reasmei Kampuchea, 2000.

Peou, Sorpong, *Intervention and Change in Cambodia, Towards Democracy?*, New York: St Martin's Press, 2000.

Pfaff, William, 'A new colonialism? Europe must go back into Africa', *Foreign Affairs* 74.1 (1995).

Ramsbotham, Oliver and Tom Woodhouse, *Humanitarian Intervention in Contemporary Conflict: A Reconceptualization*, Cambridge: Polity, 1996, p. 30.

Regaud, Nicolas, *Le Cambodge dans la Tourmente: Le Troisième Conflit Indochinois 1978–1991*, Paris: FEDN-L'Harmattan, 1992.

Reisinger, William R, 'Establishing and strengthening democracy', *Democratic Theory and Post-Communist Change*, Robert D. Grey (ed.), London: Prentice-Hall, 1997.

Renshaw, Laura Roper, 'Strengthening civil society: the role of NGOs', *Development* 1994: 46.

Risse-Kappen, Thomas (ed.), *Bringing Transnational Relations Back In: Non-State Actors, Domestic Structures and International Institutions*, Cambridge: CUP, 1995.

Roberts, David, *Political Transition in Cambodia, 1991–99*, Richmond: Curzon, 2001.

Rueschemeyer, Dietrich, Evelyne Huber Stephens and John D. Stephens, *Capitalist Development and Democracy*, Cambridge: Polity, 1992.

Schedler, Andreas, 'What is democratic consolidation?', *Journal of Democracy* 9.2 (1998): 91–107.

Scott, James C, 'The erosion of patron–client bonds and social change in rural Southeast Asia', *Journal of Asian Studies* 32 (1972): 5–37.

—— *Weapons of the Weak: The Everyday Forms of Peasant Resistance*, London: Yale UP, 1985.

Shawcross, William, *Sideshow: Kissinger Nixon and the Destruction of Cambodia*, London: Fontana, 1980.

Snitwongse, Kusuma 'Thai foreign policy in the global age: principle or profit?' *Contemporary South East Asia* 23.2 (2001): 189–212.

Solarz, Stephen J, 'Cambodia and the international community', *Foreign Affairs* 69.2 (1990): 99–115.

Sørensen, Georg, *Democracy and Democratization: Processes and Prospects in a Changing World*, 2nd edn, Boulder: Westview, 1998.

Sorensen, Theodore, 'Rethinking National Security', *Foreign Affairs* 69.3 (1990): 1–18.

Stuart-Fox, Martin and Bunheang Ung, *The Murderous Revolution*, Bangkok: Orchid Press, 1998.

Summers, Laura, 'Cambodia: the prospects for a UN-controlled solution', *Asian Review*, 5 (1991): 43–71.

Tarrow, Sidney, *Power in Movement: Social Movements, Collective Action and Politics*, Cambridge, CUP, 1994.

Taylor, Charles, 'The dynamics of democratic exclusion', *Journal of Democracy* 9.4 (1998): 143–56

Taylor, R.H. (ed.), *The Politics of Elections in Southeast Asia*, Cambridge: CUP, 1996.

Thion, Serge, *Watching Cambodia*, Bangkok: White Lotus, 1993.

United Nations, *The United Nations and Cambodia 1991–1995*, New York: UN Publications Dept., 1995.

Uphoff, Norman, 'Grassroots organisations and NGOs in rural development: opportunities with diminishing states and expanding markets', *World Development* 24 (1993): 607–22.

Vickery, Michael, *Cambodia 1975–82*, Boston: South End Press, 1984.

White, Gordon, 'Civil society, democratization and development (1): Clearing the analytical ground', *Democratization* 1.3 (1994): 375–90.

Yonekura, Yukiko, 'Partnership for whom? Cambodian NGOs' supporting schemes', *IDS Bulletin* 31.3 (2000): 35–47.

Zakaria, Fareed, 'The rise of illiberal democracy', *Foreign Affairs* 76.6 (1997): 22–43.

Reports and papers

Amnesty International, 'Cambodia: human rights developments, 1 October 1991 to 31 January 1992', London, April 1992.
—— 'State of Cambodia: update on human rights concerns', London, October 1992.
—— 'Cambodia: human rights concerns: July to December 1992', London, February 1993.
—— 'Kingdom of Cambodia. The children of Krang Kontroul: waiting for justice', London, March 1997.
—— 'Cambodia: escaping the killing fields?', news release, October 1997.
Asian Development Bank, International Monetary Fund, United Nations Development Programme, United Nations Transitional Authority in Cambodia, and World Bank. 'Cambodia: short term needs', prepared for International Conference on the Reconstruction of Cambodia, Paris, 8–9 September 1993.
Banwell, Suzanna Stout, 'Vendors' voices: the story of women micro-vendors in Phnom Penh markets and an innovative program designed to enhance their lives and livelihoods', Asia Foundation, Phnom Penh, 2001.
Boutros-Ghali, Boutros, 'Report of the Secretary-General on Cambodia Containing his Proposed Implementation Plan for UNTAC including Administrative and Financial Aspects', UN Document S/23613, 19 February 1992.
Cambodia Office of the United Nations Centre for Human Rights, 'Memorandum to the Royal Government of Cambodia, Evidence of Summary Executions, Torture and Missing Persons Since 2–7 July 1997', Phnom Penh, August 1997.
Curtis, Grant, 'Cambodia: a country profile', Stockholm: SIDA, 1990.
Economist Intelligence Unit, 'Quarterly Economic Review of Indochina – Vietnam, Laos, Cambodia', Annual Supplement (1985).
—— 'Quarterly Economic Review of Indochina – Vietnam, Laos, Cambodia', 3 (1985).
—— 'Country Report: Indochina – Vietnam, Laos, Cambodia', 1 (1986).
—— 'Country Report: Indochina – Vietnam, Laos, Cambodia', 2 (1986).
—— 'Quarterly Economic Review of Indochina – Vietnam, Laos, Cambodia', 2 (1986).
—— 'Country Report: Indochina – Vietnam, Laos, Cambodia', 3 (1986).
—— 'Country Profile: Indochina – Vietnam, Laos, Cambodia', (1989–90).
—— 'Quarterly Economic Review of Indochina – Vietnam, Laos, Cambodia', 2 (1996).
—— 'Country Report: Indochina – Vietnam, Laos, Cambodia', 3 (1998).
Environment Working Group of NGO Forum on Cambodia, 'Review of fishery conflict in Stung Treng', Phnom Penh, January 2000.
Global Witness, 'Putting Cambodia's forests on the international agenda: Global Witness and the transnational campaign against the logging trade', unpublished paper delivered to conference 'Cambodia: Towards a Better Future', Oxford, June 1999.
—— 'Chainsaws speak louder than words', London, May 2000.
Hall, John A, 'Human rights and the garment industry in contemporary Cambodia', Phnom Penh, 1999.
Hammarberg, Thomas, 'Monitoring of election related intimidation and violence: report August 19–Sept 23 1998', Report of the Special Representative of the Secretary-General for Human Rights in Cambodia. Phnom Penh, 23 September 1998.

—— 'Situation of human rights in Cambodia', Report of the Special Representative of the Secretary-General for Human Rights in Cambodia. to the UN Commission on Human Rights, UN Economic and Social Council. Geneva, 26 February 1999.

—— 'Situation of human rights in Cambodia', Report of the United Nations Special Representative for Human Rights in Cambodia to the UN Commission on Human Rights, UN Economic and Social Council. Geneva, 13 January 2000.

Hughes, Caroline, 'Strategies and impact of election observer coalitions in Cambodia', Capacity Building through Participatory Evaluation of Human Rights NGOs in Cambodia Report No. 38, Phnom Penh: SIDA, 2001.

Hughes, Caroline and Real Sopheap, 'The nature and causes of conflict in the 1998 national elections', Phnom Penh: Cambodian Centre for Conflict Resolution, 1999.

International Institute of Rural Reconstruction, 'Participatory rural appraisal output in Thlork, Chrok Motes, and Toul Ampil Villages, Svay Teap District, Svay Rieng Province, Kingdom of Cambodia, 27 February–16 March 1996', Phnom Penh: Catholic Relief Services Cambodia, 1996.

Kant, Elise, 'Comparing poverty to poverty, internally displaced persons and local villagers in Kompong Svay: results of a baseline survey in Kompong Svay District, Kompong Thom Province, Cambodia', Phnom Penh: Church World Service Cambodia, December 1993.

Karlstedt, Cecilia, 'Relationship between Cambodian and Swedish partner organizations', Capacity Building through Participatory Evaluation of Human Rights NGOS in Cambodia Report No. 39, Phnom Penh: SIDA, 2001.

Keat Chhon, 'Foreword: advances in implementing a new partnership paradigm in Cambodia', prepared for the 2001 Consultative Group Meeting for Cambodia. Tokyo, June 2001.

Kingdom of Cambodia, 'Implementing the national programme to rehabilitate and develop Cambodia', Phnom Penh, February 1995.

Kirby, Michael, 'Oral statement', delivered to Third Committee of the General Assembly, 27 November 1995.

Kus, Thida, 'Proceedings NGO–Donor workshop', John Vijghen (ed.), *Project Document*, Capacity Building Through Participatory Evaluation of Human Rights NGOs in Cambodia Report No. 23, Phnom Penh: SIDA, 2001, 56–67.

Leonhardt, Maurice and Somporn Boonyhabancha, 'An introduction to the urban poor in Phnom Penh, Cambodia', Bangkok: Action Coalition for Housing Rights, 1993.

Leuprecht, Peter, 'Situation of human rights in Cambodia', Report of the United Nations Special Representative for Human Rights in Cambodia to the UN Commission on Human Rights, UN Economic and Social Council. Geneva, 28 December 2001.

Ministry of Foreign Affairs and International Co-operation, 'Crisis in July, report on the armed insurrection: its origins, history and aftermath', White Paper, Phnom Penh, 22 September 1997.

—— 'Background on the July 1997 crisis: Prince Ranariddh's strategy of provocation', White Paper, Phnom Penh, 9 July 1997.

Ministry of Planning, 'Demographic survey of Cambodia: summary results', Phnom Penh, 1996.

—— 'Report on the Cambodian socio-economic survey 1997', Phnom Penh, 1997.

—— 'Cambodia human development report 1998: women's contribution to development', Phnom Penh, 1998.

Mysliwiec, Eva, 'Cambodia: NGOs in transition', presented to Workshop on the Social Consequences of the Peace Process in Cambodia, Geneva, 29–30 April 1993.

Neb Sinthay and Janet Ashby, 'Possibilities to reduce the number of weapons and the practice of using weapons to solve problems in Cambodia', Phnom Penh: Peace Partnership, 28 July 1998.

NGO Resource Project, daily and weekly reports. Phnom Penh, January to May 1993.

Royal Government of Cambodia, 'Cambodia: supplementary memorandum of economic and financial policies for 2000', Phnom Penh, 31 August 2000, accessed online at www.imf.org

—— 'First draft of the second Five-Year Socio-Economic Development Plan, 2001–5', presented for discussion at a High Level Forum held at Cambodiana Hotel, Phnom Penh, 22 March 2001.

Sam Rainsy, 'Cambodia: documents for International Conference on the Reconstruction of Cambodia (ICORC)', Paris, 14–15 March 1995.

Sik Boreak, 'Land ownership, sales and concentration in Cambodia: a preliminary review of secondary data and primary data from four recent surveys', Working Paper No. 16, Phnom Penh: CDRI, 2000.

Thayer, Carlyle A, 'The Soviet Union and Indochina', paper presented to IV World Congress for Soviet and East European Studies, Harrogate, 21–26 July 1990. Accessed online at ftp://coombs.anu.edu/coombspapers/

United Nations Population Fund, 'Cambodia: programme review and strategy development report', Phnom Penh, 1998.

UNTAC Human Rights Component, 'Final report', Phnom Penh, 1993.

UNTAC Office of Rehabilitation and Economic Affairs, 'Short term economic management and stabilization strategies for Cambodia', background draft prepared for Meeting of the Extended Permanent Five, Phnom Penh, 17 June 1993.

US Agency for International Development, 'South and South East Asia floods fact sheet #2', 14 November 2000, accessed online at www.reliefweb.int

Vijghen, John, 'Decision making in a Cambodian village: a study of decision making processes in a development project in Cambodia, Takeo', Report No. 15, Phnom Penh: Cambodian Researchers for Development, 1996.

—— 'Understanding human rights and democracy NGOs in Cambodia', Capacity Building through Participatory Evaluation of Human Rights NGOs in Cambodia Report No. 35, Phnom Penh: SIDA, 2001.

—— (ed), 'Impact of human rights activities in Cambodia', Capacity Building through Participatory Evaluation of Human Rights NGOs in Cambodia, Report No. 36, Phnom Penh: SIDA, 2001.

Ward, Michael, 'Constraints on re-building Cambodia's economy', delivered at 'Conference on Cambodia's Economy', University of Washington, Seattle, 3–5 November 1994.

Williams, Shaun, 'Where has all the land gone?' Cambodia Land Study Project, Vol. 2, Phnom Penh, Oxfam (GB), 1999, accessed online at http://www.camnet.com.kh/ngoforum/

World Bank, 'Background note: Cambodia, a vision for forestry sector development', paper prepared for Consultative Group Meeting on Cambodia, Tokyo, February 1999. Accessed online at www.worldbank.org.

World Bank, East Asia and Pacific Region, Country Dept. 1, 'Cambodia: agenda for rehabilitation and reconstruction', Bangkok, June 1992.

World Food Programme and Food and Agriculture Organisation, 'Statistical supplement: WFP/FAO crop and food supply assessment mission, 1996/7, Cambodia', Phnom Penh, 1997.

Yem Sam Oeun and Rebecca F. Catalla, 'I live in fear': consequences of small arms and light weapons on women and children in Cambodia', Research Series on Small Arms and Light Weapons Issues in Cambodia, Report No. 2, Phnom Penh: Working Group on Weapons Reduction, 2001.

Unpublished dissertations

Ebihara, May, 'Svay: a Khmer Village in Cambodia', PhD dissertation, Columbia University, 1968.

Hughes, Caroline, 'Human rights in Cambodia: international intervention and the national response', PhD dissertation, University of Hull, 1998.

Shatkin, Gavin, 'Claiming a piece of the city: squatting as a response to changing property relations in Phnom Penh's transitional economy', Master's dissertation, University of Hawai'i, 1996.

Yonekura, Yukiko, 'The emergence of civil society in Cambodia: its role in the democratization process', PhD dissertation University of Sussex, 1999.

Newspapers

Cambodia Daily
Cambodian Business
Far Eastern Economic Review
Koh Santepheap (Island of Peace)
Moneaksekar Khmer (Khmer Conscience)
Phnom Penh Post
Reasmei Kampuchea (Light of Cambodia)
Udam Kate Khmer (Khmer Ideal)

E-lists and websites

camnews@lists.best.com
camnews@cambodia.org
www.bharattextile.com
www.camnet.com.kh/ngoforum/
www.cdri.org.kh
www.imf.org
www.phnompenhpost.com
www.reliefweb.int
www.worldbank.org

Index

An environmentally friendly book printed and bound in England by www.printondemand-worldwide.com

This book is made of chain-of-custody materials; FSC materials for the cover and PEFC materials for the text pages.

#0032 - 110216 - C0 - 234/156/15 [17] - CB - 9780700717378